"Information through Innovation"

Acumen Series

Windows 3.1

Samantha Penrod

Purdue University at Calumet

boyd & fraser publishing company

I(T)P An International Thomson Publishing Company

Danvers • Albany • Bonn • Boston • Cincinnati • Detroit • London • Madrid • Melbourne
Mexico City • New York • Paris • San Francisco • Singapore • Tokyo • Toronto • Washington

Publishing Process Director: Carol Crowell
Series Editor: Linda Ericksen
Development Editor: Mary Terese Cozzola
Production Editor: Jean Bermingham
Composition: Gex, Inc.
Interior Design: Gex, Inc.
Cover Design: Richard Pepper/Flying Pepper Design
Manufacturing Coordinator: Carol Chase
Marketing Director: William Lisowski

Printed in the United States of America

This book is printed on recycled, acid-free paper that meets Environmental Protection Agency standards.

For more information, contact boyd & fraser publishing company:

boyd & fraser publishing company
One Corporate Place • Ferncroft Village
Danvers, Massachusetts 01923, USA

International Thomson Publishing Europe
Berkshire House 168-173
High Holborn
London, WCIV 7AA, England

Thomas Nelson Australia
102 Dodds Street
South Melbourne 3205
Victoria, Australia

Nelson Canada
1120 Birchmount Road
Scarborough, Ontario
Canada M1K 5G4

International Thomson Editores
Campose Eliseos 385, Piso 7
Col. Polanco
11560 Mexico D.F. Mexico

International Thomson Publishing GmbH
Konigswinterer Strasse 418
53227 Bonn, Germany

International Thomson Publishing Asia
221 Henderson Road
#05-10 Henderson Building
Singapore 0315

International Thomson Publishing Japan
Hirakawacho Kyowa Building, 3F
2-2-1 Hirakawacho
Chiyoda-ku, Tokyo 102, Japan

1 2 3 4 5 6 7 8 9 10 MT 9 8 7 6 5

ISBN 0-87709-965-0

Brief Contents

Contents

Preface

Welcome to the boyd & fraser family of *ACUMEN* authors, educators, and students who are participating in this vanguard of computer education. The *ACUMEN* series is both a well-integrated solution to the demands of the classroom and the foundation for the essential computer skills that today's students require for economic survival in the modern business world.

Computer literacy is essential in education and a growing number of professions. In the course of their careers, most individuals will have to learn more than a single application and, eventually, new versions of those applications. They will need to know how to integrate the applications to produce complex documents. They will need to work with other individuals to produce unified team projects.

The primary goals of the *ACUMEN* series are to instill confidence, build the skills and insight necessary to master the software application, develop a basic understanding of the concepts behind each task, and comprehend how different applications are often used interactively to complete a variety of tasks.

To meet these goals, *ACUMEN* introduces the concept of *active learning* that links all of the books in strategic and important ways. While other computer books isolate students in the world of a single application, *ACUMEN* students enter the real world of interactive computer technology.

Each text can be taught as a stand-alone course or combined in a unified syllabus. For example, the letters and plans written in the word processing application can be performed alone or combined with the financial projections and charts from the spreadsheet application. This information can then be applied to the product database from the database application to produce a complete business plan. In addition, optional group projects teach students how to work together in teams to produce the unified projects.

The *ACUMEN* structure, objectives, content, exercises, projects, and design are the product of extensive research, interviews, and field studies on what computer educators need to effectively teach both individual applications courses and fully integrated, comprehensive courses that cover a variety of applications.

The ACUMEN Solution: from Concept to Comprehension

- **Quick Preview.** Each *ACUMEN* begins with a short, pre-written program that demonstrates the application to the students and introduces a confidence-building real-world example.

- **Progressive Chapters.** The chapters of each book are grouped into three distinct parts, with each chapter in a part progressively building on the preceding chapter.

- **Fundamentals.** Part I introduces the application and the basic skills required for competency. All of the chapters in this part cover the essential tasks necessary for using the program.

- **Critical Thinking.** Part II combines problem solving and critical thinking while adding skills required to produce useful work.

- **Advanced Features.** Part III combines advanced skills designed to improve productivity and proficiency.

- **Conceptual Introductions.** Each chapter begins with a list of objectives, a list of key terms and definitions, and a short, conceptual overview that clearly tell the student what will be covered in that chapter.

- **Objectives Covered.** The chapter objectives are each covered individually and are introduced with a brief why-this-is-important or explanatory paragraph. Each objective includes at least one hands-on exercise.

- **Key Terms.** New terms are printed in italic when first introduced. The term also is printed in bold in the margin of the text so that the student can make the connection between the definition in the *Key Terms* box and the use of the term in context.

- **Self Evaluation.** Each chapter ends with self-evaluation review questions, four Quick Projects, and two In-Depth projects. Projects are written so that two are specific to the chapter, two are continuing projects specific to the part, and two are *stretch* projects that require critical thinking.

- **Part Projects.** Each of the three parts ends with two comprehensive applications projects that combine the knowledge and skills learned in that part. One is an individual project and one is a team project.

- **Linked Case Studies.** Each applications title includes Case Studies that, while specific to the particular application covered in that book, are also part of an overall series project. The Case Studies can be used to link different applications and create actual business projects, with source materials drawn from the various applications.

- **Boxed Sidebars and Special Features.** To maintain student interest and show the effectiveness of the application in practical situations, each chapter contains at least one boxed sidebar and one special features box. Boxed sidebars provide human interest and real-world examples, while special features boxes emphasize an advanced or particularly interesting skill.

- **Appendix on Windows.** A special appendix introducing Windows to novice users is included at the back of each *ACUMEN* text. This Introduction to Windows gives the user an overview of basic Windows features and includes a hands-on tutorial.

Instructor's Materials

A comprehensive *Instructor's Manual* containing topic overviews, key terms, and solutions to all exercises and problems is available for each book. An *Instructor's Resource Disk* containing exercise and problem files, as well as all solutions files, is also available. The *Instructor's Resource Disk* contains data files that can be distributed to the user via disk or over a computer network. It also contains the integrated Case Studies and accompanying solutions, and a complete text-based copy of the *Instructor's Manual.*

Software Upgrades

ACUMEN adopters are eligible to participate in boyd & fraser's software upgrade program. Contact your sales representative for specific details.

Acknowledgments

The following reviewers helped shape this text by providing valuable comments:

Sandra S. Hagman	Forsythe Technical Community College
Tiga Muntean	Western Business Academy
Debbie Weberg	University of Phoenix

Special thanks go to Linda Ericksen, Series Editor, for her work on the entire list of *ACUMEN* series titles.

ACUMEN Series Titles

boyd & fraser is proud of the diversity, variety, and quantity of the computer education resources we offer designed to meet your instructional needs. New titles will be added for major software applications as the programs are released in new versions. Our current offerings include:

DOS:

DOS 6.22 ISBN 0-87709-971-5

WordPerfect 6.0 for DOS ISBN 0-87709-956-1

Windows:

Windows 3.1 ISBN 0-87709-965-0

Windows 95 ISBN 0-7895-0349-2

Ami Pro 3.1 for Windows ISBN 0-87709-962-6

Word 6.0 for Windows ISBN 0-87709-959-6

WordPerfect 6.1 for Windows ISBN 0-87709-953-7

Excel 5.0 for Windows ISBN 0-87709-980-4

Lotus 1-2-3, Release 5 for Windows ISBN 0-87709-974-X

Access 2.0 for Windows ISBN 0-87709-983-9

Paradox 5.0 for Windows ISBN 0-87709-968-5

QuattroPro 6.0 for Windows ISBN 0-87709-977-4

Combined Applications:

Acumen: Target Edition:
DOS 6.2 Essentials, Windows 3.1 Essentials,
Word 6.0 for Windows, Excel 5.0 for Windows,
Access 2.0 for Windows ISBN 0-7895-0199-6

Quick Preview

Windows 3.1

Windows 3.1 is an operating environment that works with the MS-DOS and PC-DOS operating systems. With Windows 3.1 you can run multiple applications; share text, data, and graphics among applications; and perform a variety of disk- and file-maintenance tasks. Windows 3.1 is a graphical user interface (GUI) that contains icons, or pictures, and menus that can be manipulated by a mouse to perform various tasks. The icons and menus facilitate easy communication between the application and user because the user doesn't have to recall hard-to-remember commands to perform each task. Windows 3.1 also comes equipped with other programs to help you handle everyday tasks such as tracking appointments, performing calculations, creating documents, and communicating with other computers.

This Quick Preview shows you some of these features.

Activity 1: Starting Windows

To start the Windows program, do the following:

1. At the C:>\ prompt, type CD\WINDOWS.

   You are now at the Windows subdirectory on the hard disk.
2. At the C:\Windows> prompt, type WIN.

The Windows desktop, which is the screen background, is displayed, and the Program Manager is displayed in a smaller window frame within the desktop (see Figure QP-1). (The Main window may or may not also be displayed depending on the configuration of the settings of your machine.) The Program Manager is responsible for all Windows applications. In the same way you rearrange items on a desktop, Windows enables you to rearrange electronic files, icons, and other windows on its visual desktop.

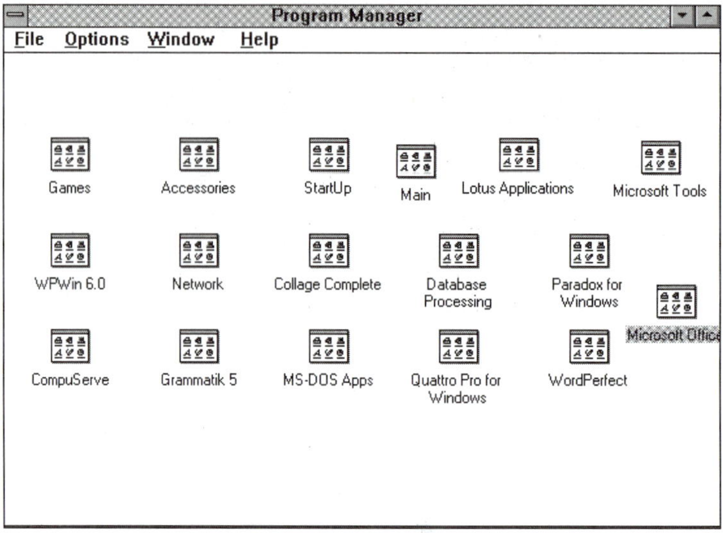

Figure QP-1 The initial Windows desktop screen and group window icons

Activity 2: Moving Through the Windows Desktop

1. Position the mouse pointer, which looks like an arrow, over the Program Manager title bar.
2. To move the window, click and drag the window one-half inch down. Release the mouse button.
3. Position the mouse pointer over the left border of the Program Manager window; the pointer changes to a double-headed arrow.
4. To resize the window, click and drag the left border one-half inch to the right.
5. Point to the menu bar of the Program Manager window and click File to activate a pull-down menu. Menu options can be used to carry out various tasks (see Figure QP-2).
6. Click the File option from the menu bar again to remove the pull-down menu.
7. To activate the Program Control menu box pull-down menu, click the Program control menu box, which is the hyphen in the upper, left corner of the window. This pull-down menu contains options that are consistent for all Windows application programs and can be used to close, move, and resize windows.
8. Click the Program Control menu box again to remove the pull-down menu.
9. Click the Maximize button, which is the upward pointing arrow in the upper, right corner of the window.

The Program Manager fills the entire screen, and you can no longer see the desktop area.

10. Click the Restore button, which is the double-headed arrow in the upper, right corner of the window. The Program Manager window returns to its previous, smaller frame size on the desktop.
11. Click the Minimize button, which is the downward pointing arrow inthe upper, right corner, to reduce the current window to the size of an icon.
12. Double-click the Program Manager icon to restore it back to a window.

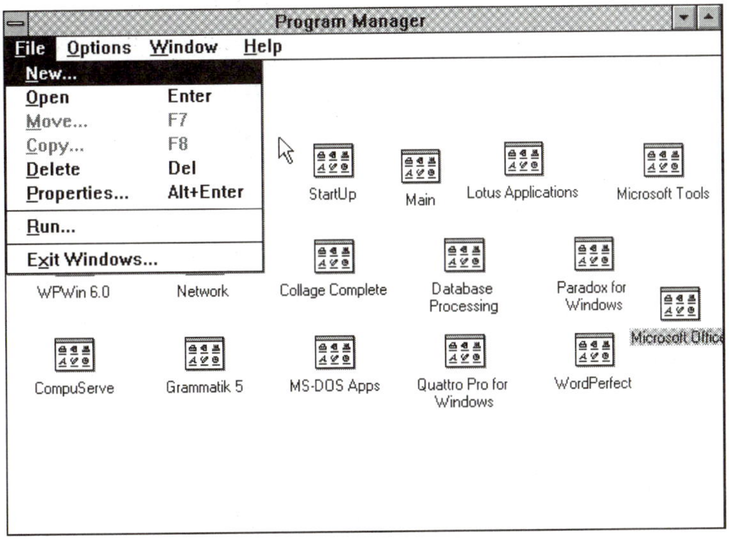

Figure QP-2 The File pull-down menu

Activity 3: Opening and Arranging Multiple Windows

You can open and arrange multiple windows on the desktop at one time. There are two methods for opening windows: double-clicking the group window icon or using the Window pull-down menu. The group window icons are the small boxes within the Program Manager that contain program icons. The name of the corresponding window is under each group window icon.

1. Double-click the Accessories group window icon to open the Accessories window.

   The Accessories window is opened within the Program Manager window.
2. Choose the Window option on the menu bar of the Program Manager window.

3. Choose the Games option from the listing to open the Games window. (If you don't see the Games option in the numbered list, click More Windows... at the bottom of the list to view additional options.

   The Games window opens.

   The last window that you opened is the active window and is displayed at the forefront of your screen. If the Main window is not open, open it at this time. You should have three windows open within the Program Manager window at this time: Main, Accessories, and Games (see Figure QP-3).

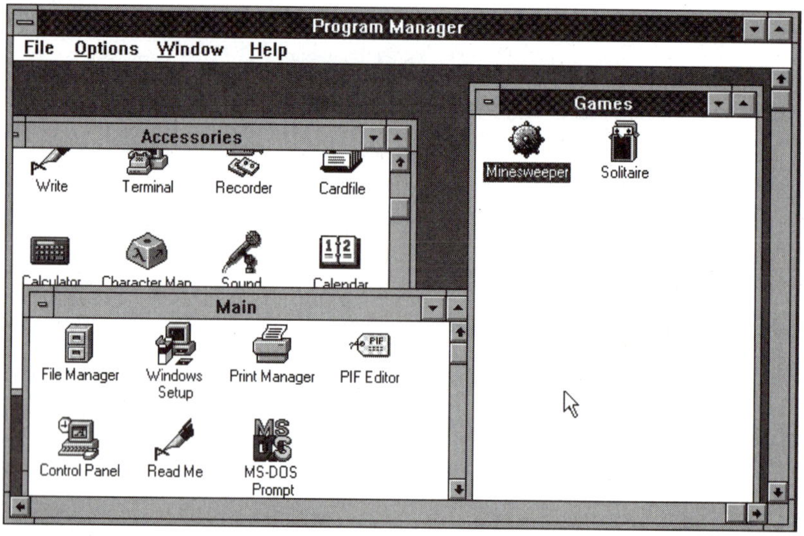

Figure QP-3 Multiple windows opened within the Program Manager window

4. To rearrange the windows, choose Window from the menu bar.
5. Choose Cascade.

   The three windows overlap one another, and the active window is on top.
6. Choose Window from the menu bar.
7. Choose Tile.

   The three windows are next to one another, and you can see the icons that reside in each one (see Figure QP-4).

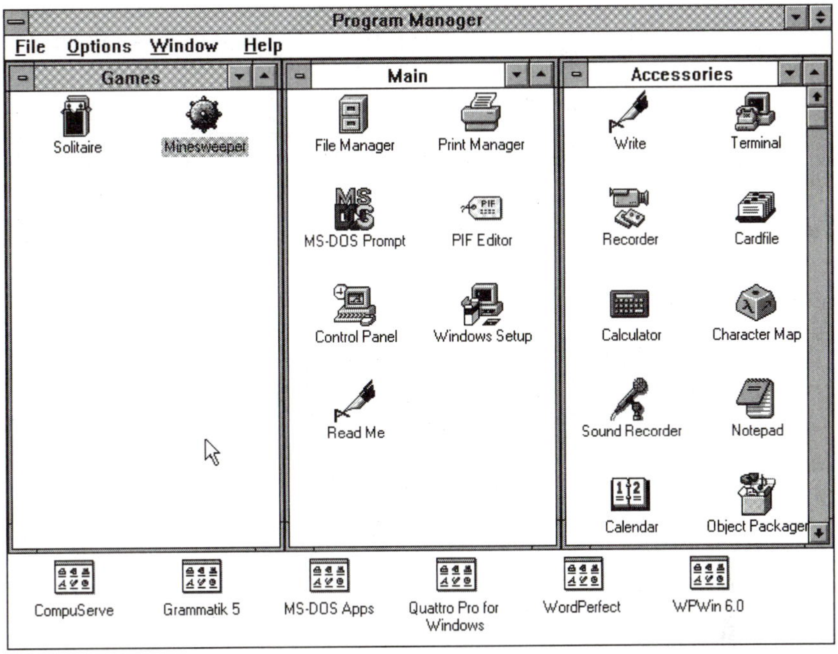

Figure QP-4 Tiled windows with icons

Activity 4: Activating, Closing, and Scrolling through a Window

Although many windows can be open at one time, only one can be active.

1. To make the Accessories window active, click anywhere within the Accessories window.

   The title bar of the Accessories window is highlighted, indicating that it is active.

2. To make the Main window active, click anywhere within the Main window.

   The title bar of the Main window is highlighted, indicating that it is active. Scroll bars are provided on each window when all the window's information will not fit within the window frame. A window can have a vertical scroll bar that appears on the right side of the window, a horizontal scroll bar that appears on the bottom of the window, or both (see Figure QP-5).

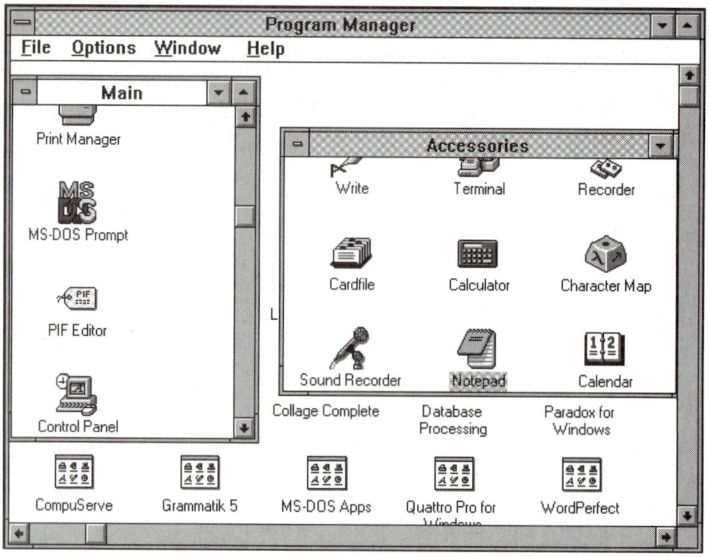

Figure QP-5 The Program Manager window with both vertical and horizontal scroll bars

3. Using the double-headed arrow mouse pointer, resize the Main window, making it smaller until the vertical and horizontal scroll bars appear.
4. Click the right or left arrow in the horizontal scroll bar to move the window display to the right or the left.
5. Click the top or bottom arrow in the vertical scroll bar to move the window display up or down.

   Each scroll bar contains a scroll box that can be used to move the window display.
6. Click and drag the scroll box on the horizontal or vertical scroll bar to scroll through the display quickly.

   You can close a window when you are finished using it.
7. Click anywhere on the Games window to make it the active window.
8. Double-click the control menu box in the upper, left corner of the Games window.

   The Games window closes.

Activity 5: Customizing the Windows Screen

You can customize the way Windows looks and behaves by changing the settings in the Control Panel. The Control Panel is a window that contains several applications you can use to customize Windows.

1. Open the Main window, if it is not already open.
2. Double-click the Control Panel icon 
.

The Control Panel window is displayed. The Control Panel manages many settings, including screen colors, fonts for printing, background screen patterns, and the arrangement of icons on the desktop (see Figure QP-6).

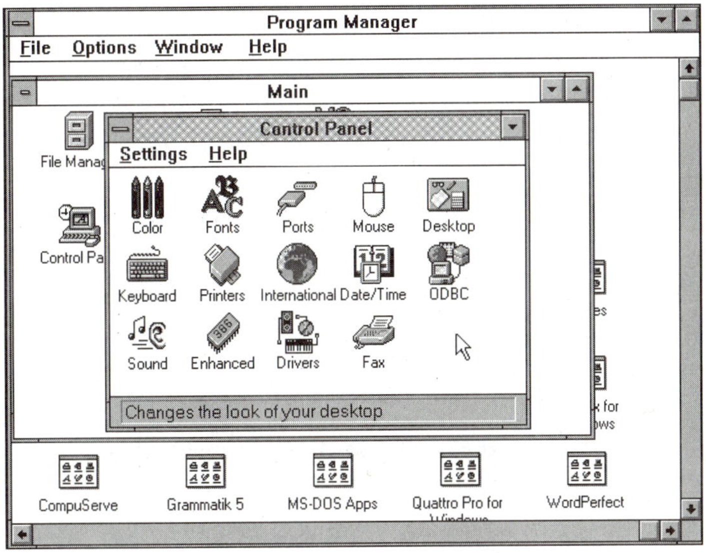

Figure QP-6 The Control Panel window

3. Double-click the Desktop icon  in the Control Panel window.
   The Desktop dialog box is displayed (see Figure QP-7).

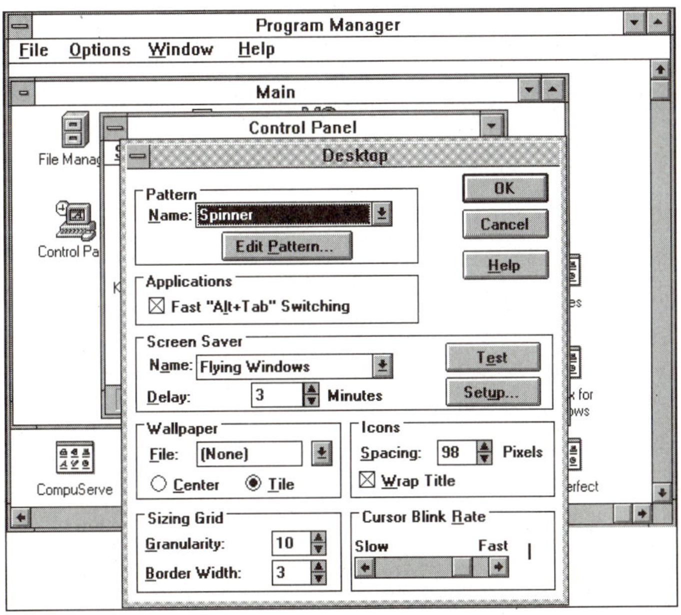

Figure QP-7 The Desktop dialog box

4. To change the background pattern of the desktop, click the down arrow next to the Pattern Name text box and choose Spinners from the drop-down list.
5. To see a sample of the Spinners pattern, click the Edit Pattern command button.

   A sample box displays the chosen pattern.
6. Click OK from the Edit Pattern window.
7. To change the screen saver, click the down arrow next to the Screen Saver Name text box.
8. Choose Flying Windows from the drop-down list.
9. Click OK in the Desktop dialog box to accept the changes you have made.
10. To close the Control Panel window, double-click the control menu box in the Control Panel menu window.

Activity 6: Using a Windows Accessory—The Clock

Windows provides you with a number of different accessories that can act as productivity tools to help you with everyday tasks. One of these tools is the clock. The clock enables you to display the time in a digital or analog format on your screen while you work in other programs.

1. Open the Accessories window, if it is not already open.
2. Double-click the Clock icon  to open the Clock window.

   The clock may be displayed as a digital or analog clock depending on the setting that was used last (see Figures QP-8 and QP-9).

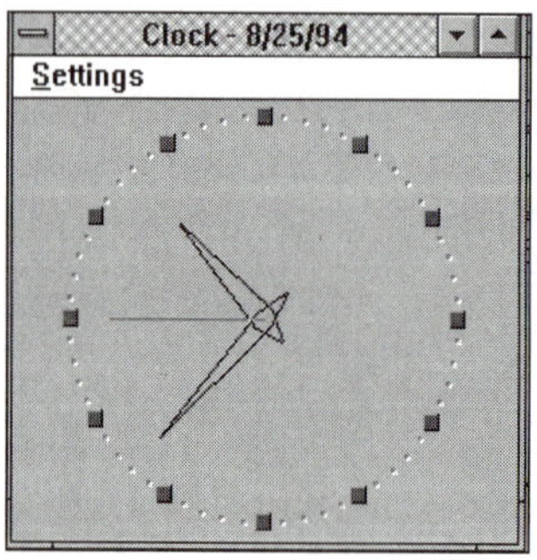

Figure QP-8 An analog display of the clock

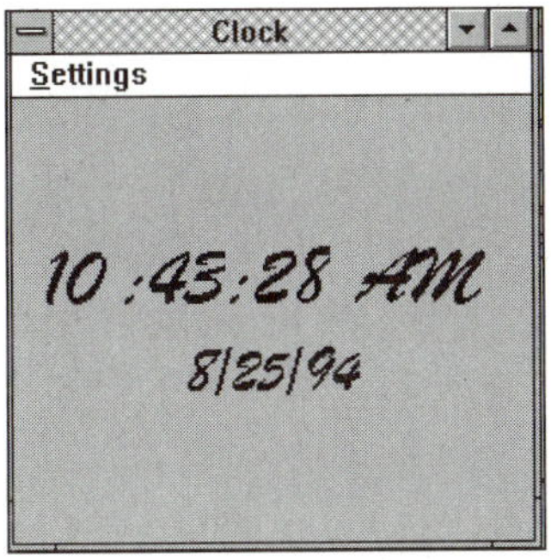

Figure QP-9 A digital display of the clock

3. To set the clock to a digital setting, click Settings in the Clock menu bar, and then choose Digital from the pull-down menu.
4. To have the seconds display on the clock, click Settings in the Clock menu bar, and then choose Seconds from the pull-down menu.
5. To have the date display on the clock, click Settings in the Clock menu bar, and then choose Date from the pull-down menu.
6. To change the display to analog, click Settings in the Clock menu bar, and then choose Analog from the pull-down menu.
7. To shrink the clock display to an icon on the desktop, click the Minimize button in the Clock window.

   The Clock icon is displayed on the desktop.

Activity 7: Exiting the Windows Program

To exit the Windows program and return to the disk operating system:

1. Double-click the control menu box in the Program Manager window.

   A message box appears informing you that the Windows session will end.
2. Click OK.

   You will be returned to the DOS prompt.

Part 1

Fundamentals

Chapter 1

Understanding Windows

Objectives

- Starting Windows
- Using the Mouse and Keyboard
- Looking at the Windows Screen
- Working with Menus
- Closing a Window and Exiting the Program

Key Terms

TERM	DEFINITION
Desktop	the background area of the screen in the Windows environment representing a workspace upon which all other items—such as applications and documents—are arranged
Window	a rectangular area on the screen containing program icons, a single program, or a single program document
Graphical User Interface	an operating system environment that contains menus and icons that facilitate communication between the user and the computer
Icon	a small, graphical representation of a program, file, window, or command
Mouse Pointer	a small graphic that moves across the screen as you move the mouse; the mouse pointer takes on different shapes depending on its position on the screen and the task that is being performed
Document Window	a framed area found inside an application window that shows the contents of a document

TERM	DEFINITION
Application Window	a framed area that displays a type of software program—for example, an application window may contain a word processing, spreadsheet, database, or graphics program
Program Manager	a program within Windows that controls all other applications that run under the Windows environment

This chapter introduces the fundamental concepts and skills necessary to work productively in the Windows environment. While reading this chapter, you will familiarize yourself with the components of the Windows screen, learn how to start the program, understand what an icon is (a graphical symbol used in the Windows environment), use the mouse and keyboard, understand the use of dialog boxes, and exit the Windows program.

Objective 1: Starting Windows

Depending on the configuration of your computer system, Windows may automatically start up when you turn the computer on. If this is not the case, you will need to tell the operating system where to find Windows.

Exercise 1: Starting Windows

To start Windows from the DOS prompt, do the following:

1. At the C:>\ prompt, type CD\WINDOWS.

   This command places you in the Windows subdirectory.
2. At the C:\Windows> prompt, type WIN.
3. Press ↵ ENTER.

   The Windows logo appears, followed by the initial Windows screen (see Figures 1.1 and 1.2).

TIP Your screen may look like either Figure 1-1 or Figure 1-2. But if your opening screen does not look exactly like these figures, don't worry. Windows normally returns to previous display settings, which may have been customized to suit an individual's preferences in a previous Windows session. Also the group icons, which are the little boxes that contain icons shown at the bottom of the Program Manager window, may vary according to the particular applications that are currently installed on your computer. The Program Manager always runs while you are in Windows; it is responsible for managing all other Windows applications.

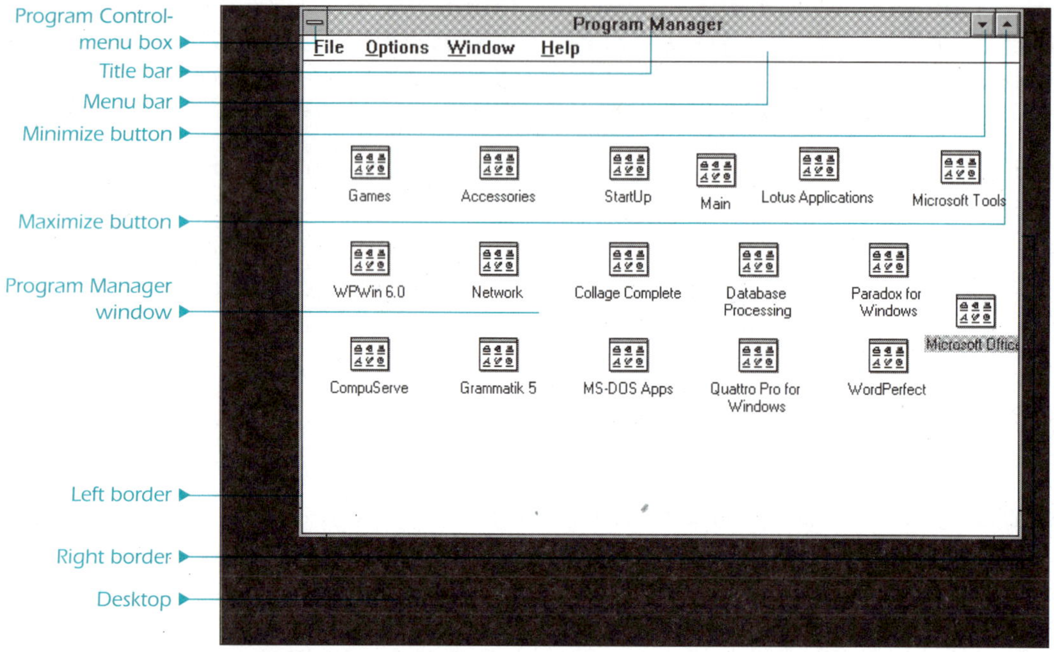

Figure 1-1 **The Program Manager window and group window icons**

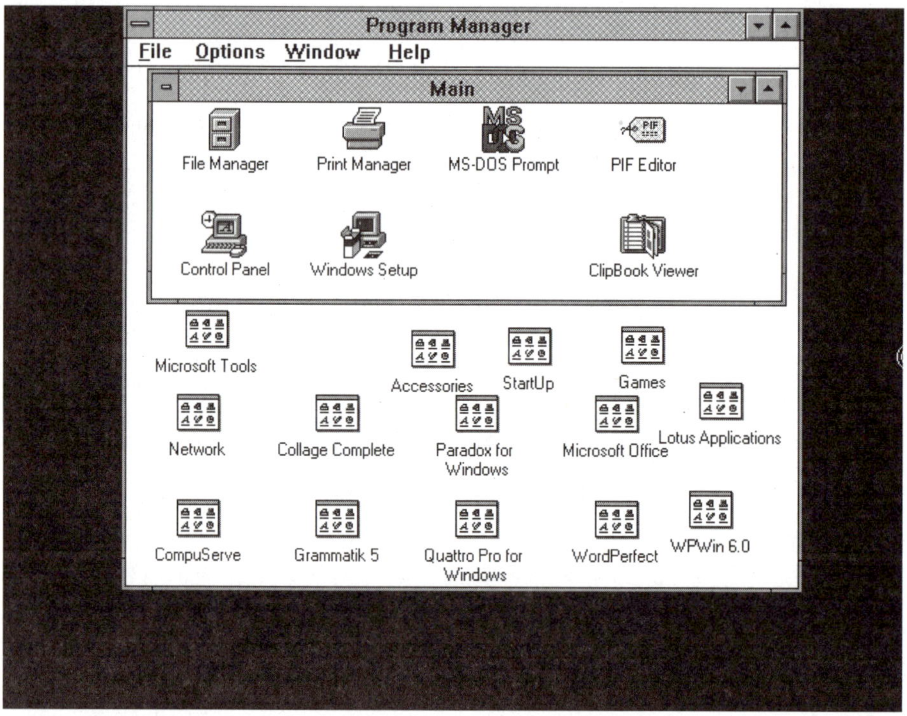

Figure 1-2 **The Program Manager window, the Main group window, and group window icons**

Types of Windows

application window Windows provides two basic types of windows: application windows and document windows. An *application window* is used to display an application that is currently running and can include more than one document window. An application window has a menu bar that controls elements in a document window. The Program Manager window is an example of an application window.

document window A *document window* is a window inside an application window. The Main and Accessories windows are document windows within the Program Manager application window. Document windows are easy to identify because they do not include their own menu bars; they use the menu bar of the application that is running them. Document windows can also be group windows because they can contain a set of applications. For example, the Accessories window could be considered a group window because it contains various applications such as Write, Paintbrush, Cardfile, and Notepad.

Objective 2: Using the Mouse and Keyboard

Both the mouse and keyboard can be used in the Windows environment to perform various tasks, although the mouse is usually the preferred method. The mouse is a pointing device that enables you to quickly move from one document to another, activate commands, and choose options by clicking, double-clicking, and dragging. The keyboard does not have as many capabilities as the mouse and can be clumsy and difficult to work with in Windows. This book focuses on using the mouse for most of the exercises.

Using the mouse

A mouse can have one, two, or three buttons, depending on its manufacturer. The left mouse button is used most often. The following list describes the typical mouse actions.

MOUSE ACTION	DESCRIPTION
Clicking	Pressing and releasing the left mouse button once
Double-clicking	Pressing and releasing the left mouse button twice in rapid succession
Dragging	Pressing and holding down the left mouse button as you move the mouse pointer across the screen

mouse pointer The mouse controls the *mouse pointer*, a small graphic that moves across your screen as you move the mouse across a flat surface. The mouse pointer changes its shape depending on its position on the screen and the task that you are trying to perform. A summary of the various mouse shapes and what each represents is given in Table 1-1.

Table 1-1 Mouse pointer shapes

MOUSE POINTER SHAPE	ACTION
	A single arrow used to point to various screen elements
	A double-headed horizontal arrow use to drag the left or right border of a window to increase or decrease the width of the window
	A double-headed vertical arrow used to drag the top or bottom border of a window to increase or decrease the height of the window
	A diagonal double-headed arrow used to drag the corner of a window to increase or decrease the width and height of a window at the same time
	A four-headed cross used to drag a window to a new location

Exercise 2: Moving the mouse across the Windows screen

In this exercise, you will move the mouse across the screen to explore the different components of the screen.

1. Move the mouse back and forth across a flat surface.

   The mouse pointer is displayed as a single arrow  , which moves according to the movements of the mouse.
2. Point to a group icon in the Program Manager window and click once to select it.

   The name beneath the group icon is highlighted, indicating that it is active.

Using the keyboard

The keyboard can also be used to manipulate the Windows. With the keyboard, you can press various keys and key combinations to invoke different commands. The corresponding keyboard shortcut can be found to the right of any option on a pull-down menu. Function keys—such as F1, F2, F3—as well as key combinations—such as Alt+F, Ctrl+S—can be used to invoke a command. In this book, key combinations are shown with a plus sign (+) between keys. The plus sign means that the user is to (1) press and *hold down* the first key indicated, (2) press the second key, and (3) release both keys.

Objective 3: Looking at the Windows Screen

The world of Windows brings with it many new and exciting concepts. One of the major features of the program is the various graphical components that are part of the Windows screen. Before you begin using the program, you need to be able to identify certain key elements on the screen.

This section defines the different components that you will find on the Windows screen. Refer to Figure 1-2 to see the items listed below.

The Windows desktop

desktop The Windows *desktop* is a visual representation on your computer screen of an actual desktop at which you might work. Just as you might have various papers, documents, and files on top of a desk, you may place documents, programs, and icons on your Windows desktop. These items are displayed **windows** in rectangular boxes called *windows*. Windows can be moved, sized, stacked, or cleared off the desktop. The greatest advantage of the desktop is that it can hold several unrelated items at the same time, enabling you to switch back and forth between programs and documents.

The title bar

Each window displayed on the screen has its own title bar. The title bar appears at the very top of a window and contains the name of the document or application it represents. A screen can display multiple windows, but only one window is active at one time. The title bar of the active window appears in a highlighted color.

The menu bar

The menu bar is found beneath the Program Manager's title bar. The menu bar contains options that are specific to the window that is active.

The control menu box

In the upper, left corner of the screen, on the same line as the title bar, is the control menu box, which is a small box with a horizontal line through it. The control menu box can be used to close a window or activate a drop-down menu with commands to move, size, minimize, maximize, close, and switch between windows.

Maximize, Restore, and Minimize buttons

The Maximize button is found in the upper, right corner of a window and appears as an upward pointing arrow. You can use this button to enlarge a window to fill the screen. Once the window is enlarged to full-screen size, the Maximize button turns into a Restore button, which can be used to return the window to its previous size.

The Minimize button is found in the upper, right corner to the left of the Maximize/Restore button and is used to reduce a window to an icon.

Borders

Each window has top, bottom, and side borders. Borders can be used to make a window narrower or wider.

Application and document icons

icons

A window can contain small, graphical pictures called *icons*. Icons represent programs, files, windows, or commands. Application and document icons can be maximized to utilize the entire Windows screen or can reside on the desktop as icons that keep the application or document available while you perform various other tasks.

The Program Manager

Program Manager

Once you start the Windows program, the Program Manager appears at the top of the screen. The *Program Manager* is responsible for managing all other application programs that run under the Windows environment. The Program Manager must be running at all times while you are using Windows. If you close the Program Manager window, the Windows program terminates and returns you to the DOS prompt. We will discuss the Program Manager in Chapter 3.

Group icons

Inside the Program Manager window are icons that resemble small boxes with icons inside of them. These are called group icons and they represent other application programs or other windows.

Scroll bars

Scroll bars appear on a window when the contents of the window will not fit completely within the window's frame. A window may display a vertical scroll bar on the right side of the window, a horizontal scroll bar on the bottom of the window, or both. Each scroll bar has a scroll box to enable you to scroll quickly.

Exercise 3: Moving through components in the Windows screen

In the following exercise, you will point to components of the screen and perform tasks with the mouse pointer.

1. Position the mouse pointer over the title bar of the Program Manager window and drag the pointer down one inch. This action moves the entire window.
2. Position the mouse pointer on the right border of the Program Manager window. The pointer becomes a double-headed arrow . Drag the border of the window one inch to the left. This technique enables you to resize a window's width.

Environmentally Friendly

People are becoming more environmentally conscientious—as a reaction to this growing awareness, businesses are forming throughout the United States and Europe to design and create ways to recycle and reuse PC components.

One of the newest ideas is the echomachine, for manufacturing clean chips, disassembling PCs, recycling plastic components such as floppy disks and CD ROMS, and finding procedures to guarantee the safe disposal of waste from circuit-board products.

3. Position the mouse pointer in the lower, right corner of the Program Manager window until it becomes a diagonal, double-headed arrow. Drag the corner of the window one inch diagonally upward and to the left to resize the window's length and width.
4. Resize the window (making it smaller) until both vertical and horizontal scroll bars appear. *You may have to reduce the size of the window significantly.*
5. Click ↓ on the vertical scroll bar.

   The contents of the window scroll up one line.
6. Continue clicking the vertical scroll bar arrow until you reach the bottom of the window.
7. Click ↑ on the vertical scroll bar to return to the top of the window.
8. Click → on the horizontal scroll bar.

   The contents of the window scroll to the left.
9. Click ← on the horizontal scroll bar.

   The contents of the window scroll to the right.
10. Position the mouse pointer on the vertical scroll box and drag it up and down.

    Notice how the contents of the window scroll quickly to a new position.

Objective 4: Working with Menus

Windows uses three types of menus: menu bars, pull-down menus, and control menus.

Menu bars and pull-down menus

Menu bars are found beneath the title bar of a window. They include options that pertain to the particular window being used. When selecting an option from a menu bar, additional related options are displayed on a pull-down menu (see Figure 1-3). The Program Manager menu bar, which is found directly beneath the Program Manager title bar, is an example of a menu bar. This menu bar includes the options File, Options, Window, and Help. Pressing a menu bar option causes a pull-down menu to appear.

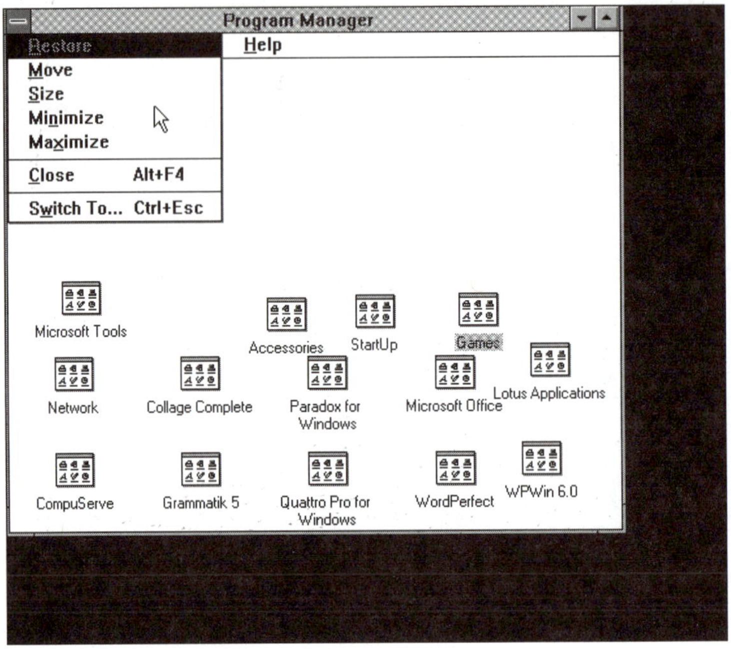

Figure 1-3 A pull-down menu

The following list describes what an option found on a pull-down menu may be.

OPTION	DESCRIPTION
A dimmed option	These are currently unavailable for use.
An option followed by an ellipsis	This option requires additional information to carry out a command.
A checkmark option	This option acts as a toggle switch. A checkmark beside the option indicates that the option is active. When you select the option again, the checkmark disappears indicating the option has been deactivated.
An option followed by text	The text is the keyboard shortcut used for that particular option.

A right triangle next to a command when clicked on activates an additional submenu that contains commands pertaining to the command on the pull-down menu.

Exercise 4: Using the menu bar and pull-down menus

To activate the menu bar and generate pull-down menus, do the following:

1. Click the File option in the Program Manager menu bar.

   The File pull-down menu appears.

2. Click the File option in the menu bar again to cancel the pull-down menu.
3. Click the Options option in the Program Manager menu bar to activate the pull-down menu.
4. This time, press ESC on the keyboard to cancel the pull-down menu.
5. Use → on the keyboard to move to the Window option in the Program Manager menu bar. Press W, which is the underlined letter, to activate the pull-down menu.
6. Press ESC or click Window from the menu bar to cancel the pull-down menu.

Exercise 5: Using the keyboard and the mouse to activate menus

In the following exercise, you will use keyboard shortcuts to activate a menu.

1. Press ALT+F to access the File pull-down menu.
2. Press ALT+↵ ENTER to access the Properties dialog box. (Dialog boxes will be discussed in Chapter 3.)
3. Press ESC to remove the dialog box.
4. Press ALT to activate the menu bar.

   Notice the File option is highlighted.
5. Use → and ← on the keyboard to move from one menu option to the next.
6. Press ESC to deactivate the menu bar.

Control menus

A control menu box containing a hyphen is located in the upper, left corner of every window. When activated, the control menu box displays a control menu, a pull-down menu that includes options for closing, moving, and controlling the size of the window (see Figure 1-4). Options for control menu boxes are covered in more detail in Chapter 2.

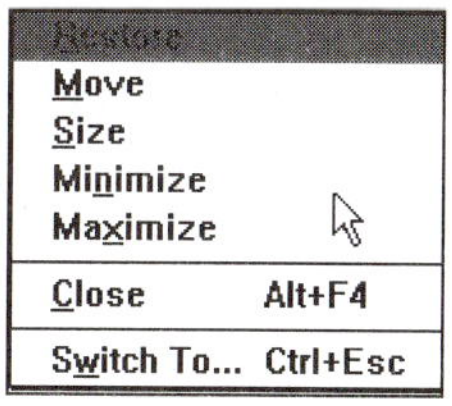

Figure 1-4 **The control menu**

Exercise 6: Activating a control menu box

1. Click the control menu box found in the upper, left corner of the title bar of the Program Manager window to display the pull-down control menu.

   The options for controlling a window are displayed.

2. Click on the control menu box again to cancel the pull-down menu.
3. Press ALT.

   The control menu box hyphen becomes dimmed.
4. Press → over each of the menu options in the menu bar until the Program Manager hyphen becomes dimmed.
5. Press SPACEBAR.

   The control menu appears. You can activate menu options using the keyboard by pressing the underlined key of the desired menu option.
6. Press ESC to cancel the pull-down menu for the control menu box.

Objective 5: Closing a Window and Exiting the Program

When you no longer need a window, you should close it so that the desktop remains uncluttered. You will find it easier to work on a clean desktop in Windows. The procedures for closing both document and application windows are the same. You can double-click the control menu box or click the control menu box and select the Close option from the pull-down menu. When you close a program window, any document windows within it will also close. If any changes have been made to a document, you will be prompted to save the changes before closing.

Exercise 7: Closing a window

To close the Main window from the Program Manager window, do the following:

1. Click the control menu box in the Main group window to activate the pull-down menu.
2. Choose Close.

   The Main group window disappears.

Exercise 8: Exiting the Windows program

There are two different methods you can use to exit Windows. To practice each of these methods, do the following:

1. Double-click the Program Manager control menu box.

   The End Windows Session message box is displayed.
2. Choose OK to exit the program.

   The system returns to the DOS prompt.
3. Type win and press ↵ ENTER.

   You are returned to the Program Manager window.
4. Choose File, and then choose Exit Windows.

   You are returned to the DOS prompt.

Chapter Summary

In this chapter, you learned how to start the Windows program and recognize the different parts of the Windows screen. You also learned how to use the mouse, work with menus, close windows, and exit the program.

Review Questions

True/False Questions

_____ 1. A document window can contain more than one application at a time.

_____ 2. A document window is found inside an application window.

_____ 3. The Program Manager must be running in order for other Windows applications to run.

_____ 4. More than one option button can be selected at one time.

_____ 5. Keyboard shortcuts are found to the left of an option in a pull-down menu.

Multiple-Choice Questions

_____ 6. Options on a pull-down menu that are dimmed

A. are unavailable at the current time.

B. have an associated dialog box.

C. act as toggle switches.

D. none of the above

_____ 7. To activate the pull-down menu for the File option in the Program Manager menu bar, press

A. ALT+F

B. CTRL+F1

C. ALT+F1

D. CTRL+F

_____ 8. The control menu box includes all the following options except

A. Move.

B. Size.

C. Edit.

D. Close.

____ 9. The Maximize button looks like a(n)
   A. down arrow.
   B. up arrow.
   C. double-headed arrow.
   D. hyphen.

____ 10. Document windows do not include their own
   A. title bar.
   B. scroll bars.
   C. menu bar.
   D. control menu box.

Fill-in-the-blank Questions

11. To start the Windows program, type ____________ at the DOS prompt.
12. The two basic types of windows are ____________ and ____________.
13. The graphical symbols used by Windows are called ____________.
14. To press and release the left mouse button twice in rapid succession is to ____________ ____________.
15. To narrow or widen a window, the mouse pointer must be in the shape of a ____________ arrow.

Acumen-Building Activities

Quick Projects

1. Using the Main window

1. Double-click the Main group icon to open the window.
2. Drag the borders of the Main window to resize it.
3. Click the control menu box of the Main window to display the pull-down menu.
4. Press ESC to cancel the pull-down menu.

2. Comparing desktops

Write a paragraph comparing a physical desktop with papers, files, and folders on it to the Window's visual desktop. Explain how they resemble one another.

3. Resizing a window

Resize the Program Manager window until both the vertical and horizontal scroll bars can be seen.

4. Closing a window

1. Close a window using the mouse.
2. Reopen the window and close it using the keyboard.

In-Depth Projects

1. Using Windows

1. Start the Windows program.
2. Using the mouse, activate a pull-down menu, and then cancel it.
3. Using the keyboard, activate the menu bar and a pull-down menu.
4. Exit the program.
5. Record the steps used to perform these actions.

2. Observing the changes in the mouse pointer

1. With the mouse pointer, point to the following components of the Windows screen and describe what shape the mouse pointer becomes as you do so:

    title bar
    borders
    corner of a window

Chapter 2

Working in Windows

Objectives

- Minimizing, Maximizing, and Restoring Windows
- Using Control Menu Box Options
- Using Icons
- Getting Help

Key Terms

TERM	DEFINITION
Control Menu Box	a boxed hyphen in the upper, left corner of a window that is used to close a window and also provides a menu to close, move, size, minimize, and maximize a window
Program-Group Icon	a graphical symbol appearing as a small window in the Program Manager window that contains a set of related applications or programs
Program-Item Icon	a graphical symbol that represents a program that is currently not running; clicking an icon launches a program or opens a document file
Program Document Icon	a graphical symbol on the desktop representing a program that is currently running but has been minimized
Hypertext	Help screen text that, when clicked with the mouse, activates an additional screen of information about the subject in question

Windows is a highly versatile environment that enables you to customize the screen to your liking. This chapter teaches the various ways to maximize, minimize, and restore windows and how to work with icons. It also introduces the many Help features available in Windows so that you can work effectively in this environment.

Objective 1: Minimizing, Maximizing, and Restoring Windows

Since the Windows program enables you to display multiple windows at one time, you may find yourself working on a cluttered screen with too many windows displayed at once. Or you may want to fill the screen with a single window. To address these issues, Windows provides the Minimize, Maximize, and Restore buttons.

The Minimize button

The Minimize button is found in the upper, right corner of the title bar as a downward-pointing arrow. You can use the Minimize button to reduce a program or document window to an icon on the desktop, thus freeing up space on the screen.

Exercise 1: Minimizing a window

To minimize the Program Manager window, do the following:

1. Click the Minimize button  in the upper, right corner of the Program Manager window.

   The Program Manager is reduced to an icon at the bottom of the desktop (see Figure 2-1).

Figure 2-1 The Program Manager window reduced to an icon on the desktop

2. Double-click the Program Manager icon to enlarge it to its previous window size.

The Maximize and Restore buttons

The Maximize button, which appears as an upward-pointing arrow, is found to the right of the Minimize button in the upper, right corner of the title bar. If a window does not fill the screen, the Maximize button is available. Clicking the Maximize button in a document or application window causes the window to fill the entire screen.

Whenever a window is maximized to use the full screen, the Maximize button becomes the Restore button. The Restore button appears as a double-headed arrow and is used to restore the window to its previous display size (see Figure 2-2).

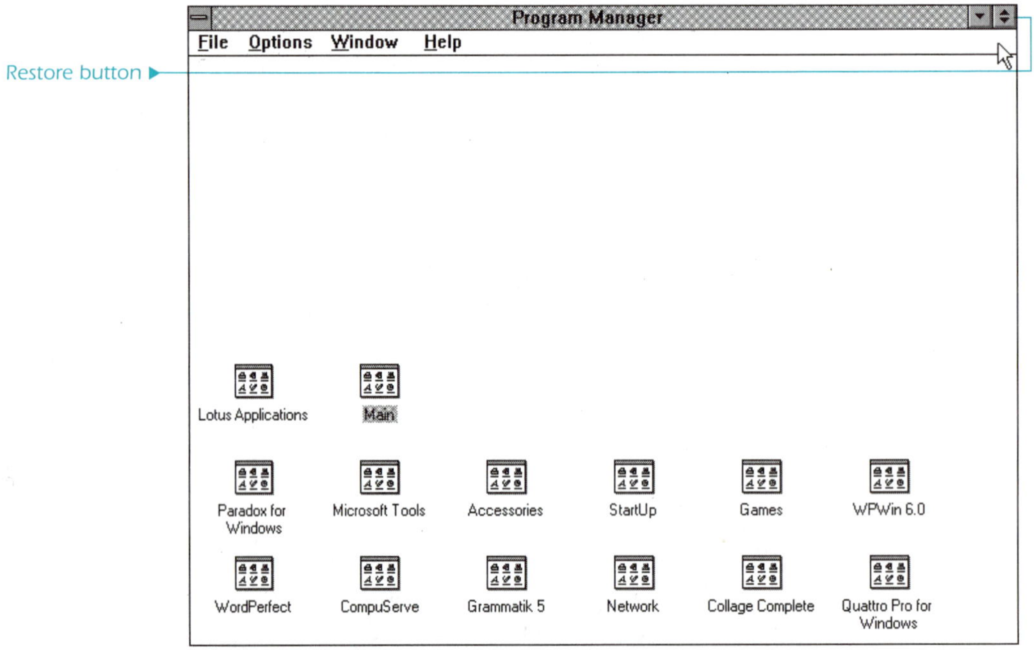

Figure 2-2 The window is enlarged to fill the entire screen

Exercise 2: Maximizing and restoring a window

To demonstrate maximizing and restoring a window, perform the following steps:

1. Click the Maximize button , which is the upward-pointing arrow in the Main window.

   The Main window enlarges to fill the screen. Notice also that the word `[Main]` is now displayed in the Program Manager's title bar.

Remember that the Program Manager must always be running in order for the Windows program to work; therefore, the Program Manager is still running, but the Main window is using the full screen.

2. Click the Restore button in the upper, right corner of the Main window title bar.

   The Main window is restored to its previous size within the Program Manager window.

TIP You can maximize and restore a window by double-clicking the window's title bar.

Objective 2: Using Control Menu Box Options

control menu box A *control menu box* is a boxed hyphen in the upper, left corner of a window that is used to close a window. It also provides a pull-down menu with the following options: Restore, Move, Size, Minimize, Maximize, Close, and Switch To. Table 2-1 defines each option in the control menu box pull-down menu.

Table 2-1 The control menu box options

OPTION	DESCRIPTION
Restore	Restores a window to its previous size after minimizing it or maximizing it.
Move	Enables you to use the keyboard to relocate a window on the desktop.
Size	Enables you to use the keyboard to change the size of a window on the desktop.
Minimize	Reduces the window to an icon.
Maximize	Enlarges a window to fill the screen.
Close	Closes a window.
Switch To	Displays the Task List dialog box that enables you to quickly switch from one running application to another. This option is especially useful when there are applications running that are not visible because they are hidden by other windows.
Next	Enables you to switch from one open document to the next. This option is found only on a document control menu box.

The Move and Size options

The Move and Size options on the pull-down menu of the control menu box enable you to move and resize a window using the keyboard. When these options are activated, the mouse pointer turns into a pointed cross. You can then use the arrow keys on the keyboard to move the window to a different location on the screen or resize the window.

Exercise 3: Moving and sizing a window

To move and size a woindow, do the following:

1. Click the control menu box in the Program Manager window and choose Move.

   The mouse pointer turns into a pointed cross .
2. Press each of the arrow keys in turn to move the window to the right, left, up, and down.
3. Press ENTER to accept the window's new position.
4. Click the control menu box in the Program Manager window and choose Size.

   The mouse turns into a pointed cross.
5. Press each of the arrow keys in turn to make the window wider, narrower, shorter, or longer.
6. Press ENTER to accept the new size.

Objective 3: Using Icons

Windows uses icons extensively. Icons can be moved and arranged using the mouse or the menu bar. Icons can also be created and deleted from a window; this is discussed in Chapter 3.

Program-group icons

program-group icon

When you first start the Windows program, the Program Manager usually appears displaying various program-group icons within it (see Figure 2-3). A *program-group icon* is a graphical symbol appearing as a small window in the Program Manager window that contains a set of related applications or programs. The name of each group of applications is found below each program-group icon. A program-group icon can be opened up into a group

FEATURE

The Auto Arrange option

If you have trouble moving icons around on the screen because they keep repositioning themselves, check to see if the Auto Arrange option (found on the Options pull-down menu of the Program Manager menu bar) has a checkmark to the left of it. This option acts as a toggle switch and can be activated by clicking it once and then deactivated by clicking it again. When the Auto Arrange option is activated, it positions icons at the top of the window you are using. regardless of where you try to position them with the mouse.

window by double-clicking it from the Program Manager window or clicking it once and then choosing Restore from the pop-up menu. Once the window is open, you can reduce it to a program group-icon by pressing the Minimize button on the opened group window.

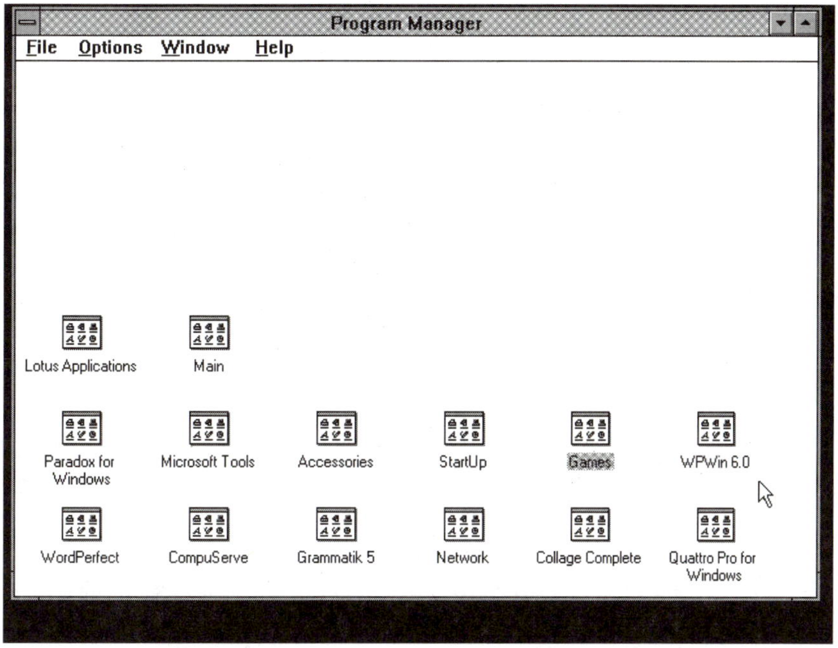

Figure 2-3 Program-group icons within the Program Manager window

Exercise 4: Opening group windows using icons

Icons can be used to open group windows that contain sets of programs. To open the Accessories and Games windows, perform the following steps:

1. Find the Accessories group icon in the Program Manager window.
2. Double-click the Accessories group icon .

   The Accessories window opens within the Program Manager window.
3. Find the Games group icon in the Program Manager window.
4. Click the Games group icon .

   A pop-up menu appears.
5. Choose Restore.

   The Games window opens within the Program Manager window.
6. Click the Minimize buttons  of the Accessories and Games windows to reduce both to their group icons in the Program Manager window.

Program-item icons

program-item icon

A *program-item icon* is a graphical symbol that represents a program that is currently not running. Program-item icons are used to launch programs into main memory. There can be several program-item icons in one group window. By double-clicking a program item icon from a group window, you can begin running the program. While the program is running, its window can fill the screen or be minimized to an icon on the desktop.

Exercise 5: Using a program-item icon to start a program

To practice starting a program using an program-item icon, you will use the Write program, which comes with the Windows program and is found in the Accessories group window.

1. Double-click the Accessories group icon 

from the Program Manager window to open the Accessories window.
2. Double-click the Write program item icon 

to start the Write program (see Figure 2-4).

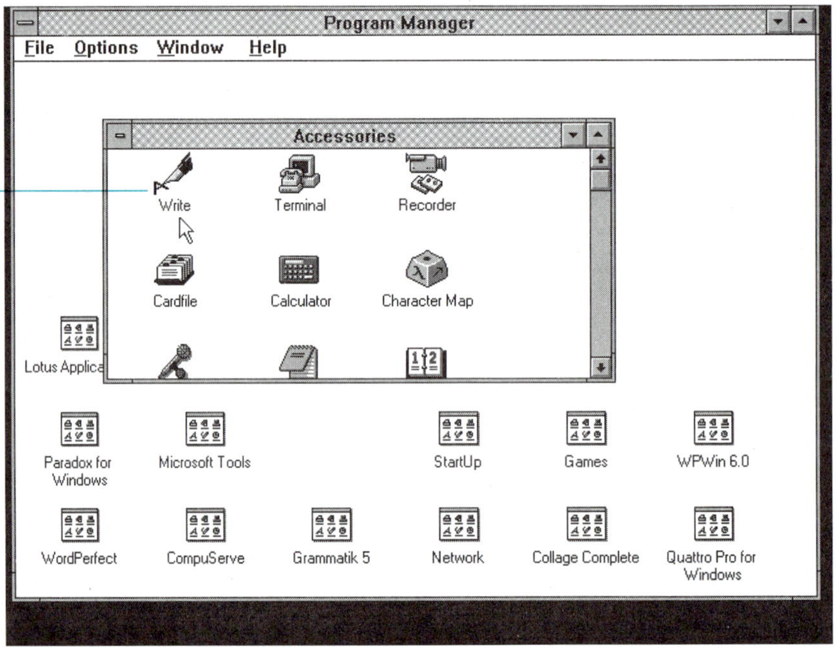

The Write program item icon

Figure 2-4 The Write program-item icon

An hourglass appears as the program is started. After the program has successfully started, the Write program title bar and a blank document window are displayed on the screen.

3. Double-click the Notepad program-item icon 

in the Accessories window.

The Notepad program is started, and the Notepad document window is displayed (see Figure 2-5).

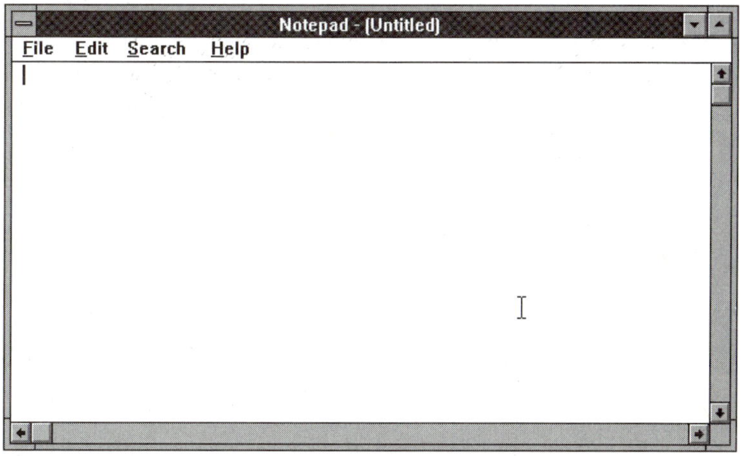

Figure 2-5 The Notepad program document window

Exercise 6: Moving icons in a window

Icons can be moved within a window using the mouse. To move icons using the mouse, do the following:

1. Find the Accessories group icon  in the Program Manager window.
2. Use the mouse to drag the Accessories group icon to a different area in the Program Manager window.
3. Find the Games group icon  in the Program Manager window.
4. Use the mouse to drag the Games group icon to a different area in the Program Manager window.
5. Open the Main window and use the mouse to drag the File Manager icon  and the Control Panel icon  to the right side of the window.

   The group icons should appear scattered in the Program Manager window and the program-item icons (File Manager and Control Panel) should be located on the right side of the Main window.

Using the Arrange Icons option

As you have seen, you can move icons from one place to another by dragging them with the mouse. When you arrange icons with the mouse, you may accidentally obscure an icon from view. To remedy this situation, you can use the Arrange Icons option on the Window pull-down menu on the Program Manager menu bar. The Arrange Icons option rearranges group window icons across the bottom of the Program Manager window and program-item icons across the top of their group window.

Exercise 7: Automatically rearranging icons in a window

To rearrange icons automatically within a window, perform the following steps:

1. Make the Main window the active window.
2. Choose the Window option from the menu bar.
3. Choose Arrange Icons.

   The program-item icons rearrange themselves evenly across the top of the Main window.
4. Close the Main window.

   The Program Manager window is the only active window.
5. Choose Window from the menu bar, and then choose Arrange Icons (see Figure 2-6).

   The group icons in the Program Manager window rearrange themselves evenly across the bottom of the window.

Arrange Icons option ▶

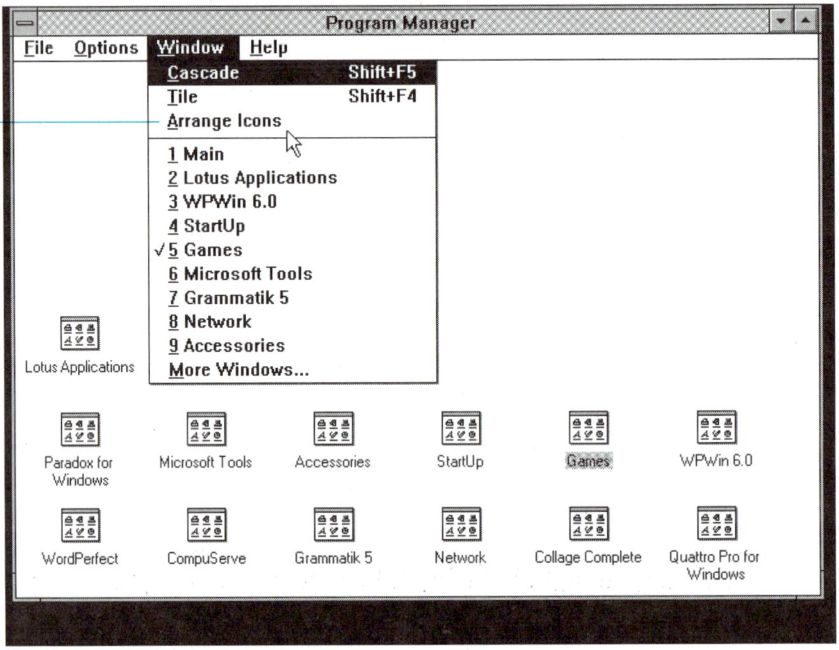

Figure 2-6 The Arrange Icons option

Program-document icons

program-document icon

A *program-document icon* is a graphical symbol on the desktop representing a program that is currently running but has been minimized. Many programs allow you to open several documents at a time. By reducing a document to an icon, you are able to free up screen space, thus enabling you to perform other tasks. Imagine that you are preparing a report in a word processing program. You decide to refer in your report to information that has been compiled in a spreadsheet program. With Windows, you can temporarily switch to the spreadsheet document to view the information you need without having to exit the word processing document. You simply reduce the word processing document to an icon and bring up the spreadsheet document to get the needed information. When you are finished viewing the spreadsheet document, you can return the word processing document to the screen by clicking the word processing program-document icon.

Exercise 8: Reducing document icons on the desktop

To reduce the two currently open windows (Notepad and Write) to program document icons, do the following:

1. Click the Minimize button on the Write program title bar to reduce the program document to an icon on the desktop.
2. Click the Minimize button on the Notepad document window to reduce it to a program document icon on the desktop (see Figure 2-7).

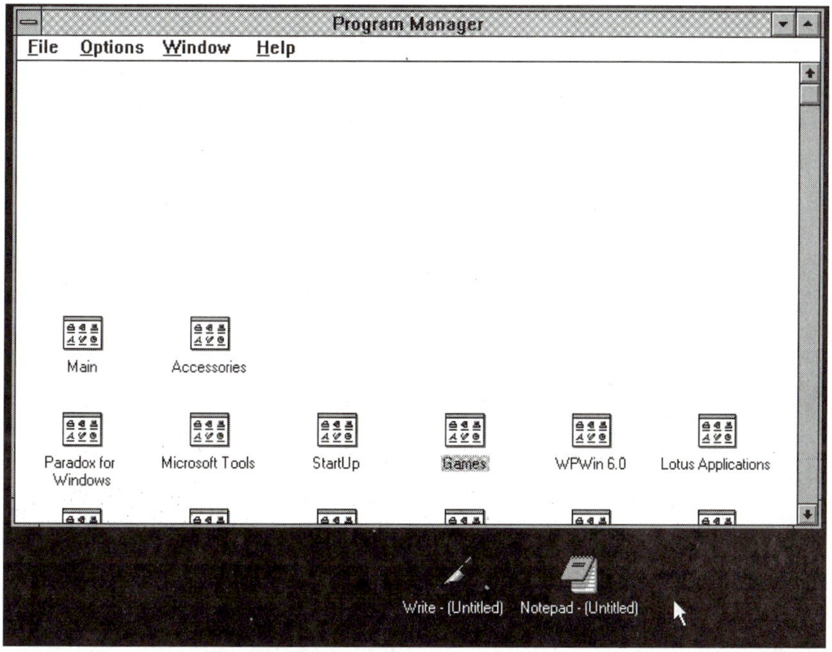

Figure 2-7 The Write and Notepad program-document windows reduced to icons on the desktop

The icons for the Write and Notepad program-document windows are displayed on the desktop under the Program Manager window with the document name Untitled next to each icon. If you cannot see the icons, resize the Program Manager window to a smaller size so that more of the desktop is visible.

3. Click the Write program-document icon Write to display the pop-up menu.
4. Choose Close.

5. Click the Notepad program document icon to display the pop-up menu.
6. Choose Close.

   The Write and Notepad programs are closed and the icons are removed from the desktop. By closing the windows, you exit the programs. Once you exit a program, it is no longer running; only currently running program windows are displayed as icons. If you had typed information in either document window, you would have been prompted to save the information before closing the window.

TIP The word *Untitled*, which may appear next to a program document icon, indicates that the document has not yet been given a unique name and saved. Once a document is saved, the name that is given to the document appears next to the program document icon on the desktop.

Objective 4: Getting Help

Windows offers an extensive on-line Help system to answer your questions and to aid you while working in the program. The Help option is always found on the far right of a Windows menu bar. Each Windows application has its own Help menu system; information provided by each Help system varies. All Help options operate in the same manner, regardless of the application in which each is found.

Options on the Help pull-down menu

The following options are found on the Program Manager Help menu:

OPTION	DESCRIPTION
Contents	Provides a listing of help topics for the current application.
Search for Help on...	Displays the Search dialog box. You can type the name of a help topic or scroll through a list of help topics and choose one.
How to Use Help	Displays a list of help topics from which you can choose. Each topic explains how to use a specific feature of the Help system.
Windows Tutorial	Takes you through step-by-step procedures for performing different functions of the Windows program.
About Program Manager	Lists the version number of the software, the registered user's name, the mode the software is running in, the amount of available memory, and the amount of available system resources. When you request technical support for Windows from the manufacturer, Microsoft, you will often be asked to provide the information on this screen.

Exercise 9: Using the Help menu

To use the Windows Help menu, do the following:

1. Click Help in the Program Manager menu bar.

TIP You can also press F1 to access the Help system.

The Help pull-down menu is displayed (see Figure 2-8).

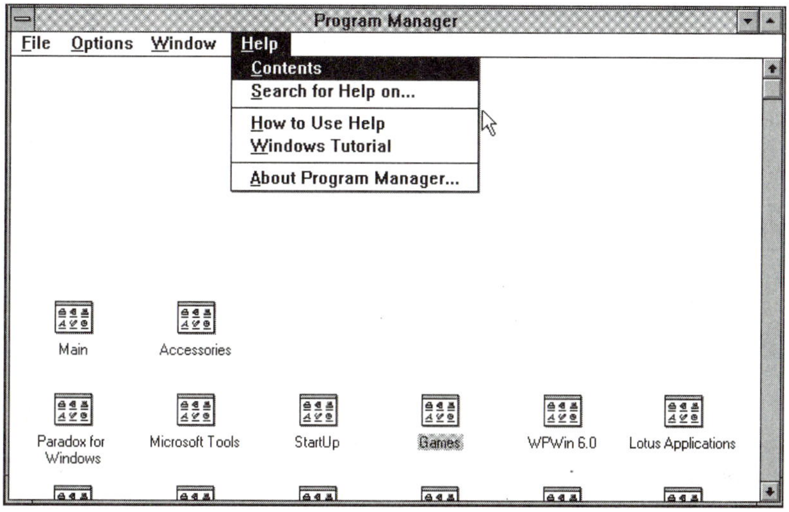

Figure 2-8 The Program Manager Help menu

2. Click Contents.

   The Contents for Program Manager screen appears (see Figure 2-9).

Click on solid underlined items to activate additional screens of information

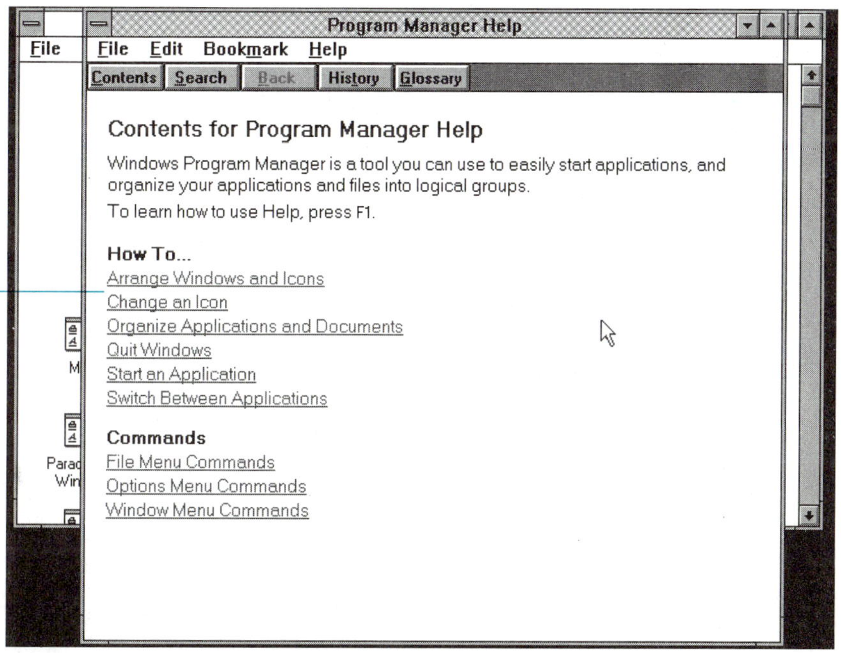

Figure 2-9 The Contents for Program Manager screen

Hypertext

hypertext Help screens often display text as hypertext. *Hypertext* is text that, when clicked with the mouse, activates an additional screen of information about a query topic. Hypertext words and phrases appear with a solid or dashed underline. When you click hypertext that has a solid underline, a screen of additional information on that topic appears. When you click hypertext that has a dashed underline, a small definition box pops up on the screen to explain what the word or phrase means. On a color monitor, hypertext appears in green.

Exercise 10: Using hypertext

Make sure the Contents for Program Manager screen is displayed. To use hypertext to learn more about a topic or term, do the following:

1. Click Arrange Windows and Icons.

   The mouse pointer changes to a pointing finger , and a new help screen appears with information on arranging windows and icons.
2. Click title bar.

   A small pop-up box is displayed containing the definition of title bar.
3. Click the definition box to remove it from the screen.

Using Help buttons

Each help window displays five command buttons that are used to perform various tasks. These buttons are the Contents, Search, Back, History, and Glossary buttons.

The Search Button

When activated, the Search Command button displays the Search dialog box, which prompts you for information. You may respond by typing a word that refers to the topic you want to view or highlighting a topic from a list of help topics.

Exercise 11: Searching for information

To activate the Search dialog box from the Arranging Windows and Icons help screen, do the following:

1. Choose the Search command button.

   The Search dialog box appears displaying a list of topics in the top box (see Figure 2-10).

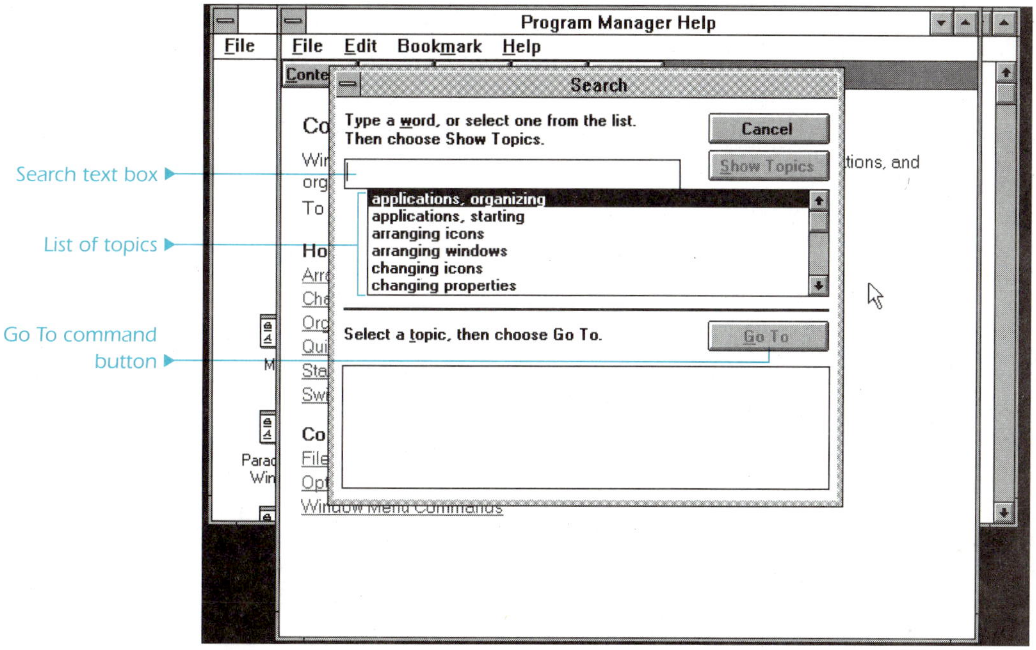

Figure 2-10 The Search dialog box

2. Select Changing Icons.
3. Choose the Show Topics command button.

   The lower box displays the topics related to changing an icon.
4. Select Changing an Icon, which is located in the lower box.
5. Choose the Go To command box.

   A help screen on changing an icon is displayed.

The Back command button

The Back command button is found in each help screen; when chosen, it returns you to the previous help screen. Each time you press the Back command button, it takes you back one screen until all previous screens have been displayed.

Exercise 12: Moving back to a previous screen

To practice using the Back command button, do the following:

1. Choose the Back command button.

   The previous screen (Arranging Windows and Icons) is displayed.
2. Continue choosing the Back command button until you have viewed all previous help screens. The command button will appear dimmed once you have displayed all previous screens.

The History command button

The History command button can be used to access a listing of previously viewed screens, in the order in which they were viewed. You can then select a topic from the list to return automatically to the help screen of your choice.

Exercise 13: Locating a previous screen

To use the History command button, do the following:

1. Choose the History command button.

   The Windows Help History window displays a listing of previously viewed help topics in the order in which they were viewed (see Figure 2-11).

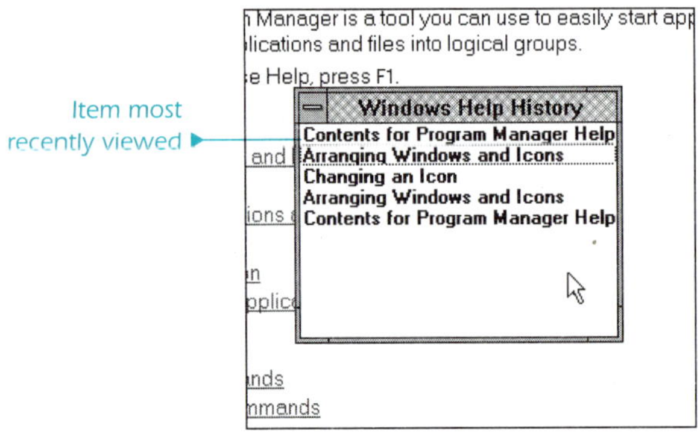

Figure 2-11 The Windows Help History window

2. Double-click the Arranging Windows and Icons topic.

   You are returned to the help screen related to that topic.

The Glossary command button

The Glossary command button can be used to look up words or phrases. Words and phrases are listed in alphabetical order in the Glossary window. When you select a word from the Glossary window, a definition box appears defining the word.

Exercise 14: Looking up words

To find the definition of the word *icon*, do the following:

1. Choose the Glossary command button.

   The Glossary window is displayed (see Figure 2-12).

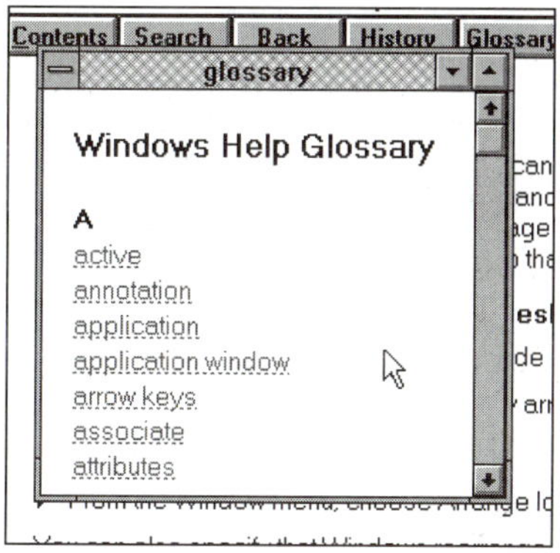

Figure 2-12 The Glossary window

2. Scroll through the list until you find the word *icon* and select it.

   A pop-up definition box appears.

3. Click the definition box to remove it from the screen.
4. Close the Glossary window.

Using the Help menu bar

Help screens are application windows; therefore, they contain their own menu bars. The options in the Help menu bar are File, Edit, Bookmark, and How to Use Help and are described in the following table.

Table 2-2 The Help menu bar options

OPTION	DESCRIPTION
File	Used to access another application's Help system from the Windows Help system.
Edit	Activates a pull-down menu, which includes the Copy and Annotate commands. The Copy command enables you to copy the information from a help screen and store it on the Clipboard. This information resides in the Clipboard until you copy something else to the Clipboard or quit Windows. You can copy information from the Clipboard and paste it to another file. The Annotate command enables you to add your own comments and reminders to an existing help topic.
Bookmark	Enables you to place a bookmark on frequently used topics so that you can return directly to them.
How to Use Help	Displays the contents for How to Use Help.

Using the Annotation feature

The Annotation feature enables you to add comments or notes to a help screen. For example, you may frequently reference help screen information on arranging icons in a group window because you often need to arrange icons in a certain way on your computer. You could add a comment to this help screen regarding the way the icons should be set up—for example, certain groups for different departments. Help screens that include annotations appear with a paper clip symbol next to the help topic.

Exercise 15: Adding an annotation to a help topic

To place an annotation next to a help topic, do the following:

1. Display the Arranging Windows and Icons help screen in the Help window.
2. Choose Edit from the menu bar.
3. Choose Annotate.

   The Annotate dialog box is displayed (see Figure 2-13).

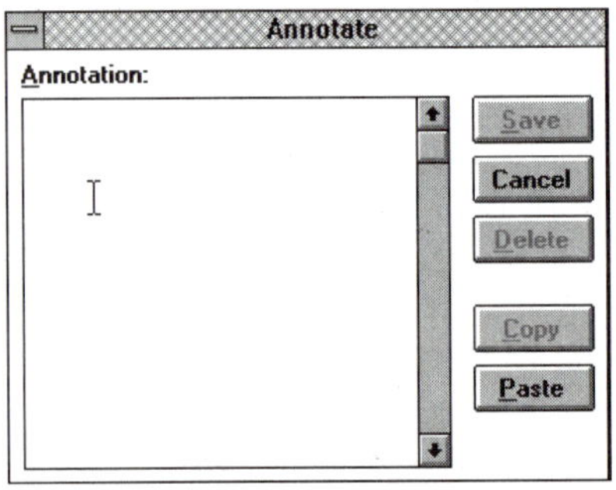

Figure 2-13 The Annotate dialog box

4. Type the following note: Be sure to name each group window according to the department that uses it, per supervisor's orders.

   The mouse pointer changes to an I-beam.
5. Choose Save from the Annotate dialog box.

   A paper clip symbol appears next to the title of the Help screen window, letting you know that there is a note attached to the help screen (see Figure 2-14).

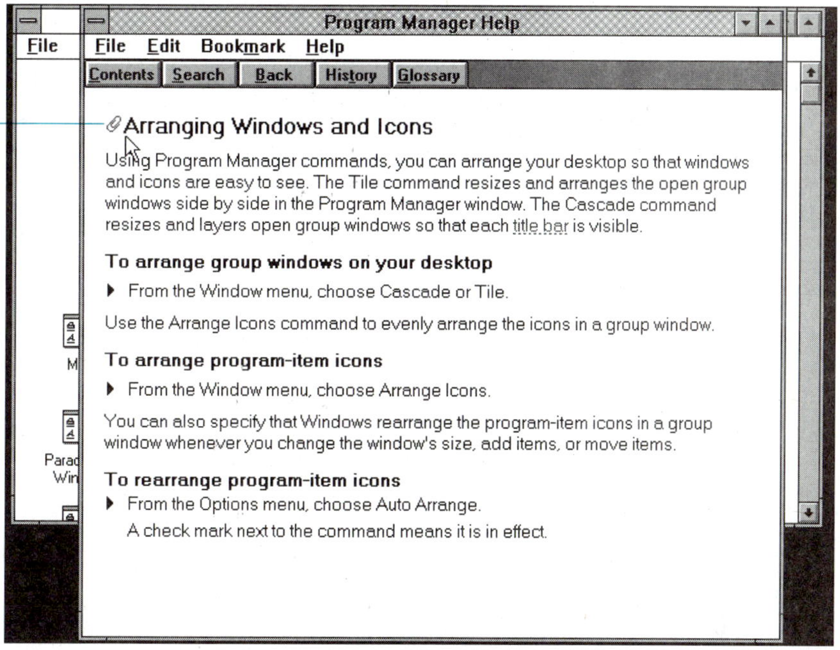

Figure 2-14 The paper clip symbol appearing next to the help screen title

Exercise 16: Viewing an annotation

To view a note attached to a help screen, do the following:

1. Double-click the paper clip .

   The note is displayed.
2. Close the Annotate window.

Printing help topics

If you refer to a help screen frequently, you may find it useful to print a copy of the help screen so that you can always have it on hand. You can print the help screen currently displayed by choosing File from the Windows Help Screen menu bar and then choosing Print Topic.

Exercise 17: Printing a help topic

To get a printed copy of the Arranging Windows and Icons help screen, do the following:

1. Choose File from the Help menu bar.

   The File pull-down menu appears.
2. Choose Print Topic.

   The Arranging Windows and Icons help screen prints out.

Getting Caught in the Web

For people who enjoy traveling on the information super highway, there is a new attraction. It's called the World Wide Web (WWW), and it's an on-line server that is accessed via the Internet with a modem. Since the Web is hooked up directly to the Internet, you can access information from all over the world.

The Web is primarily run by college students who take an interest in telecommunications. One of the prerequisites of running a Web server is that you provide information on yourself, your organization, and the type of information you will be furnishing to those accessing the Web.

The information that can be accessed includes an enormous variety of academic and scientific papers, as well as answers to frequently asked questions on almost any topic you can think of. The Web has a huge collection of graphics as well. In fact, the greatest appeal of the Web is the fact that it offers an incredible number of scanned pictures on a variety of topics.

The Bookmark menu option

The Bookmark option is found on the menu bar of the help screen. When you have a help topic to which you often refer, you can place a bookmark on that particular topic to enable you to return to it quickly.

Exercise 18: Assigning a bookmark

To assign a bookmark to a help topic, do the following:

1. Open the Help menu and choose the Contents button.
2. Choose Start An Application from the How to... listing.

   The Starting an Application help screen is displayed.
3. Choose Bookmark from the menu bar.
4. Choose Define.

   The Define dialog box appears (see Figure 2-15).

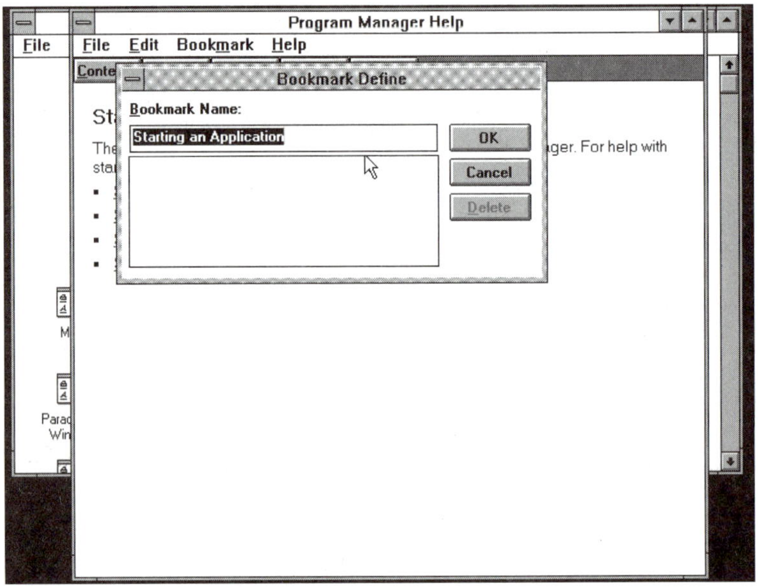

Figure 2-15 The Define dialog box

5. Choose OK to accept the default name for the bookmark.
6. Choose the Back button to return to the previous screen.
7. Choose Bookmark from the menu bar.

   A drop-down list appears, displaying the name of the bookmark you created (see Figure 2-16). Bookmarks are numbered sequentially in this list.

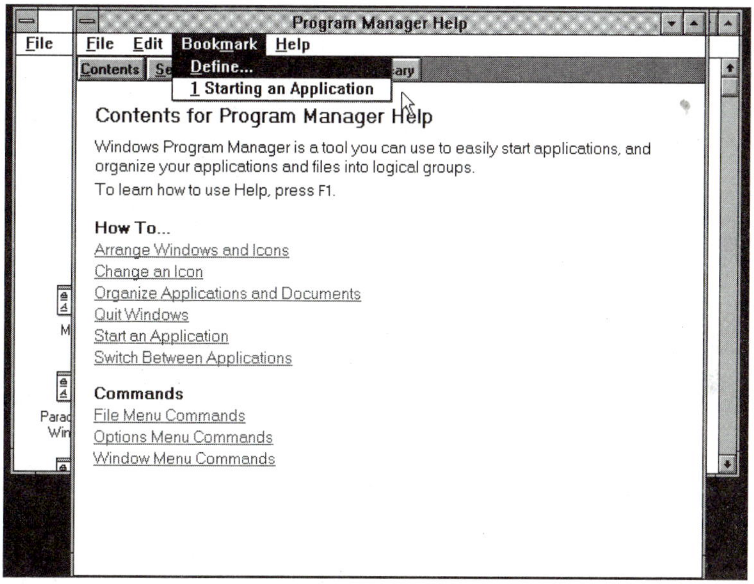

Figure 2-16 The drop-down list of bookmarks

8. Click on the bookmark name (Starting Applications) to return to the help screen for that topic.

Exercise 19: Deleting a bookmark

To remove a bookmark topic, do the following:

1. Open the Bookmark menu.
2. Choose Define.

   The Define dialog box is displayed.
3. Choose the name of the bookmark that you want to delete (Starting Applications).
4. Choose Delete, and then choose OK.

Chapter Summary

This chapter has introduced you to some of the many ways the Windows program can be manipulated. You have learned the advantages of minimizing and maximizing windows. You learned how to use the options on control menu boxes and to identify the different types of icons that are available in the Windows program. You also learned about the many help screen options that the Windows environment provides for you.

Review Questions

True/False Questions

_____ 1. When a screen is maximized, the Maximize button becomes a double-headed arrow.

_____ 2. The Move option in the pull-down menu of the control menu box enables you to move the window around the screen with the mouse.

_____ 3. By restoring a window, you reset it to its previous screen size.

_____ 4. Pressing the History button moves you back to the previous screen.

_____ 5. A group icon contains a set of related programs.

Multiple-Choice Questions

_____ 6. A small box found in the Program Manager window that contains icons and displays a name underneath is called a

A. document icon.

B. program-item icon.

C. group icon.

D. none of the above

_____ 7. The Restore option is found on the pull-down menu of the

A. control menu box

B. the Window option on the Program Manager menu bar.

C. the File option of a help screen menu bar.

D. none of the above

_____ 8. When pointing to hypertext on a help screen, the mouse pointer changes to a

A. double arrow.

B. pointing finger.

C. hourglass.

D. pointed cross.

_____ 9. When you click the Minimize button of a document window, the window

A. closes.

B. shrinks to a document window icon.

C. reduces to a smaller frame on the desktop

D. causes a prompt to appear, asking you if you want to save any changes.

_____ 10. To attach your own comments or notes to a help topic, choose the following option:

A. Bookmark.

B. Annotate.

C. Copy.

D. History.

Fill-in-the-blank Questions

11. The ______________ ______________ ______________ is a boxed hyphen in the upper left corner of a window.
12. When a window fills the entire screen, the Maximize button turns into ______________ button.
13. ______________ ______________ ______________ are used to start programs.
14. The ______________ ______________ option will cause group icons in the Program Manager window to arrange themselves evenly across the bottom of the window.
15. To access a list of previously used Help screens, click on the ______________ command button.

Acumen-Building Activities

Quick Projects

1. Using Windows

Start the Windows program and complete the following tasks:

1. Open the Accessories and Main windows.
2. Maximize the Accessories window using the appropriate command button.
3. Restore the Accessories window to its previous size.
4. Record the steps you used to perform the above tasks.

2. Using the keyboard

Complete the following exercise:

1. Use the keyboard to move the Main window to the bottom, left corner of the desktop.
2. Use the keyboard to change the size of the Main window.

3. Arranging icons

Complete the following exercise:

1. Maximize the Main window to fill the screen.
2. Using the mouse, drag the icons in the Accessories window to the middle of the window and place them very close to one another.
3. Reposition the icons automatically across the top of the screen, using the option discussed in this chapter.
4. Record the steps you used to perform the above tasks.

4. Starting an application

Complete the following exercise:

1. Open a program-group window and start an application. (You will have to choose from the software applications—such as Lotus 1-2-3, WordPerfect, Microsoft Word, Excel—that are currently installed on your computer.
2. Minimize the resulting document window to an icon.
3. Restore the document window to full-screen size and close the window.
4. Record the steps you used to perform the above tasks.

In-Depth Projects

1. Learning about Windows

Start the Windows program and do the following:

1. Search for information on quitting Windows.
2. Attach the following annotation to the Quitting Windows help screen: Make a backup disk of all newly created files after you exit the Windows program and before leaving at the end of each day.
3. Print the Quitting Windows help topic.
4. Close the help window.

2. Learning more about Windows

Complete the following exercise:

1. Start the Windows program.
2. Open the Main, Games, Accessories, and StartUp windows.
3. Use the mouse to resize and move the windows so that you can see all four windows on the screen at once.
4. Scroll to see the contents of each window.
5. Using the Help system, look up the word *font* and write down the definition that is provided.
6. Create a bookmark for the help topic Arranging Windows and Icons. Use the default name for the bookmark.
7. Remove the bookmark.

3. Practicing using Windows

Complete the following exercise:

1. Start the Windows program.
2. Have the Program Manager fill the entire screen.
3. Open the Main, Accessories, StartUp, Games, and Group windows. Place all five windows in the upper half of the Program Manager window.
4. Place all other group icons in the lower, left corner of the Program Manager window.
5. Use the command to rearrange the group icons evenly across the bottom of the Program Manager window.
6. Start the Write program and the Paintbrush program. Reduce both program windows to document icons on the desktop.
7. Restore the Program Manager screen.
8. Restore the Write and Paintbrush documents.
9. Close the Write and Paintbrush documents.
10. Close all group windows.
11. Exit Windows.

Chapter 3

Using the Program Manager

Objectives

- Understanding Program Groups
- Arranging Multiple Windows
- Creating Program Groups
- Working with Program-Item Icons
- Starting Programs Automatically and Switching between Programs
- Deleting Group Windows and Program-Item Icons

Key Terms

TERM	DEFINITION
Cascade	a Windows command that causes multiple windows to be displayed overlapping one another, each showing its own title bar.
Tile	a Windows command that causes multiple windows to be displayed so that they are arranged evenly next to one another, each showing its contents.

In Chapters 1 and 2, we began exploring the various elements of the Program Manager. The different types of icons found in the Program Manager window were introduced, and you learned how they could be manipulated. In this chapter, you will learn how to control and organize windows using the Program Manager. You will learn how to add and delete program-group icons and program-item icons in a window, move and copy icons from one window to another, and use the options on the Program Manager menu bar.

Objective 1: Understanding Program Groups

The Windows package comes equipped with four program groups: the Main, Accessories, Games, and StartUp program groups. Your screen may contain many other program groups besides these, depending on the programs that have been installed on your system. The following list briefly describes each program-group window and its purpose. The program-item icons found in each of these windows will be covered in more depth in later chapters.

The Main group window

The program icons in the Main group window help you control and manage files and printers, as well as customize the Windows desktop. They include the following icons: File Manager, MS-DOS Prompt, Print Manager, Control Panel, Clipboard Viewer, Windows Setup, and PIF Editor (see Figure 3-1).

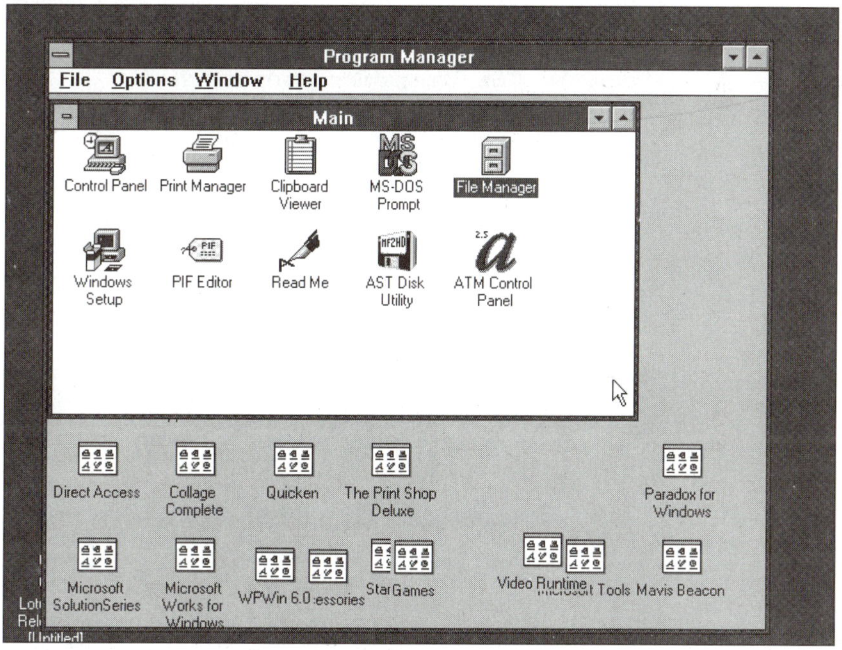

Figure 3-1 The Main group window

The Accessories group window

The icons located in the Accessories group window perform a variety of specialized tasks that can help you with your daily work. The Accessories group window includes the following programs: Write, Paintbrush, Calendar, Clock, Cardfile, Notepad, Calculator, Character Map, Media Player, Object Packager, Recorder, Sound Recorder, and Terminal (see Figure 3-2).

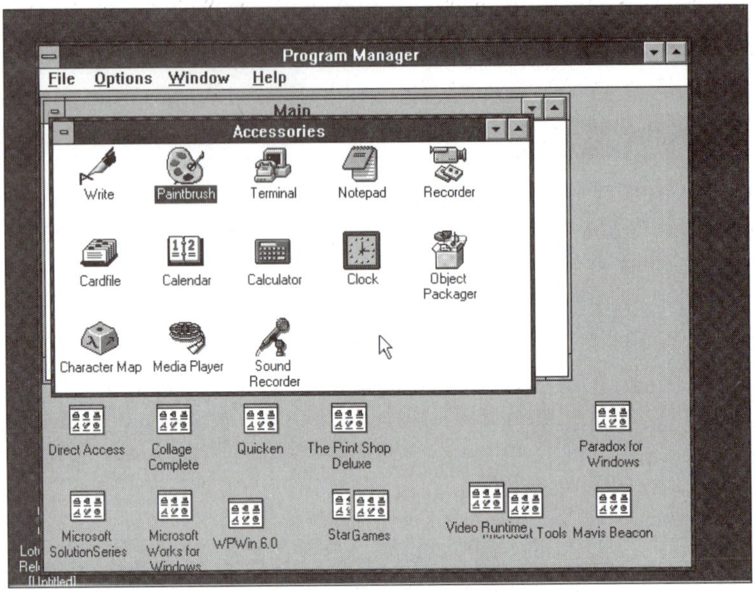

Figure 3-2 **The Accessories group window**

The Games group window

The Games group window includes two games: Solitaire and Minesweeper. Solitaire is a computerized version of the card game Solitaire, and Minesweeper is a computerized board game. Many people use these two games to familiarize themselves with the mouse and Windows components such as the menu bars and scroll bars (see Figure 3-3).

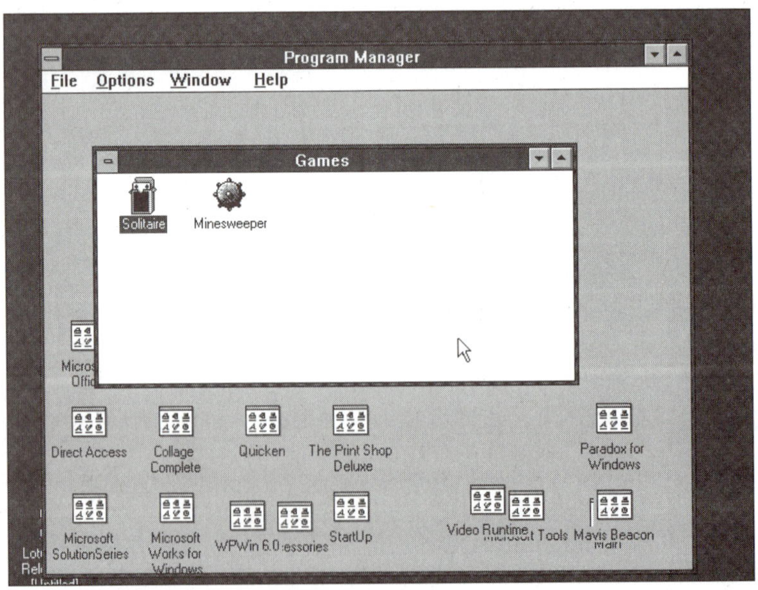

Figure 3-3 **The Games group window**

The StartUp group window

You can add program icons to the StartUp group window by moving or copying them from other windows. Once an application is added to the StartUp window, it launches automatically every time the Windows program is loaded into memory. You can also determine whether an application will appear as a window or an icon at the startup of the Windows program (see Figure 3-4).

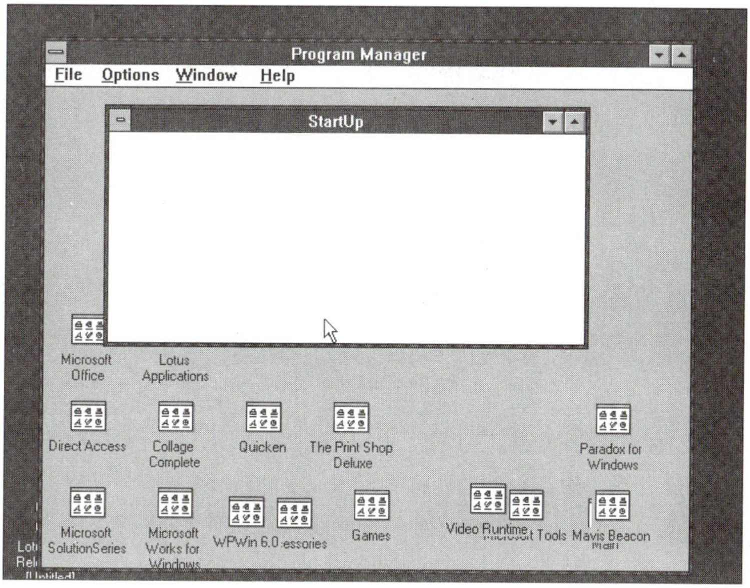

Figure 3-4 **The StartUp group window**

Objective 2: Arranging Multiple Windows

Since you can have more than one window open at a time, Windows provides two techniques for arranging multiple windows on the desktop. The Tile and Cascade options can be accessed from the Program Manager menu bar; they give you the opportunity to change the arrangement of multiple windows.

Exercise 1: Using the Cascade and Tile options

Cascade
Tile

The *Cascade* option displays windows overlapping one another, with the active window's title bar highlighted. The *Tile* option places windows next to one another so that you can see the contents of each window. To practice using the Cascade and Tile options, do the following:

1. Open the Main, Accessories, and Games windows.

   All three windows should be displayed on the screen.

2. Choose the Window option on the Program Manager menu bar.

   The pull-down menu is displayed.

3. Choose the Cascade option.

   The three windows are displayed, overlapping one another. The last opened window (Games) is the active window and appears in the foreground with its title bar highlighted (see Figure 3-5). Note that the contents of the other windows are obscured by the active window.

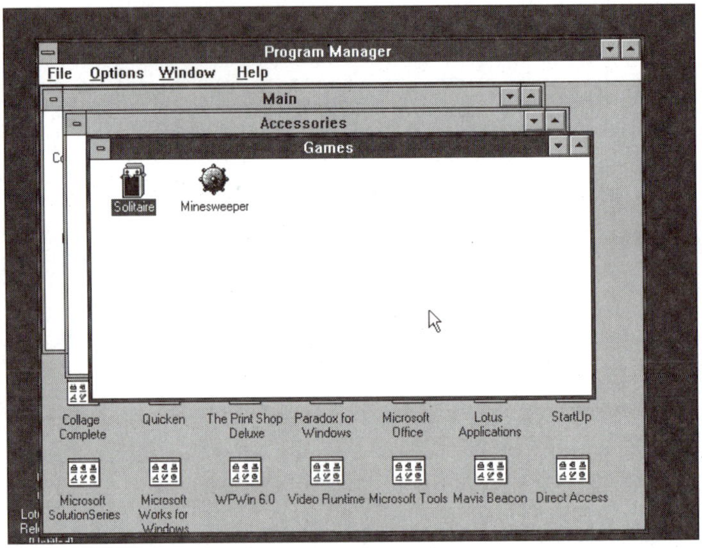

Figure 3-5 Cascaded windows

4. Choose the Window option from the menu bar. Choose Tile.

   The three windows are arranged next to one another with their contents displayed (see Figure 3-6).

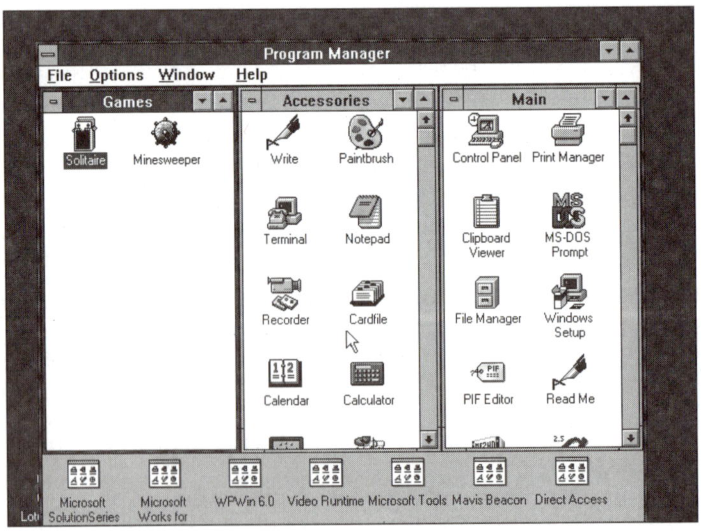

Figure 3-6 Tiled windows

5. Click any one of the three windows to activate it.

   When you activate a window, the title bar becomes highlighted.

6. Close all the windows except the Program Manager window.

Objective 3: Creating Program Groups

You've learned that the Windows package includes a set of program groups. The Windows program also enables you to create your own program groups so that you can readily access the applications and documents you use most frequently.

Exercise 2: Creating a new program group

To create a new program group, perform the following steps:

1. Click File in the Program Manager menu bar.
2. Choose New.

   The New Program Object dialog box appears (see Figure 3-7).

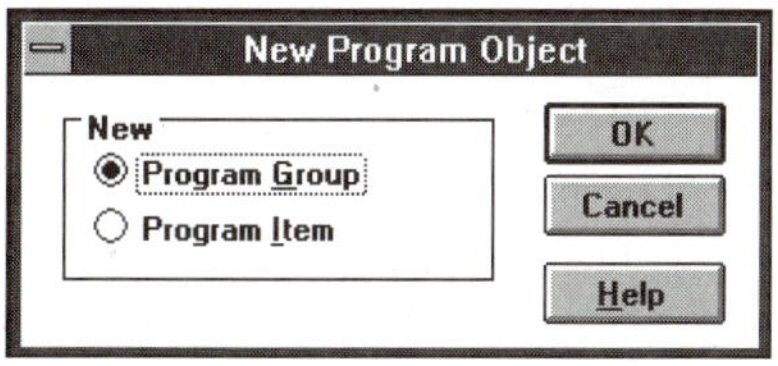

Figure 3-7 The New Program Object dialog box

   There are two program objects that Windows lets you create: a program group, which represents a set of related applications, and a program item, which represents a single application found within a program group.

3. Choose the Program Group option, if it is not already selected.
4. Choose OK.

   The Program Group Properties dialog box is displayed. A flashing cursor is displayed in the Description text box where you will assign a name to the program group you are creating (see Figure 3-8). The Group File text box will be filled in by Windows after you choose OK.

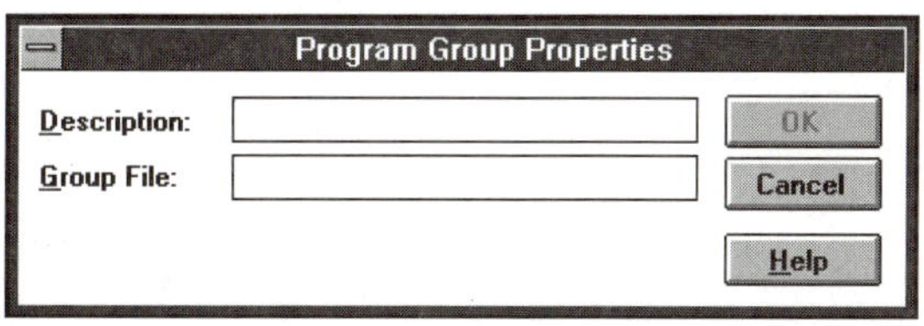

Figure 3-8 The Program Group Properties dialog box

5. Type Programs Used Daily in the description text box.
6. Choose OK.

   The new Programs Used Daily window is displayed in the Program Manager window. It is empty (see Figure 3-9).

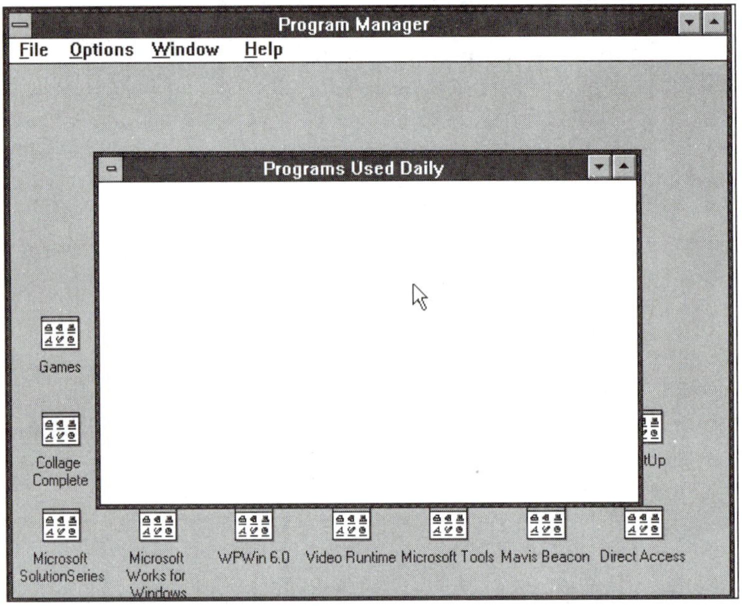

Figure 3-9 The newly created Programs Used Daily window

7. Click File from the menu bar and choose Properties.

   The Program Group Properties dialog box is displayed. Note that the Group File text box now includes the current directory path, `C:\Windows`, the first word of the description you provided for the description text box, `Programs`, and an extension, `.grp`.
8. Choose Cancel to close the Group Properties dialog box.
9. Minimize the Programs Used Daily group window.

   The Programs Used Daily group window is reduced to an icon in the Program Manager window.

Changing the name of a group window

If you want to change the name of a program group, you can do so easily using the Program Items Properties dialog box.

Exercise 3: Renaming a group window

To rename the Programs Used Daily group window, perform the following steps:

1. Click the Programs Used Daily group icon in the Program Manager window.

   A pop-up menu appears, and the name beneath the group icon is highlighted.
2. Click anywhere on a blank area of the window to remove the pop-up menu.
3. Choose the File option from the Program Manager menu bar.
4. Choose Properties.

   The Program Group Properties dialog box is displayed.
5. In the Description text box, type Daily Applications and choose OK.

   You are returned to the Program Manager window with the new name of the group icon displayed.

Objective 4: Working with Program-Item Icons

In addition to creating your own program groups, you can create new program-item icons that represent programs and documents you use frequently. You can also have multiple icons that run a single program. You can change an icon's appearance and name, and you can copy and move icons from one window to another.

Moving and copying program icons between group windows

You can place programs that you use frequently in a single group window. In Exercise 3, you created a program group called Programs Used Daily. The programs that you use every day may be ones that are included with the Windows program, such as Write, Cardfile, and Notepad, or other application programs, such as Lotus 1-2-3, Microsoft Word, and WordPerfect. It's a good idea to group these programs in one window so they can be accessed easily. You can use Copy to place a duplicate copy of a program-item icon in another window and Move to move an icon from one window to another.

TIP Moving or copying program objects does not change where these objects reside on the hard disk. It simply enables you easier access to these objects in the Windows environment.

Exercise 4: Moving an icon between group windows

To move the Write program-item icon into the group window Daily Applications, do the following:

1. Open the Accessories window, if it is not already open.
2. Open the Daily Applications window.
3. Tile the windows so all the program item icons are visible.
4. Drag the Notepad program item icon  in the Accessories window over to the Daily Applications window.

   The Notepad program item icon appears in the Daily Applications window and is no longer displayed in the Accessories window (see Figure 3-10).

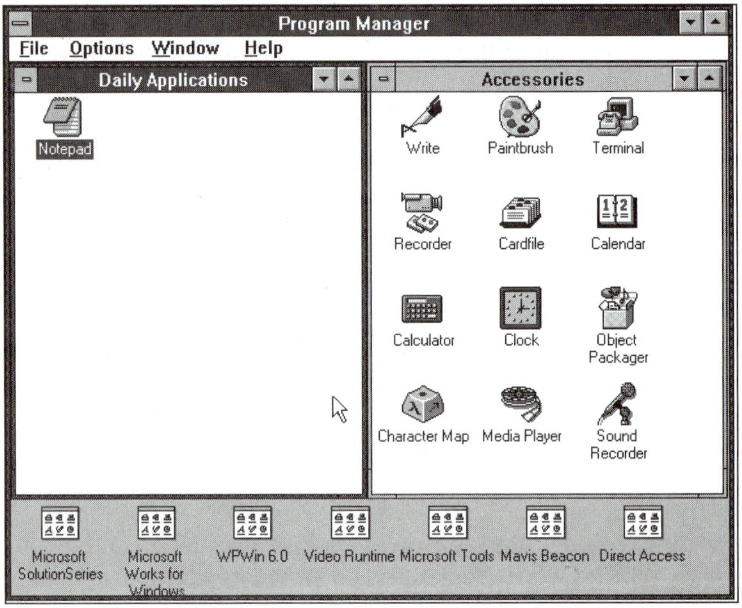

Figure 3-10 The Notepad icon in the Daily Applications window

Exercise 5: Copying an icon to a group window

To make a copy of the Write icon and place it in the Daily Applications window, do the following:

1. Open the Accessories window, if it is not already open.
2. Press and hold down CTRL while you drag the Write icon  to the Daily Applications group window.
3. Release CTRL and the mouse button (see Figure 3-11).

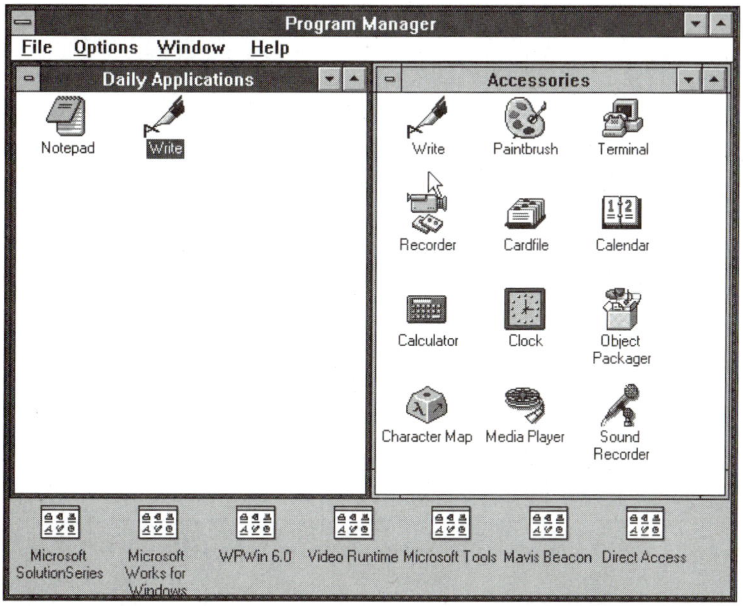

Figure 3-11 The Write icon in both the Accessories and Daily Applications windows

The Write icon is now in both the Accessories and Daily Applications windows.

Adding and changing program-item icons

You can create more than one icon to represent an application or change the icon that currently represents an application to a different icon of your choice. But before adding or changing a program-item icon, you must know the directory on the hard disk where the program is stored and the name of the executable file that is used to run the program.

Exercise 6: Changing the name of an icon

In the following exercise, you will change the name of a copy of the Write program-item icon.

1. Open the Daily Applications window, if it is not already open.
2. Choose the File option from the Program Manager menu bar.
3. Choose the New option.

   The New Program Object dialog box is displayed with the Program Item option selected.
4. Choose OK.

   The Program Item Properties Dialog box appears (see Figure 3-12). Table 3-1 describes the elements of the Program Item Properties dialog box.

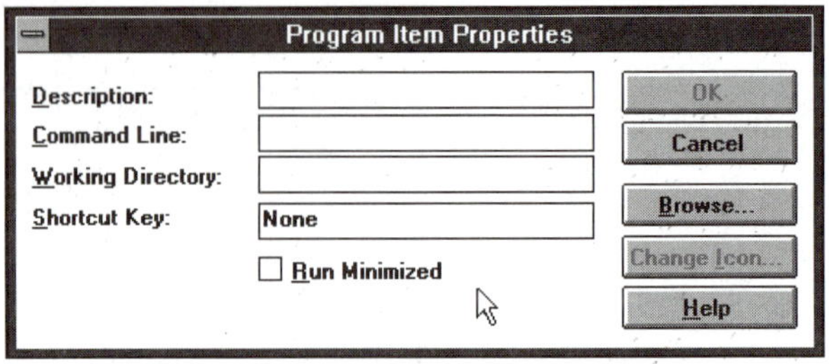

Figure 3-12 The Program Item Properties dialog box

5. In the Description text box, type Word Processing and press TAB.

   You have assigned the name *Word Processing* to the icon.

6. Choose Browse.

   The Browse dialog box appears (see Figure 3-13).

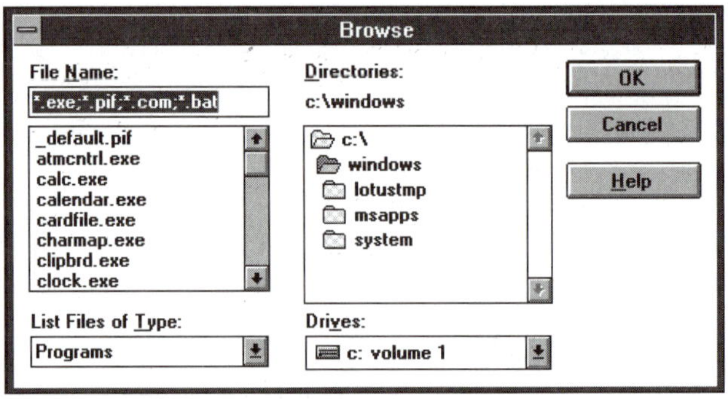

Figure 3-13 The Browse dialog box

7. Make sure that the Browse dialog box displays the correct drive and directory for the file you want to execute. In this example, the file is in the Windows directory of drive C (C:\Windows).

8. Scroll through the list of file names in the file name list box until you find write.exe and select it. Note that the write.exe file, which runs the Write program in the Accessories window, will be assigned to the new Word Processing icon you create.

TIP If you know the name of a file, you can type the file name in the file name text box instead of scrolling through the file listing.

9. Choose OK.

   The selected path and file name are inserted in the Command Line text box of the Program Item Properties dialog box.

Table 3-1 Elements of the Program Item Properties dialog box

ELEMENT	FUNCTION
Description	Enter the name of the new program-item icon.
Command Line	Enter the directory path and the name of the executable file that loads the program into memory. Only files with extensions .exe, .com, .bat, or .pif can be included in the command line.
Working Directory	Enter the directory name where you want files saved for this application.
Shortcut key	Enter a key combination that can be used to activate a running application. Shortcut keys include SHIFT, CTRL, and ALT in combination with function or character keys.
Browse	Choose a file from the Browse dialog box list, and it will be inserted into the command line text box.
Change Icon	Select an icon for an application. Windows provides 45 icons from which you can choose.
Run Minimized	Choose to reduce an application to an icon upon startup of the application.

Using a keyboard shortcut to start an application

It is often easiest to press a few keys to activate a program. By using a keyboard shortcut, you can bypass having to open the window in which a program resides and then click the appropriate icon.

Exercise 7: Assigning a keyboard shortcut

You will now assign a keyboard shortcut to the write.exe file. Make sure that you have completed Exercise 6 before attempting the following exercise.

1. Click the Shortcut Key text box in the Program Item Properties dialog box.
2. Press CTRL+SHIFT+W to assign a keyboard shortcut to the write.exe file.

   The Program Item Properties dialog box is completed (see Figure 3-14).

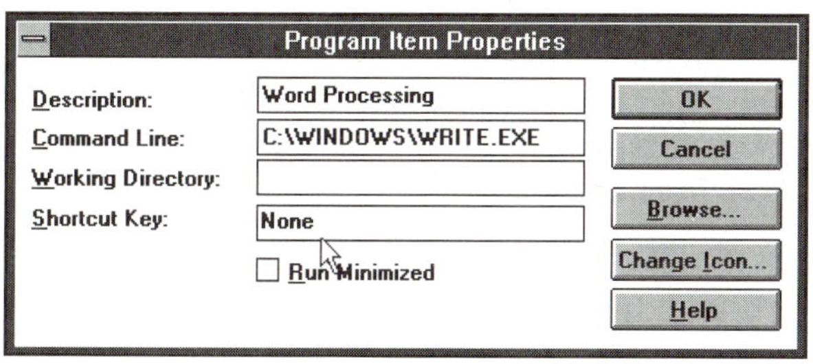

Figure 3-14 The Completed Program Item Properties dialog box

3. Choose OK.

   You are returned to the Program Manager window. Note that the Daily Applications window now shows the same icon twice. One icon is the

Write program icon that you copied from the Accessories window earlier; the other is the icon representing the Word Processing icon you created (see Figure 3-15).

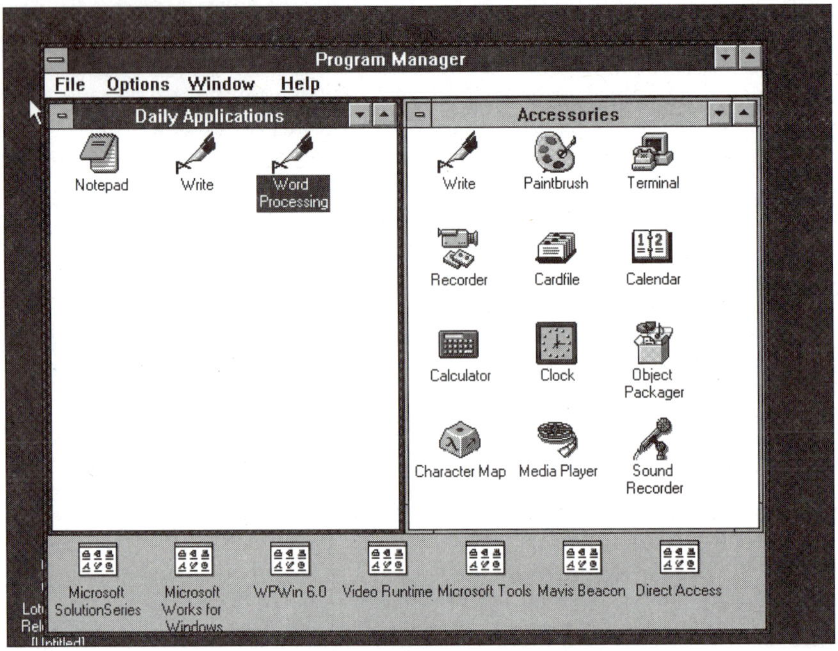

Figure 3-15 Identical icons in a window

4. Press CTRL+SHIFT+W.

   The Write application is started, and the document screen is displayed.
5. Choose File, and then choose Exit to close the Write document window.

Selecting from available icons

Windows provides a number of extra icons you can use to represent the applications you are running. Windows stores these extra icons in a special file named moricons.dll. To choose from the set of available icons, you must access the moricons.dll file, which is usually found in the Windows subdirectory.

Exercise 8: Changing the default icon for a group window

You can select an icon other than the default icon. For this exercise, we will change the look of the Word Processing icon in the Daily Applications window. Make sure that you have completed Exercises 6 and 7 before beginning this exercise.

1. Choose File; then choose Properties.

   The Program Item Properties dialog box is displayed.

2. Choose Change Icon.

   The Change Icon dialog box is displayed (see Figure 3-16). The dialog box displays the default icon that is used for the Write program.

Figure 3-16 The Change Icon dialog box

3. In the file name text box, type C:\Windows\moricons.dll as the directory path in the Change Icon dialog box.

4. Choose OK.

   The moricons.dll file is displayed in the file name text box with a horizontal display of available icons to choose from in the Current Icon display box (see Figure 3-17).

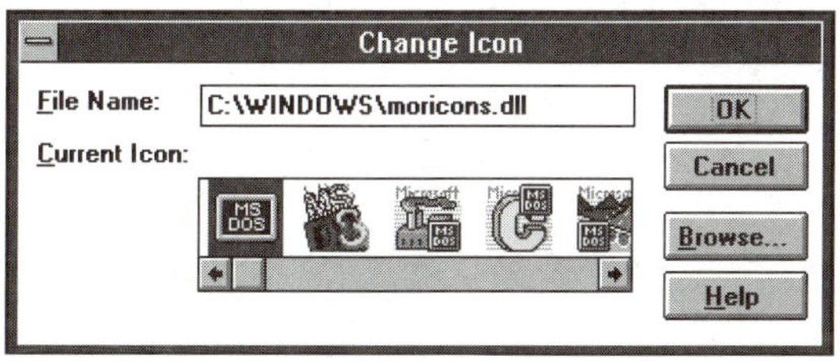

Figure 3-17 The Current Icon display box showing available icons

5. Scroll through the display box until you find the icon depicting a hand with a pen.

6. Double-click the icon .

   You are returned to the Program Item Properties dialog box. The new icon is displayed on the left side of the box (see Figure 3-18).

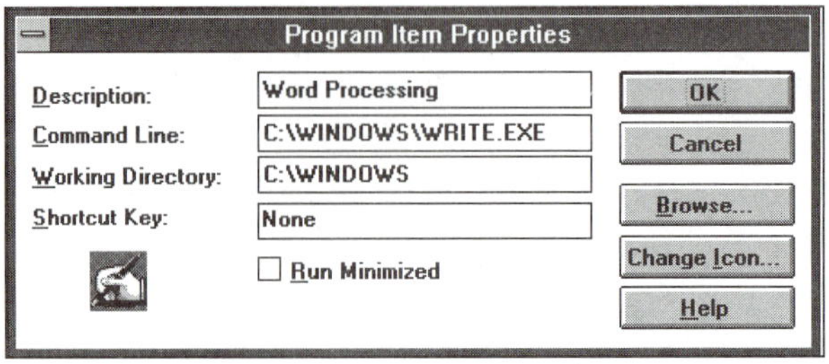

Figure 3-18 The Program Item Properties dialog box displaying the new icon

Exercise 9: Minimizing a document window at startup

Document windows can be reduced immediately to an icon on the desktop once you start a program. To minimize the Write document window using the Word Processing icon upon startup, do the following:

1. Click the Run Minimized box in the Program Item Properties dialog box.
2. Choose OK.

   The dialog box is removed, and you are returned to the Daily Applications group window with the new icon displayed (see Figure 3-19).

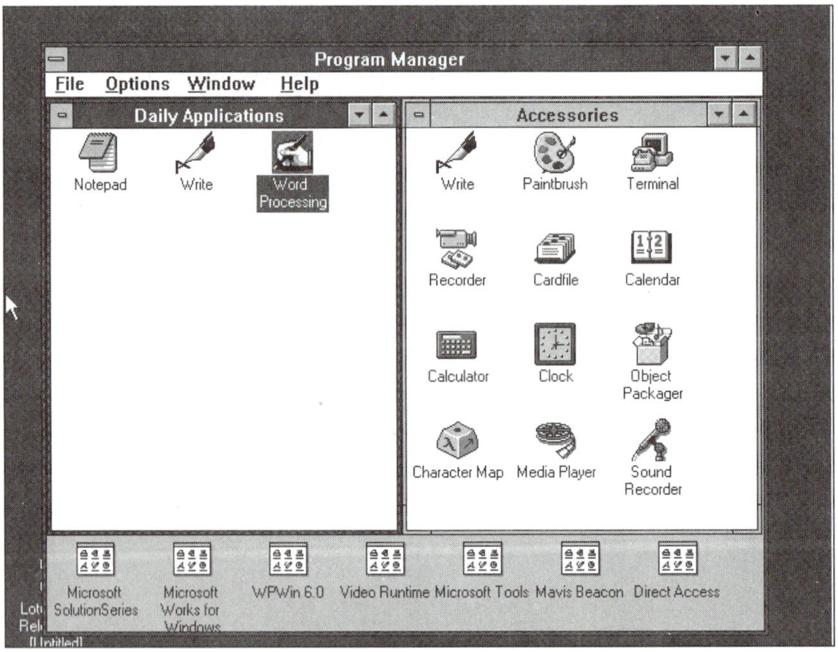

Figure 3-19 The Daily Applications group window with its new icon

3. Double-click the Word Processing icon  to start the Write program and have its document window minimized on the desktop (see Figure 3-20).

Figure 3-20 **The Write document window minimized to an icon**

TIP To see the minimized icon, you may have to make the Program Manager window smaller.

4. Double-click the minimized icon to open the Write document window (see Figure 3-21).

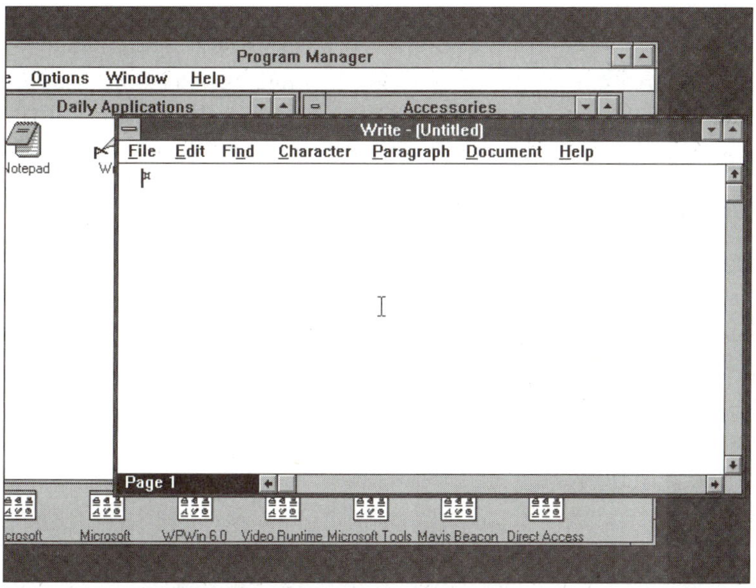

Figure 3-21 **The Write document window**

5. Choose File from the Write menu bar; then choose Exit.

   The Write window closes, and you are returned to the Program Manager window.
6. Close all open windows except the Program Manager.
7. Maximize the Program Manager window.

Adding a new icon to a group window

Exercise 9 shows how you can change the look of an existing icon. You can also add a new icon to a group window to run a program. Normally, when you install a Windows program on your system, an icon will be created automatically for you by the program you are installing. If an icon isn't created for you, or if you accidentally delete a program item from a window, you can create your own icon. Adding a new icon is similar to changing an existing icon.

Objective 5: Starting Programs Automatically and Switching between Programs

The Windows package includes a StartUp program that can be used to start a program automatically whenever the Windows program is loaded into memory. Also, you can switch easily from one running program to another by using the Task List dialog box.

Electronic Books: A New Way to Read

Several software companies are currently brainstorming to think of ways to make electronic books (called e-books) appeal to consumers. An *e-book* is the electronic version of a printed book that is stored on a disk and read from the computer screen. The problem with e-books is that people become bored and restless sitting in front of a screen. To make e-books more appealing, companies have employed new strategies to enhance the e-book concept. These include how-to books that enable the reader to watch a project from start to completion, as well as books with interactive activities.

E-book topics include home improvement, managing your finances, gardening, entertaining, and decorating. Personal hobbies are another area that developers are exploring in the hopes of building consumer interest.

Starting programs automatically

You may have specific applications that you need every time you use your computer. For example, you may work exclusively with a word processing program and a spreadsheet program. Instead of having to navigate through the Program Manager window to start up these applications, you can place them in the automatic StartUp program group.

Exercise 10: Using the StartUp group

To start up the Write and Solitaire programs automatically every time you start Windows, perform the following steps:

1. Open the Daily Applications window.
2. Open the StartUp window.
3. Open the Games window.
4. Arrange and resize them so that you can view the contents of each.
5. Copy the Word Processing program icon  from the Daily Applications window to the StartUp window using the methods covered in Exercises 4–6.

6. Copy the Solitaire program icon 

from the Games window to the StartUp window.

   The Word Processing program icon and the Solitaire program icon are displayed in the StartUp window (see Figure 3-22).

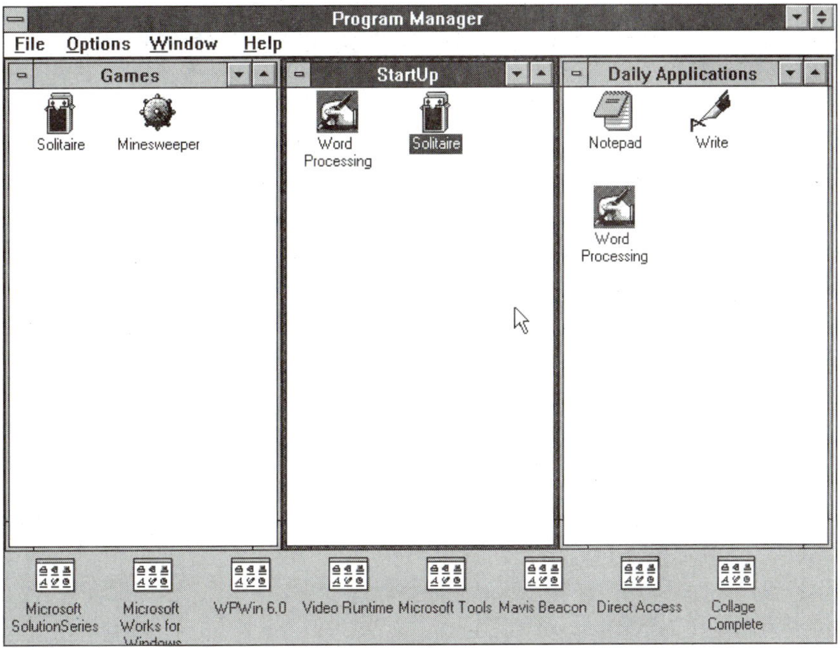

Figure 3-22 The Solitaire and Word Processing program icons in the StartUp window

7. Exit the Windows program to return to the DOS prompt.

   To see how the StartUp window works, you must exit and restart the Windows program.

8. Start the Windows program.

   The Solitaire program window is displayed on the screen automatically.

9. Double-click the control menu box of the Solitaire window to close it.

   The Word Processing icon is displayed as a minimized icon on the desktop.

10. Close all windows and applications with the exception of the Program Manager.

Switching between applications

When many windows are open at once, the one you need may not be visible. To display a window that is hidden by another or to switch from one application to another, you can use the Switch To option in the control menu box of the Program Manager. The Switch To option displays a list of all your currently running programs and enables you to quickly switch between them. By selecting the program of your choice from the Task List dialog box, the program's window is brought to the foreground of your screen.

Exercise 11: Using the Switch To option

To switch from one running application to another, do the following:

1. Open the Accessories window and start the Calendar, Cardfile, and Paintbrush programs.
2. Minimize the Program Manager window.

The application windows of the three programs that you started (Cardfile, Calendar, and Paintbrush) are displayed on the desktop (see Figure 3-23). Arrange or resize the application windows so that you can see all three on the screen.

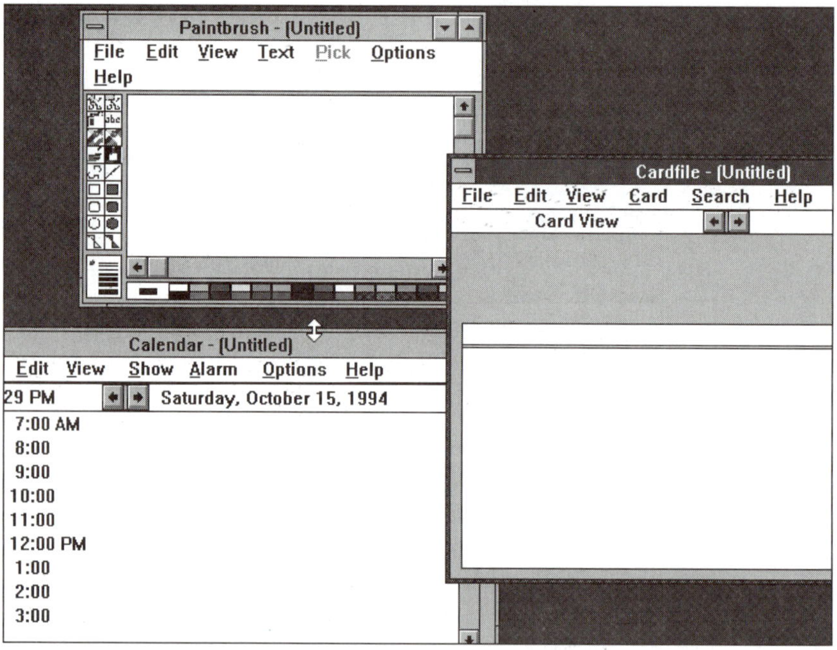

Figure 3-23 The Cardfile, Calendar, and Paintbrush windows

3. Maximize the Cardfile window.

   The Cardfile window hides the other two application windows (see Figure 3-24).

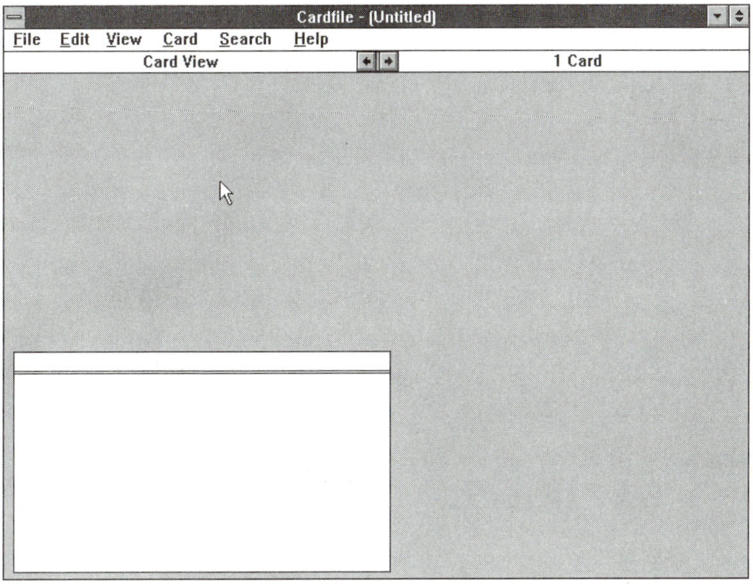

Figure 3-24 The Cardfile window hiding other running applications

4. Click on the control menu box and choose Switch To.

   The Task List dialog box appears, displaying a list of currently running application windows with the last selected application.

5. Select Calendar from the Task List and then choose Switch To.

   The Calendar application window is displayed at the foreground of your screen; it is the active window (see Figure 3-25).

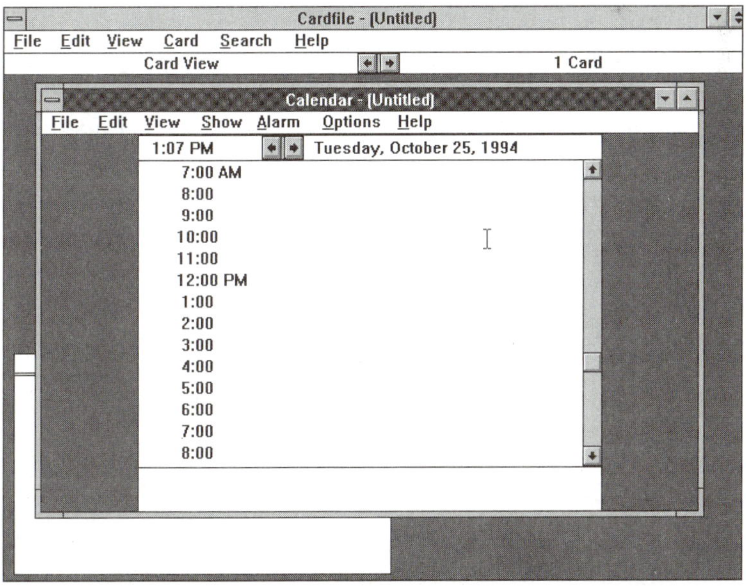

Figure 3-25 The active Calendar window

Exercise 12: Closing a window using the Task List dialog box

You can close windows you no longer need by pressing the End Task command button found in the Task List dialog box.

1. Click the control menu box in the Calendar application window.
2. Click Switch To.
3. With Calendar selected in the file listing, choose End Task to close the window.

   The Calendar application window disappears.
4. Close the Cardfile application window.
5. Close the Paintbrush application window.

Objective 6: Deleting Group Windows and Program-Item Icons

When you no longer need the icons in a group window—or the group window itself—you can easily delete both from the Program Manager window. Deleting group windows or icons has no effect on the files for those applications that are on the hard disk. It simply prevents you from accessing the applications through a window on the desktop. Once a group window (or the icons within it) is deleted, you must go through the creation process covered in the previous objectives to get it back. If you accidentally delete an icon, you can run the program by choosing File, choosing Run, and typing the program's executable name in the text box.

Exercise 13: Deleting icons from a group window

To delete the Word Processing icon from the Daily Applications window, perform the following steps:

1. Maximize the Program Manager window.
2. Open the Daily Applications window, if it is not already open.
3. Click the Word Processing icon once to select it.
4. Choose File from the menu bar; then choose Delete.

   The Delete warning box is deployed, prompting you to confirm that you want to delete the Word Processing program item (see Figure 3-26).

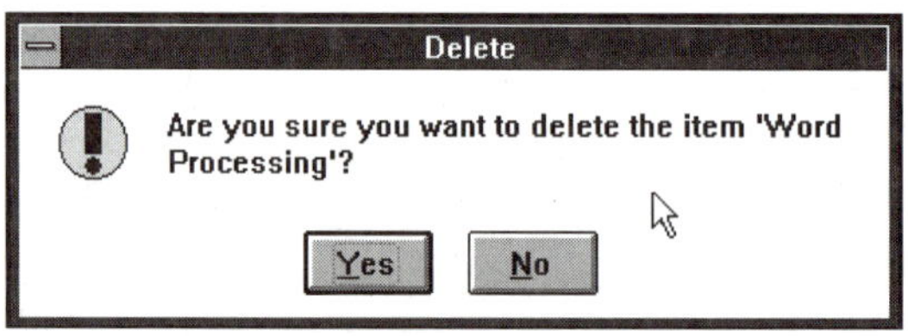

Figure 3-26 The Delete warning box

5. Choose Yes.

   The Word Processing icon is removed from the Daily Applications window.

Exercise 14: Deleting a group window

To delete the Daily Applications group window, perform the following steps:

1. Move the Notepad icon to the Accessories window.
2. Delete the extra copy of the Write icon from the Daily Applications window using the method described in Exercise 13.

   Make sure that the Daily Applications window is empty before you proceed.
3. Choose File from the menu bar; then choose Delete.

   The Delete warning box is displayed, prompting you to make sure that you want to delete the Daily Applications group (see Figure 3-27).

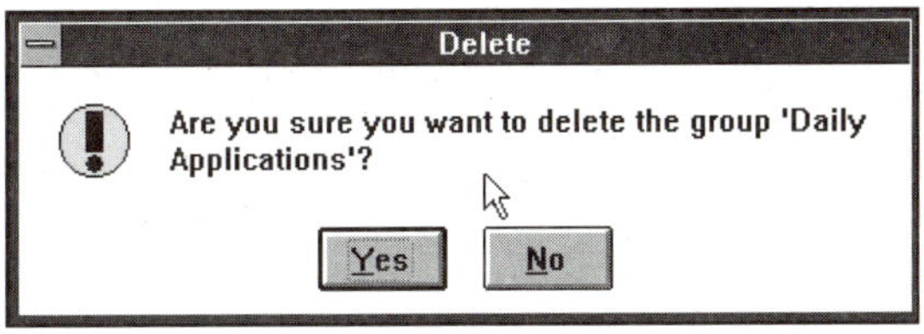

Figure 3-27 The Delete warning box for a group window

4. Choose Yes.

   The Daily Applications group window is removed from the Program Manager window.

Chapter Summary

In Chapter 3, you learned about the many functions that the Program Manager can perform. You learned how to customize the Windows environment by creating group windows and icons of your own. You learned how to copy and move icons, as well as how to change the properties of program icons and group windows. You learned about the programs included in the Windows package and how to start up a Windows application automatically whenever the Windows program is launched.

Review Questions

True/False Questions

_____ 1. To view the contents of multiple windows, you would use the Cascade option.

_____ 2. Program groups are sets of related applications.

_____ 3. You can make a group window active by using shortcut keys.

_____ 4. You can have more than one program-item icon for a program.

_____ 5. Program documents can be minimized to an icon automatically when you start the Windows program.

Multiple-Choice Questions

_____ 6. Which group window—and the program icons within it—should be used to help you with your daily work?

A. Main

B. StartUp

C. Games

D. Accessories

_____ 7. To copy an icon from one window to another, which of the following keys would you press while dragging the mouse?

A. SHIFT

B. ALT

C. CTRL + ALT

D. ALT

_____ 8. Which file can be used to display a list of available icons in Windows?

A. write.exe

B. moricons.dll

C. C:\Windows

D. program.exe

_____ 9. The Switch To option is located in which dialog box?

A. Program Item Properties

B. Task List

C. Change Icon

D. New Program Object

______ 10. To close a window from the Task List dialog box, which command button would you choose?

A. Close

B. End Task

C. Cancel

D. OK

Fill-in-the-Blank Questions

11. When a window is active, its ____________ ____________ is highlighted.
12. To create a group window of your own, you would choose File and then ____________.
13. To add or change a program-item icon, you must know which ____________ the file is stored in.
14. The information you type in the ____________ text box will appear as the name of the program-item icon you create.
15. When changing the name or look of an existing icon, you are changing its ____________.

Acumen-Building Activities

Quick Projects

1. Creating a program group

Create a program-group window called *your name* Programs. (Fill in your own first name.)

2. Copying icons

Copy the following icons to the *your name* Programs group window: Paintbrush, Notepad, and Solitaire.

3. Changing an icon

Change the Solitaire icon in the *your name* Programs window to the icon .

4. Assigning a keyboard shortcut

Assign a keyboard shortcut to run the Solitaire program found in the *your name* Programs window.

In-Depth Projects

1. Working with program groups and icons

1. Perform the steps to minimize the Paintbrush program found in *your name* Programs to an icon each time the Windows program is started.
2. Change the name of the *your name* Programs window to *your name* Applications.
3. Make the Notepad program start automatically whenever you start the Windows program.
4. Delete the icons from the *your name* Applications window, and then delete the window itself.

2. Using Windows

1. Start the Windows program and open the following windows: Main, Accessories, and Games.
2. Maximize the Games window, and then restore it to its previous size.
3. Minimize the Main window.
4. Resize the Accessories window until it is 2.5 inches wide and 2 inches long.
5. Place it in the upper, left corner of the screen.
6. Arrange the icons in the Accessories window so that all the icons are close together in the lower, right corner of the window.
7. Start the Write, Cardfile, Minesweeper, and Calendar programs from the appropriate windows.
8. Minimize Minesweeper and Cardfile to icons on the desktop.
9. Use the Task List dialog box to switch from one running program to another.
10. Cascade the windows.
11. Have the icons arrange themselves automatically within each window.
12. Use the Help feature to look up the word *font*.
13. Place a bookmark on the Switching Between Applications help screen.
14. Place a comment on the Quitting Windows help screen.
15. Make a new group window called Fun and Games.
16. Copy the Minesweeper icon into the Fun and Games window.
17. Change the icon for the Minesweeper program in the Fun and Games window to an icon of your choice from the available icons that Windows provides.
18. Change the name of the icon to Board Game.
19. Place your new icon in the appropriate group window so that it starts every time the Windows program is started.

Chapter 4

The File Manager

Objectives

- Understanding Data Storage
- Identifying the Components of the File Manager Screen
- Using the Tree Option
- Using the View Option
- Exploring Options

Key Terms

TERM	DEFINITION
Disk Drive	the hardware mechanism that reads from and writes to a floppy or hard disk
Directory	a location on a disk where sets of related files are stored; used to organize files in useful categories
Root Directory	a directory that is considered the top level in the structured organization of files and directories
Subdirectory	a directory that is under the root directory
Directory Contents List	the window within the File Manager window that displays the contents of a selected directory or subdirectory in the Directory Tree
Directory Tree	the window within the File Manager window that displays all subdirectories under a specified root
Current Drive	the drive that the system is currently addressing or accessing; when you issue relevant commands, the current drive is the default drive
Current Directory	the directory that the system is currently addressing or accessing; when you issue relevant commands, the current directory is the default directory

In the next two chapters, you are introduced to the File Manager. The File Manager is a Windows tool that enables you to organize and keep track of your information in files and directories on a hard or floppy disk. You can use the File Manager to copy, move, delete, rename, and control files. The File Manager has many of the same capabilities that DOS has but differs by supplying a visual representation of the files and directories that reside on the computer. Having to remember and type DOS commands can be frustrating. A major advantage of the File Manager is that instead of typing commands, you use the mouse and pull-down menus to perform disk maintenance.

Objective 1: Understanding Data Storage

Before beginning to work with the File Manager, you need a basic understanding of how computers keep track of information. When you enter data into a computer, the data is placed in an area called Random Access Memory (RAM). RAM is a temporary storage area for data, programs, and the disk operating system (DOS). When power to the computer is turned off, data stored in RAM is lost. To save and later retrieve information that has been entered into the computer, the data in RAM must be saved to a hard or floppy disk.

directory

root directory; subdirectory

DOS provides a way for you to keep track of and arrange information on a disk in an organized fashion. DOS uses a tree-like structure where files and directories are situated on various levels of the tree. A *directory* is a location on a disk where sets of related files are stored. The top and most basic level is the *root directory*, and all other directories beneath the root are *subdirectories* that emanate from the root-like branches on a tree.

disk drive

Data can be located on different disks in different disk drives. A *disk drive* is the hardware mechanism that reads from and writes to a floppy or hard disk. Disk drives are designated by capital letters: A, B, C, and so on. Each disk has its own files, directories, and subdirectories, which are organized on various levels of the tree structure. To understand this concept, compare these various components of the tree structure to a filing cabinet. Table 4-1 compares the parts of a filing cabinet with the way DOS organizes data on disks.

Table 4-1 Comparison of a filing cabinet and DOS components

PARTS OF A FILING CABINET	DOS COMPONENTS
The Filing Cabinet as a Whole	The collection of disks, including floppy disks and hard disks.
Drawers	Directories
Subdivisions within a Drawer	Subdirectories
Documents	Single files that may contain data or programs

Directories and subdirectories are used to hold sets of related files. For example, you could create a directory to hold all your word processing programs and documents, another for your spreadsheet programs and documents, and yet another for graphical programs and documents. It may seem that directories and subdirectories do the same thing. Essentially they do; the difference between them is that any directory that is not on the first level of the structure (the root) is considered a subdirectory.

Objective 2: Identifying the Components of the File Manager Screen

The following section describes the different parts of the File Manager window and explains the components of each. You will identify the various icons that are provided with the File Manager and learn how to use them.

Exercise 1: Starting the File Manager

The File Manager is part of the Main Window, and its icon looks like a filing cabinet. To start the File Manager, perform the following steps:

1. Open the Main group window.
2. Double-click the File Manager icon 

.

   The File Manager window appears (see Figure 4-1).

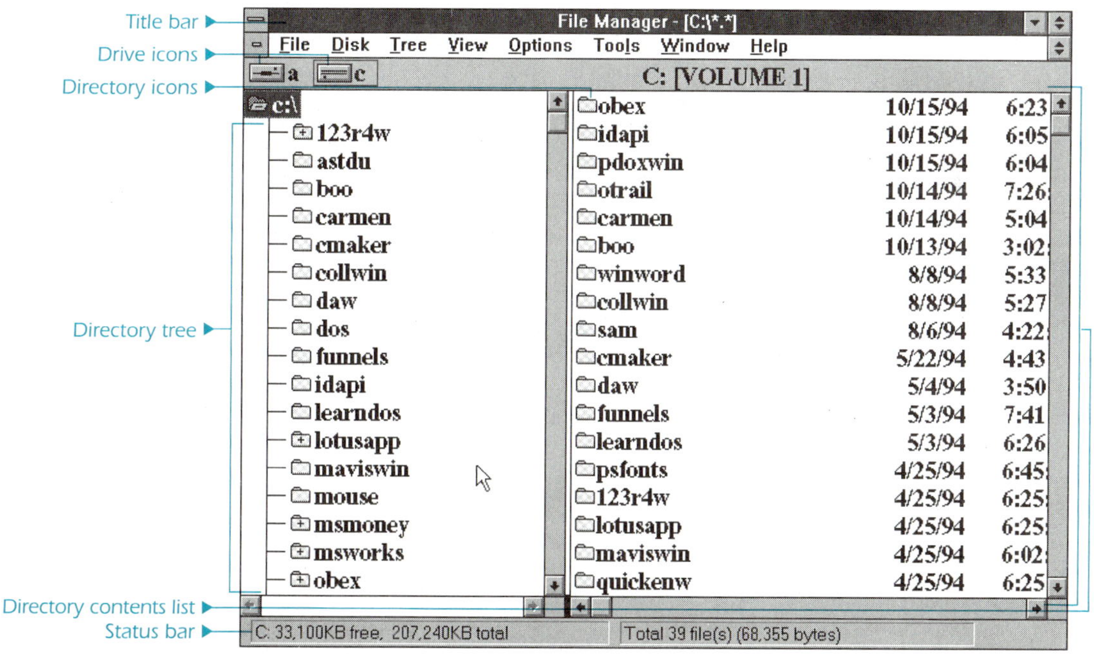

Figure 4-1 The File Manager Window

3. Maximize the File Manager window, if necessary.

Directory Tree; Directory Contents List

The File Manager screen is divided into two sections, or windows. The left window, known as the *Directory Tree*, displays directories for the current disk drive. The right window, known as the *Directory Contents List*, displays the contents of the directories that are listed in the Directory Tree. The Directory Contents List can include subdirectories of a directory, as well as program and data files.

Components of the File Manager window

The following section describes the various components of the File Manager window.

The title bar

current drive; current directory

The File Manager window has its own title bar, which displays the name of the current drive and current directory. The *current drive* is the disk drive that the system is currently addressing or accessing. The *current directory* is the directory that the system is currently addressing or accessing. When you issue relevant commands, the current drive and directory are the default drive and directory.

In this example, C:*.* indicates that the computer is addressing the disk drive C (the hard disk), the root directory (\), and the subdirectory Windows. The title bar in the File Manager tells you exactly what drive and directory your computer is currently addressing.

The menu bar

The File Manager has its own menu bar that includes commands specific to managing and viewing files on a disk. The various viewing options on this menu bar are covered later in this chapter.

The drive icon bar

The drive icon bar displays icons that represent the disk drives that your system includes. Notice that drive icons for floppy disks don't look the same as drive icons for hard disks. Some computers have more disk drives than others. You can switch from one drive to another by clicking the desired icon; the Directory Contents List in the File Manager window displays the contents (files and directories) of the chosen drive.

Icons in the Directory window

The Directory Tree displays directories as icons resembling file folders and lists them in alphabetical order. An open file folder indicates the current directory.

Icons in the Directory Contents List can include icons representing subdirectories of the current directory, programs, and documents. Table 4-2 describes each type of icon and what it represents.

Table 4-2 Types of icons displayed in the File Manager window

ICON	DESCRIPTION
Closed Folder icon	a closed directory or its subdirectories
Program File icon	a file with the extension .com, .bat, or .exe that is used to start a program
Document File icon	a files that has been created by a program
Associated Document File icon	a document file that is associated with a program

The status bar

The status bar is located at the bottom of the File Manager window. The left side of the status bar displays information when the Directory Tree is active. The information includes the total amount of disk space available for the current drive, as well as the amount of free space that is available. The right side of the status bar information displays information regarding the contents of a selected directory, including the total number of files within a directory and the number of bytes that are used.

You can view the contents of different directories and disk drives by choosing the icon that represents the disk drive or directory you want to view.

Exercise 2: Opening a Directory

To open a new directory and view the contents, perform the following steps:

1. In the drive icon bar, click the icon of the disk that contains the Windows files. This is usually the C, D, or F drive; your instructor will inform you of the correct drive.
2. Find and click the Windows folder in the Directory Tree.

TIP You may have to scroll through the listing using the vertical scroll bar if the listing is very long.

The Windows directory that resides under the root directory of the current drive opens and displays its contents in the Directory Contents List (see Figure 4-2).

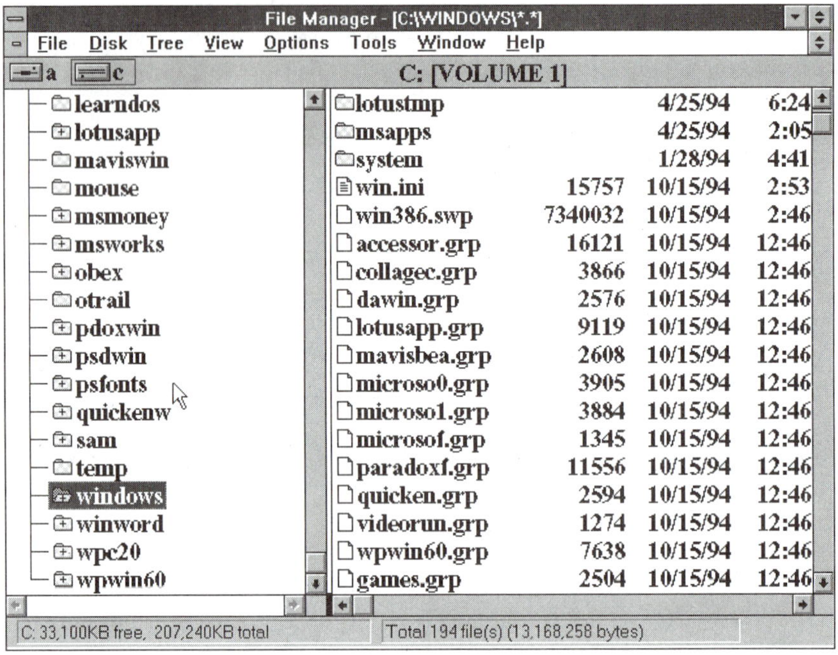

Figure 4-2 The contents of the Windows directory displayed in the Directory Contents List

3. Double-click on the System subdirectory from the list of files displayed in the Directory Contents List.

FEATURE

Wildcard characters

Many of the dialog boxes in the Windows environment allow you to use wildcard characters to pick out similarly named files from a listing. There are two types of wildcard characters: the asterisk (*) and question mark (?). The asterisk represents one or more characters in a file name, whereas the question mark represents a single character in a file name.

Wildcard characters treat the primary name of a file and the extension of a file separately. Therefore, you can specify certain characters to be included in the primary name and others for the extension. For example, to list all files with a.txt extension, regardless of the primary name of the file, you would type DIR *.txt. The asterisk means that the primary name can be any character or characters. The extension, however, must be.txt.

The question mark is used for more specific searching. For example, to list files with a five-character primary name whose third character is *A* and a three-character extension whose second character is *S*, you would type DIR ??A??.?S?.

The System subdirectory appears as an open file folder in the Directory Tree, and the files that belong to the System subdirectory are listed in the Directory Contents List. Note that the Directory Tree expands to show all subdirectories found on the same level as the System subdirectory (see Figure 4-3).

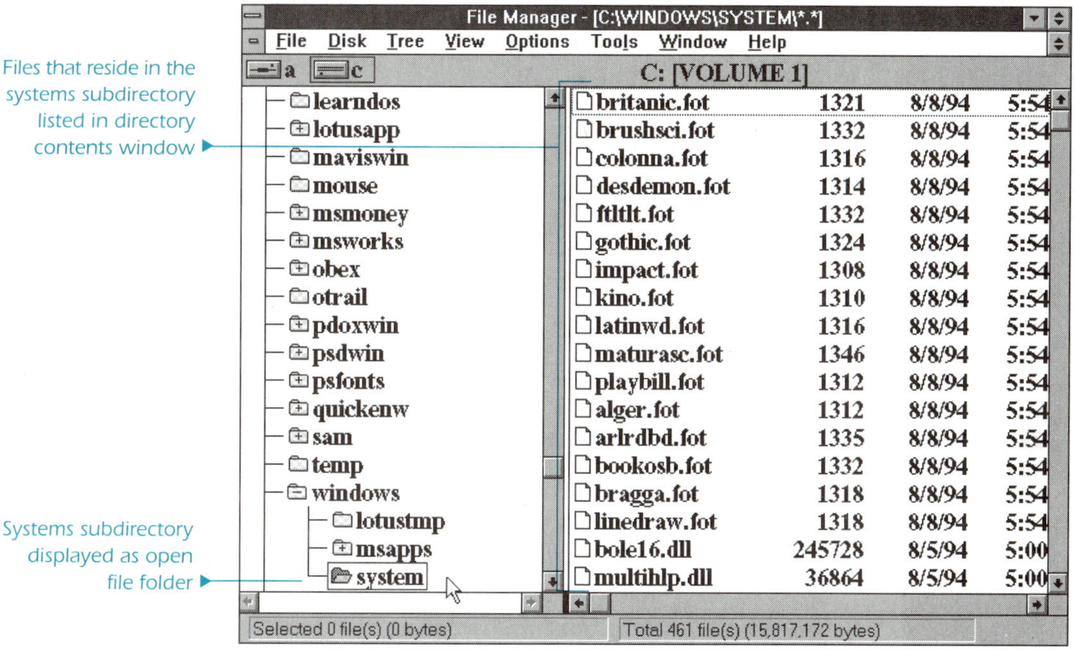

Figure 4-3 The contents of the System subdirectory listed in the Directory Contents List

TIP The double-clicking method can be used as a toggle switch to collapse and expand directory levels.

Exercise 3: Switching to a different disk drive

You can change the current drive and view its disk's contents by clicking the icon representing the desired drive in the drive icon bar.

1. Place a floppy disk in drive A.

WARNING Make sure that the disk is formatted before placing it in drive A. If you receive an error message stating that the system cannot read the disk you inserted, you may have put an unformatted disk in the drive.

2. Click drive A icon  on the drive icon bar.

   As the system addresses drive A, you should notice a small light near the drive A slot brightening, indicating that the disk is being read. A new window appears that lists the information stored on drive A (see Figure 4-4).

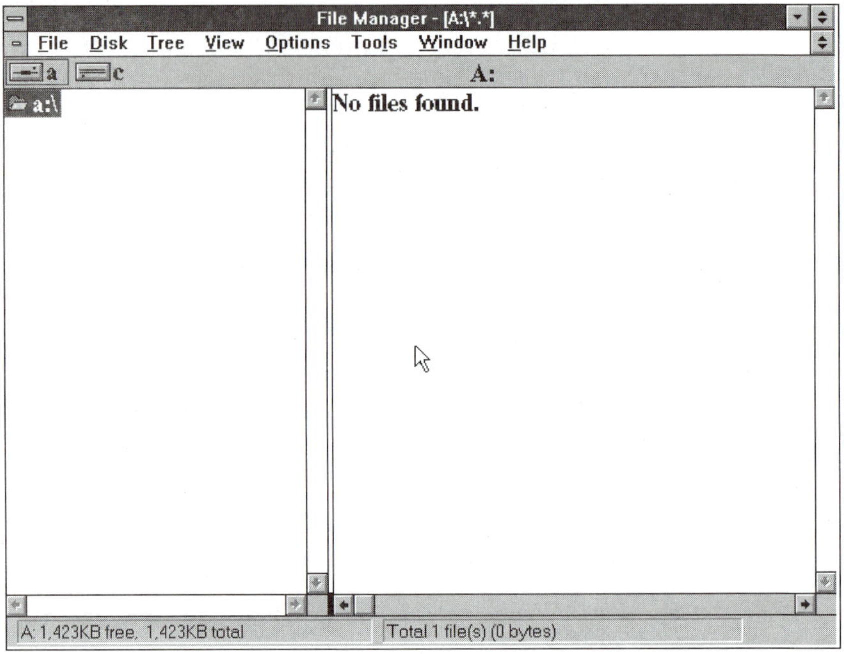

Figure 4-4 Information stored on drive A

Note that the information on the status and title bars also changes to reflect the new current drive.

3. Click the Hard Drive icon  on the icon drive bar. (Usually, this icon is the drive C icon. If it is not, ask your instructor for instructions).

   The contents of the hard disk are displayed.

Objective 3: Using the Tree Option

Since directories may contain subdirectories, the File Manager enables you to view these lower-level subdirectories easily and quickly. Subdirectories can be located on various levels in the tree structure. The Tree option—located on the File Manager menu bar—enables you to view the various levels by expanding and collapsing levels in a specific disk drive area.

Exercise 4: Expanding and collapsing the Directory Tree

To see subdirectory levels in the Directory Tree, do the following:

1. In the Directory Tree, find the icon representing your hard disk. (Usually, this icon is the drive C icon. If it is not, ask your instructor for instructions).

2. Double-click the Hard Drive icon to collapse it to an open folder icon.

   The Directory Tree displays the drive letter icon by itself—this is considered the root level. In the Directory Contents List the directories, subdirectories, and files that are located beneath the root level of the current drive are listed.

3. Choose the Tree option from the menu bar.

   The Tree menu is displayed.

4. Choose Expand One Level from the Tree pull-down menu.

   The Directory Tree displays the subdirectories that belong to the currently selected disk drive in the Directory Tree window. The Directory Contents List still displays the directories and files that are under the root directory of the currently selected drive.

5. Choose Tree; then choose Indicate Expandable Branches.

   This option acts as a toggle switch and can be turned on and off. When the option is activated, a checkmark appears to the left of the option on the menu. Note that some of the icons in the Directory Tree contain a plus sign (+), while others do not. A plus sign indicates that a directory has lower-level subdirectories within it. An empty directory icon indicates there are no lower-level subdirectories beneath it. Also, notice that the information in the title and status bars again changes as you expand and collapse levels (see Figure 4-5).

Directories indicating expandable branches

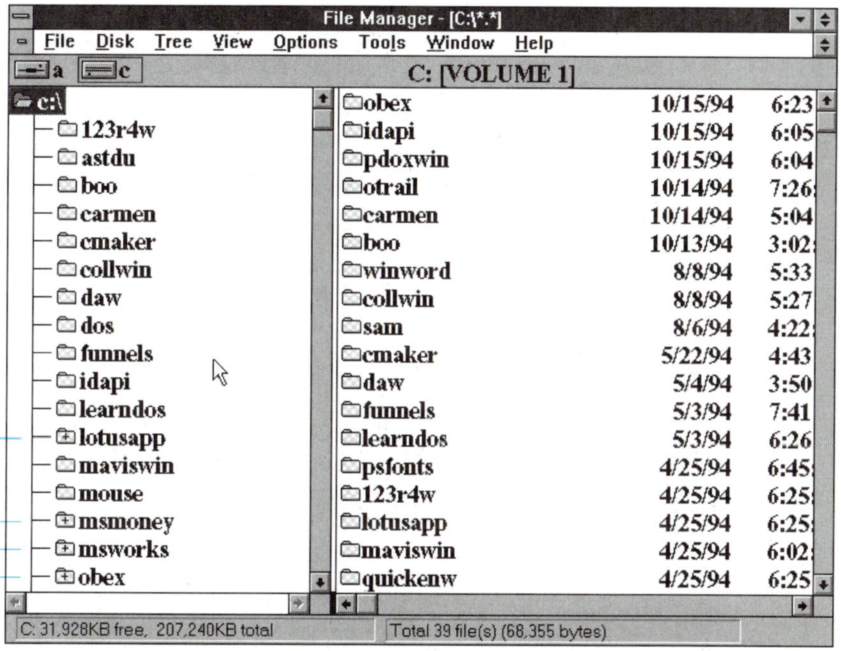

Figure 4-5 The Directory Tree indicating expandable branches

6. Scroll through the Directory Tree window until you find the Windows directory icon.
7. Select the Windows icon by clicking it once.

   It appears as an open folder.
8. Choose the Tree option and then select Expand Branch.

   The subdirectories that belong to the Windows directory are listed in the Directory Tree. Lower-level subdirectories are displayed as they cascade to the right of the Directory Tree window. The Directory Contents List displays the subdirectories of the Windows directory at the top of the Directory Contents List, as well as any existing files located in the Windows directory.
9. Scroll to the top of the Directory Contents List.

   An arrow followed by an ellipsis is displayed at the top of the Directory Contents List window. You can click this arrow to move you back to the previous level directory, which in this case would be the root directory of the current disk drive (see Figure 4-6).

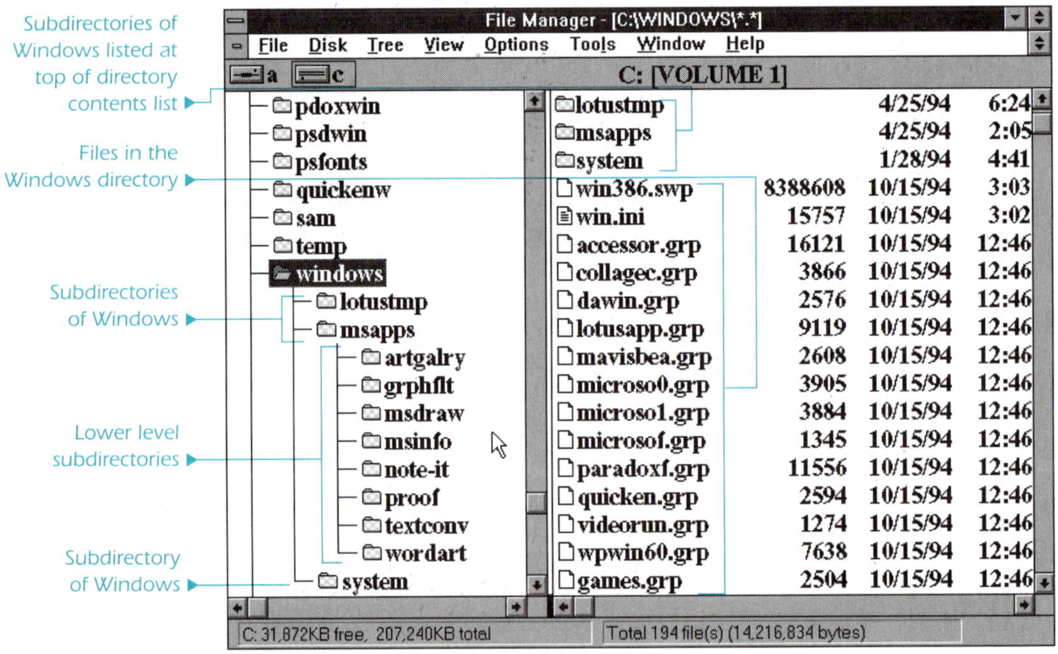

Figure 4-6 The Directory Tree displaying directories and lower-level subdirectories

10. Choose Tree; then choose Collapse Branch.

    The Directory Tree removes the expanded view of lower-level subdirectories of the Windows directory (see Figure 4-7).

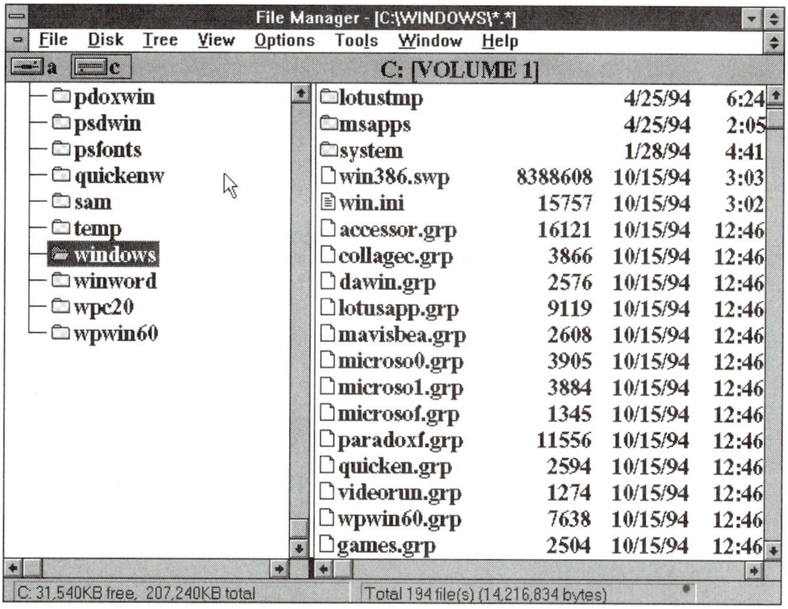

Figure 4-7 **Lower-level directories removed from the Directory Tree**

11. Choose Tree; then choose Expand All.

    All the directories found in the current disk drive area expand to show the lower-level subdirectories of each directory. A minus sign (–) inside a subdirectory means that the subdirectory can be collapsed (see Figure 4-8).

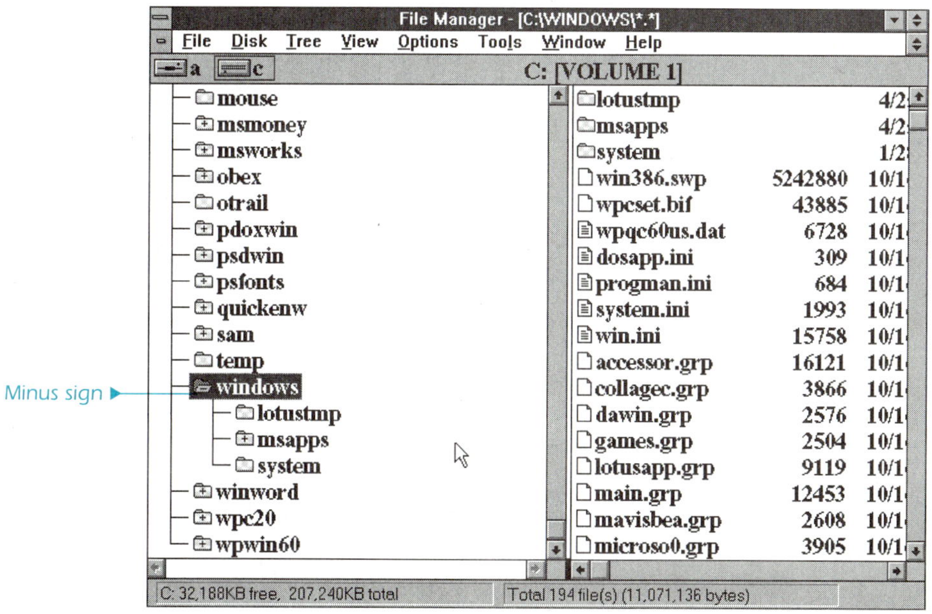

Figure 4-8 **All directories of the current drive with lower-level directories displayed**

12. Find the root level at the top of the Directory Tree window and double-click it to collapse all lower-level subdirectories.
13. Choose Tree; then choose Expand One Level.

Objective 4: Using the View Option

The File Manager provides a number of ways for you to customize the appearance of your Directory Tree and Directory Contents List. Using the View option located in the File Manager menu bar, you can increase or decrease the size of both windows, determine what elements of a file listing you want displayed in the Directory Contents List, and sort files by a variety of criteria.

Exercise 5: Sizing the File Manager windows

The Directory Tree and Directory Contents List can be increased or decreased in size to suit your individual needs. Two methods are available for resizing the windows, as this exercise demonstrates.

1. Choose the View option from the File Manager menu bar.
2. Choose Split.

   Notice that a dark vertical line is displayed (see Figure 4-9).

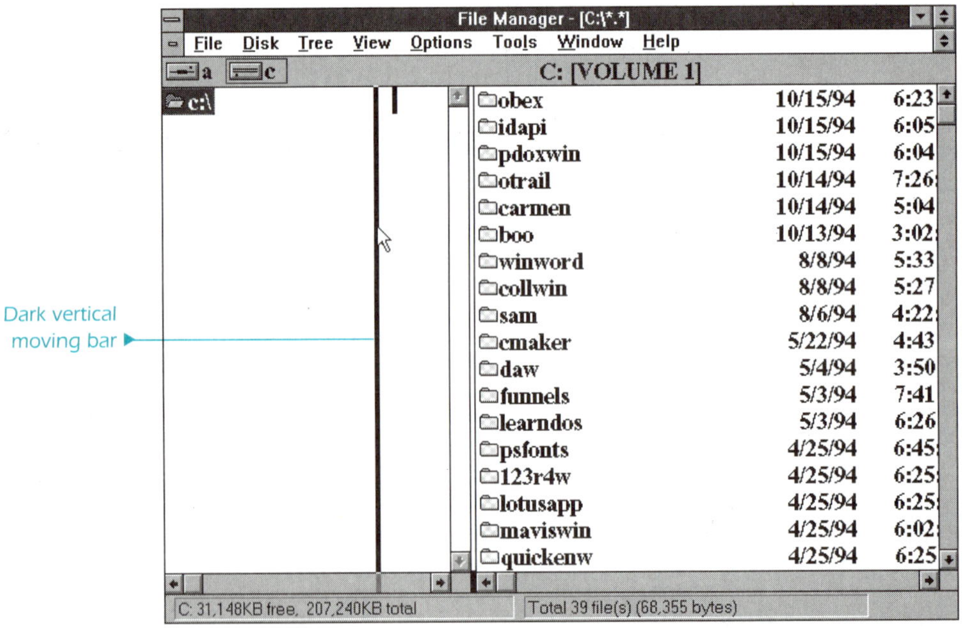

Figure 4-9 The dark vertical line in the File Manager window

3. Drag the mouse 1 inch to the right to increase the Directory Tree window and decrease the Directory Contents List window.

4. Click the left mouse button to see the change.
5. Place the mouse pointer on the double line that separates the Directory Tree and Directory Contents List windows.

   The mouse pointer turns into a double-headed arrow.
6. Drag the mouse 1 inch to the left to reposition the windows as they were before Step 3.

Choosing the windows you want to see

The View option includes several options that enable you to view the Directory Tree, the Directory Contents List, or both. These toggle-switch options are the first three options listed on the View pull-down menu.

Exercise 6: Choosing the display of the Directory Tree

To examine the different ways the Directory Tree can be displayed, do the following:

1. Choose the View option from the File Manager menu bar.

   The currently selected view has a checkmark next to it.
2. Choose Tree Only.

   The Directory Contents List disappears while the Directory Tree is still displayed (see Figure 4-10).

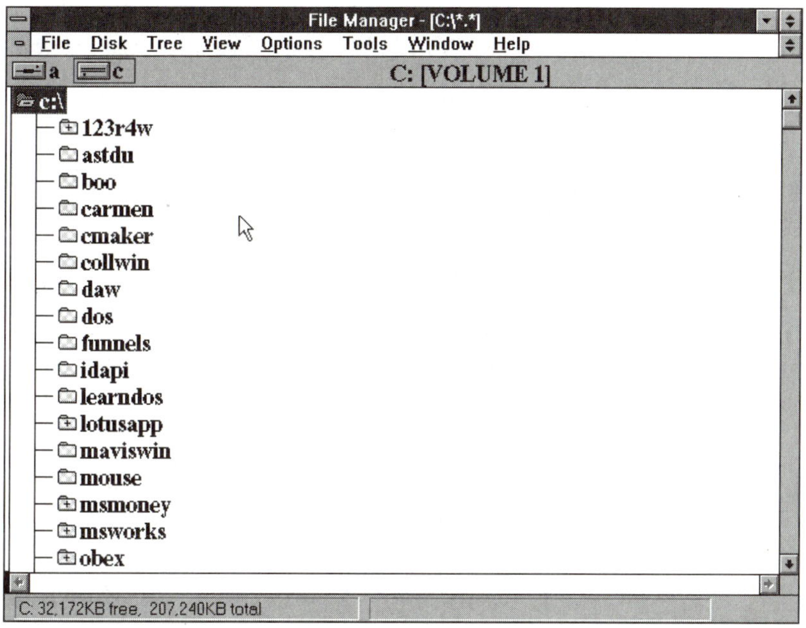

Figure 4-10 The File Manager displaying only the Directory Tree for the hard disk drive

3. Choose the View option from the menu bar; then choose Directory Only.

   The Directory Tree disappears and the Directory Contents List is displayed (see Figure 4-11).

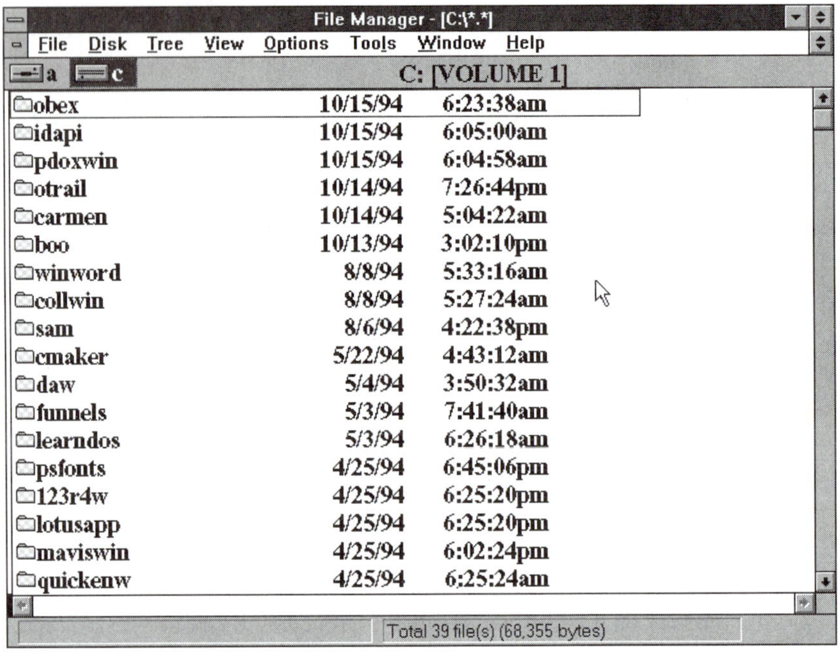

Figure 4-11 The File Manager displaying only the Directory Contents List for the hard disk drive

4. Choose the View option from the menu bar; then choose Tree and Directory.

   Both windows are displayed.

Choosing the details displayed in the Directory Contents List

You can have the Directory Contents List display different file information. You can choose to display the file names by themselves, all the detailed information regarding the files, or select specific details such as modification times and dates.

Exercise 7: Displaying different information in the Directory Contents List

To examine the different information that can be displayed in the Directory Contents List, do the following:

1. Select the Windows directory from the Directory Tree, if it is not already selected.
2. Choose View from the menu bar.

3. Choose Name.

   The Directory Contents List displays only the name of the files within the selected directory (see Figure 4-12).

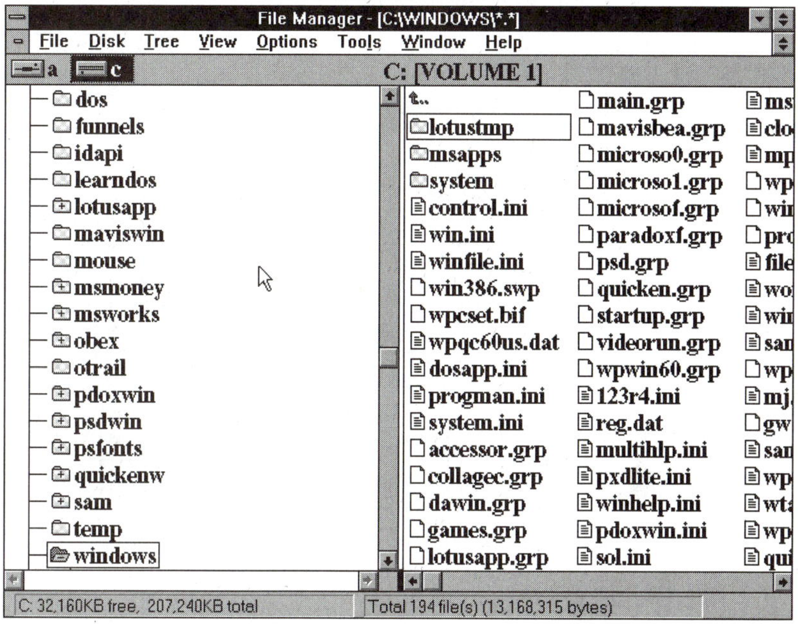

Figure 4-12 The Directory Contents List window displaying only file names

4. Choose View from the menu bar.
5. Choose All File Details.
6. Use the horizontal scroll arrows to scroll to the right side of the Directory Contents List.

   The Directory Contents List is expanded to display the file name, byte size, the date the file was created or last modified, the time the file was created or last modified, and any attributes that may have been assigned to the file (see Figure 4-13).

Virus Protection

Dark Avenger, HellRaiser, the Unforgiven. Do these names sound familiar? Maybe they're the titles of recent horror flicks or the names of bad guys in your favorite comic strip? Think again. These names are some of the more popular aliases used by virogens. *Virogens* are individuals who write code that invades your computer and wreaks disk havoc. Corrupting data files, blowing hard disks, and eating away at program files are just a few of the nasty things these codes can do. Who are these virogens? What is their motivation? How do they pull it off?

The profile of a virogen ranges from a teenager to a sophisticated computer programmer to an antivirus software developer! As far as motivation is concerned, some have said they produced computer viruses out of boredom, claiming it was thrilling to destroy information without being detected. Virogens say that antivirus developers often pay them to write and create new viruses and that antivirus developers then spread a new virus to turn a profit in their own businesses. The developers vehemently deny this, of course, but the accusations continue.

Regardless of who is at fault, there are a number of precautionary measures that users can take to prevent infection. Tips for prevention include not using pirated software, paying close attention to any inconsistencies in the operation of your system, making regular backups, being cautious about files that you download from an electronic bulletin board, and keeping secret passwords secret.

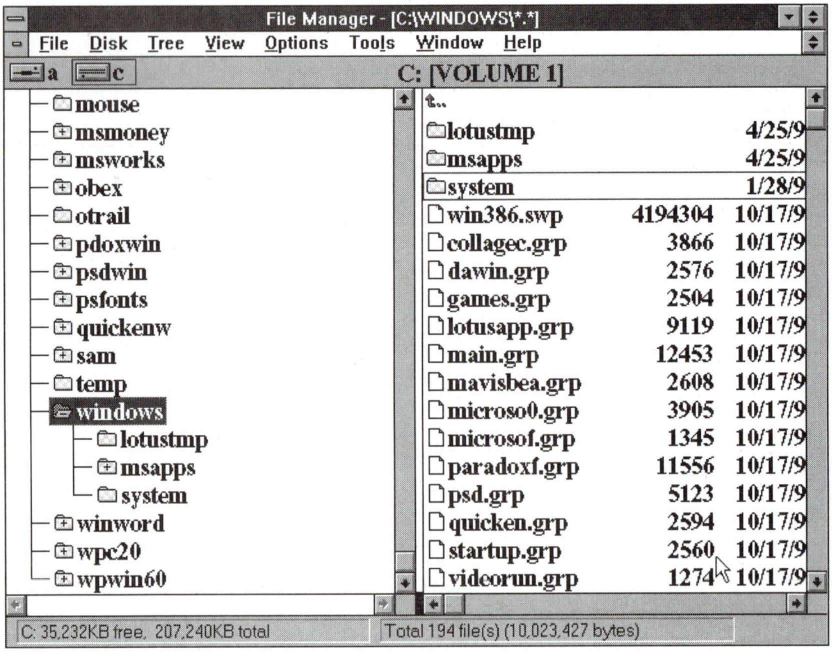

Figure 4-13 The Directory Contents List expanded to show all file details

7. Choose View from the menu bar.
8. Choose Partial Details.

   The Partial Details dialog box appears (see Figure 4-14).

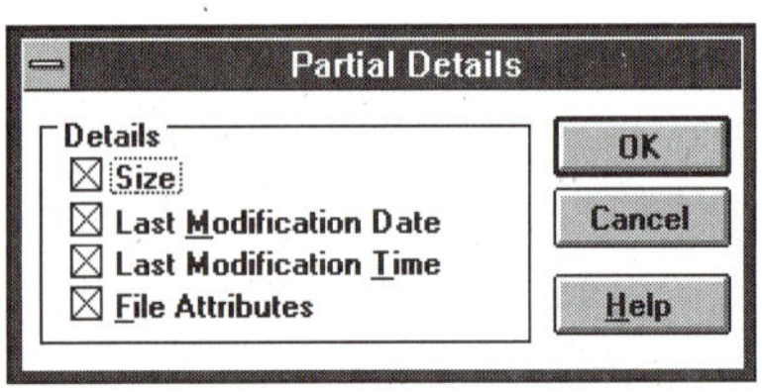

Figure 4-14 The Partial Details dialog box

   You can select any option by clicking the checkbox beside it.

9. Deselect the Size option; then choose OK.

   All the file details except size are displayed.

10. Choose View from the menu bar.
11. Choose Partial Details.

    The Partial Details dialog box appears.

12. Select Size. Choose OK.

Sorting files in the Directory Contents List

You can have the listing of files in the Directory Contents List sorted alphabetically by name or extension. You can also sort files by size, from largest to smallest, and date, from oldest to newest.

Exercise 8: Sorting a File Listing

To use the various sort options, do the following:

1. Choose the View option from menu bar.
2. Choose Sort by Name.

   The file names in the Directory Contents List appear in alphabetical order (see Figure 4-15).

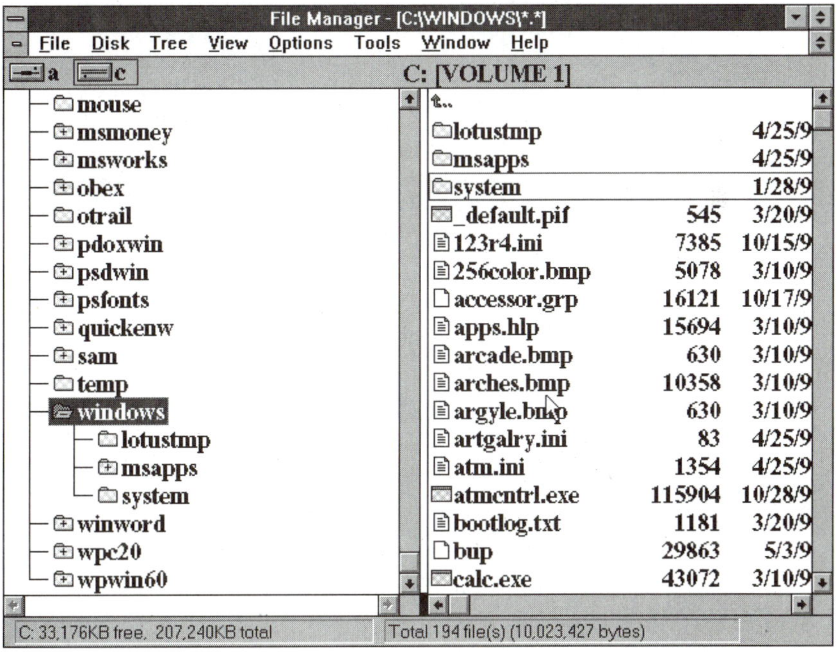

Figure 4-15 File names sorted by name in alphabetical order

3. Choose the View option; then choose Sort by Type.

   The extensions of the file names are sorted in alphabetical order (see Figure 4-16). (You may have to scroll down the list to see file names that include extensions.)

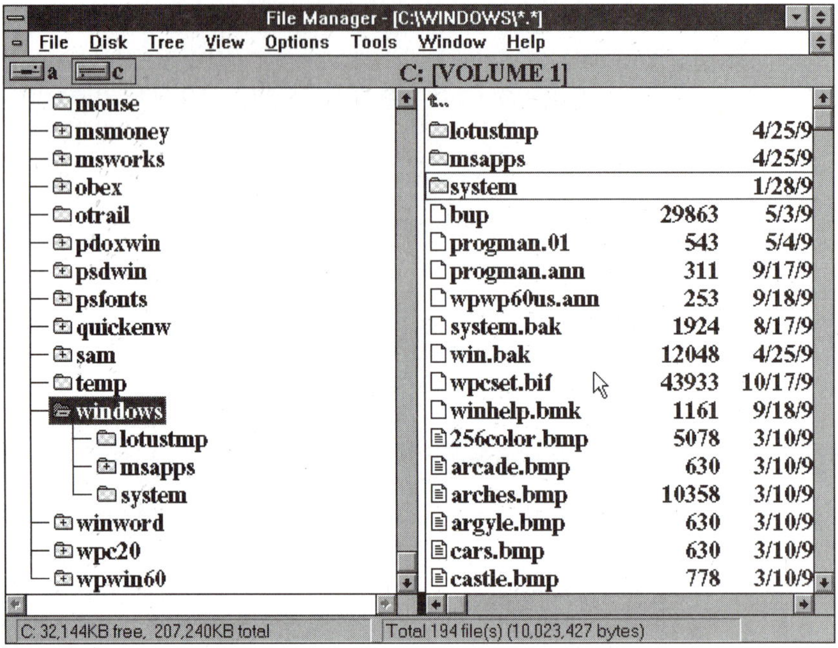

Figure 4-16 File name extensions sorted in alphabetical order

4. Choose the View option; then choose Sort by Size.

   The files are sorted by file size, from largest to smallest (see Figure 4-17).

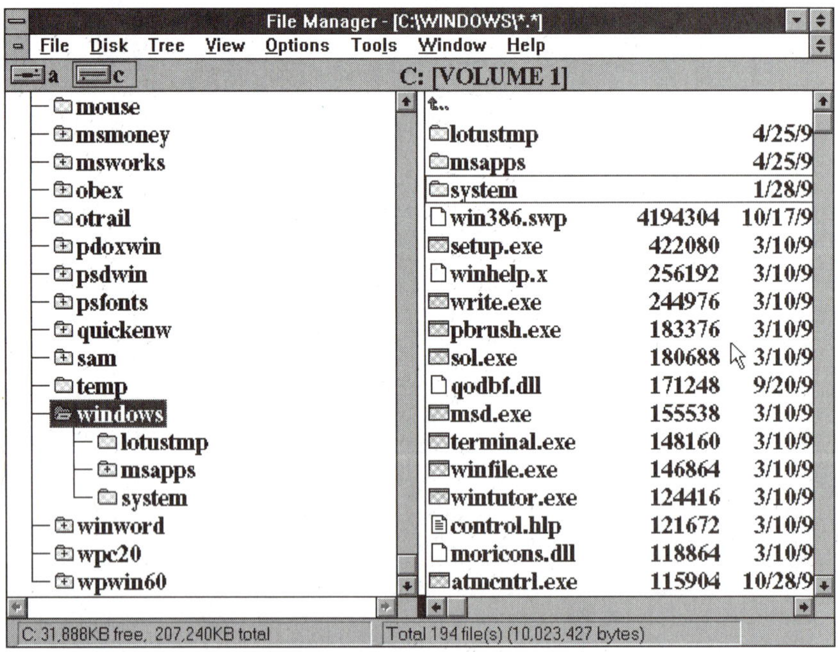

Figure 4-17 Files sorted by file size

5. Choose the View option; then choose Sort by Date.

   The files are sorted by the date of creation or last modification, from oldest date to newest (see Figure 4-18).

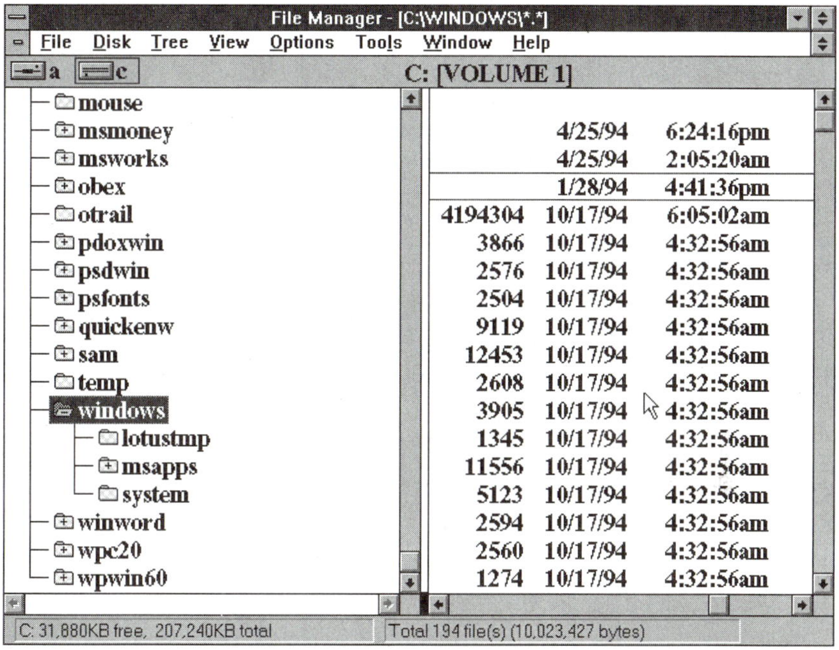

Figure 4-18 File names sorted by date

Viewing a file by type

The last option on the View menu—By File Type—enables you to select specific file types or match file names using specific parameters. Selecting from the various options affects only the active directory window.

Exercise 9: Displaying a file according to type

To view a file according to its file type, perform the following steps:

1. Choose the View option from the menu bar.
2. Choose By File Type.

   The By File Type dialog box appears offering several choices of types of files (see Figure 4-19). Table 4-3 describes the options listed in the By File Type dialog box.

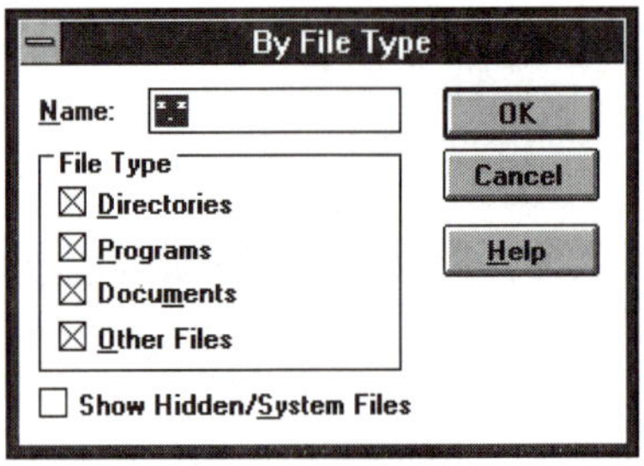

Figure 4-19 **The By File Type dialog box**

Table 4-3 **By File Type options**

OPTION	FUNCTION
Name	Type wildcard characters in the Name text box to display only those files with matching names or extensions.
Directories	Select this option to display only the directories found in the current directory.
Programs	Select this option to display all files having an extension of .exe, .com, .pif, or .bat.
Documents	Select this option to display all files that are associated with an application.
Other Files	Select this option to display files that are not associated with an application.
Show Hidden/System Files	Select this option to display hidden and system files.

3. Select Directories and Documents.
4. Deselect Programs, Other Files, and Show Hidden/System Files, if they are selected.

TIP To deselect an option, click the check box to remove the X.

5. Choose OK to return to the Directory Contents List (see Figure 4-20). Only the directories and documents of the current directory are displayed in the window.

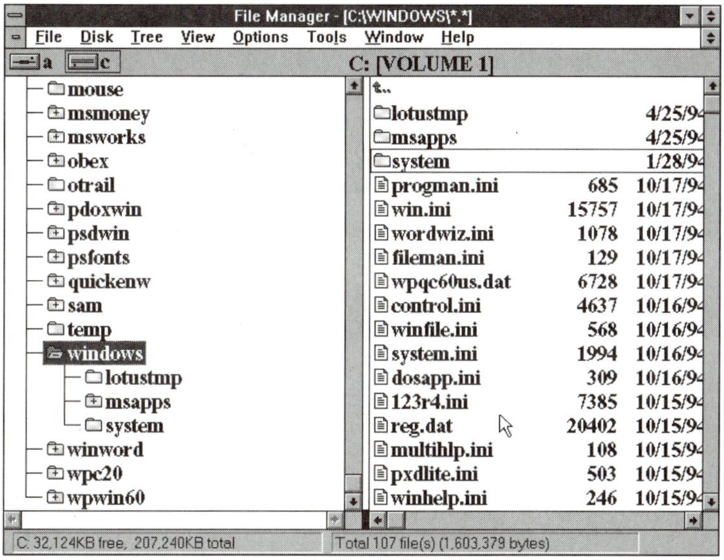

Figure 4-20 Only the directories and documents of the current directory are displayed

6. Choose View; then choose By File Type.

   The By File Type dialog box appears.

7. Select Programs and deselect all other options.
8. Choose OK.

   Only the program files for the current directory are displayed in the window (see Figure 4-21).

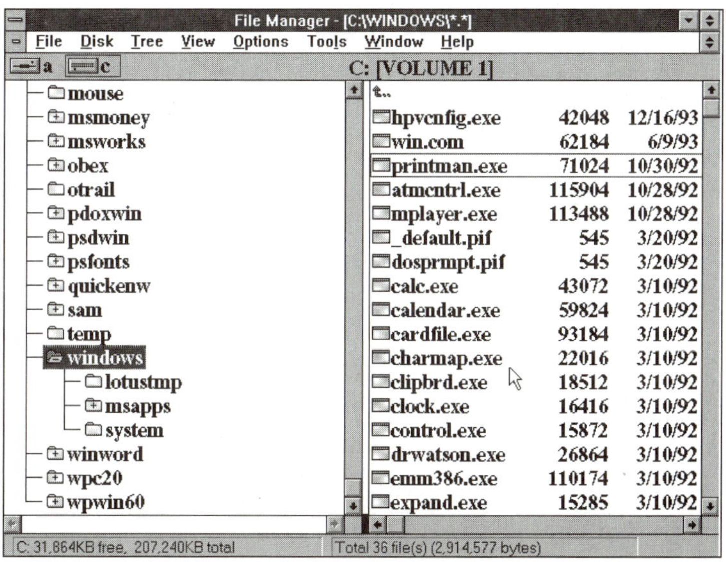

Figure 4-21 Program files displayed in the Directory Contents List

9. Choose View; then choose By File Type.

   The By File Type dialog box appears.

10. Select all options except the Show Hidden/System Files. Choose OK.

Objective 5: Using Options

By choosing Options from the File Manager menu bar, you can control a variety of visual displays that occur on the File Manager screen. The Options pull-down menu includes options for warning messages and font sizes and types, as well as toggle-switch options.

Confirming warning messages

Windows often provides a warning message that appears on your screen before you take an action that affects directories and files on a disk. You can control the display of warning messages from the Confirmation dialog box.

Exercise 10: Selecting confirmation of warning messages

To explore the use of the Confirmation dialog box, do the following:

1. Choose Options from the File Manager menu bar.
2. Choose Confirmation.

   The Confirmation dialog box appears (see Figure 4-22). Table 4-4 describes each option in this dialog box.

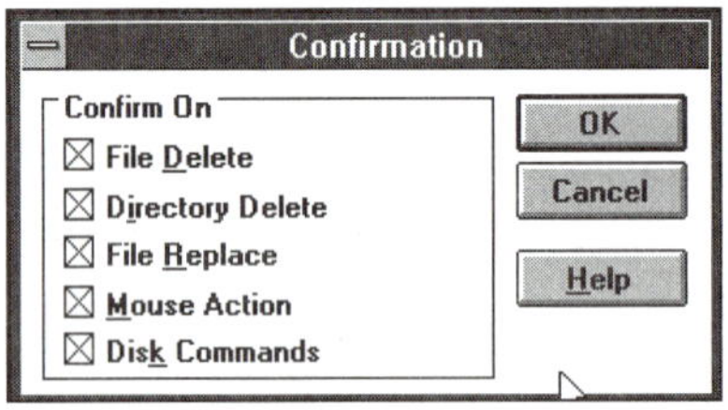

Figure 4-22 The Confirmation dialog box

3. You can select any option in this dialog box by clicking the check box beside it. Table 4-4 describes the options in the Confirmation dialog box. For now, leave all options as they appear and choose OK.

Table 4-4 Confirmation dialog box options

OPTION	DESCRIPTION
File Delete	Select this check box if you want to receive confirmation before deleting a file.
Directory Delete	Select this check box if you want to receive confirmation before deleting a directory. When you delete a directory, all its subdirectories and files are deleted.
File Replace	Select this check box if you want to receive confirmation before replacing one file name with another. (It's a good idea to select this option so that you don't write over files accidentally.)
Mouse Action	Select this check box if you want to receive confirmation before moving or copying files by dragging them with the mouse.
Disk Commands	Select this check box if you want to receive confirmation when issuing a disk command such as copying or formatting a disk.

Changing the display of the font in the File Manager windows

You can change the font size, typeface, and attributes of display text in the File Manager window. You can also specify that you want all file names or directory names to appear in uppercase or lowercase letters. To make these changes, you will use the Font option on the Options pull-down menu.

Exercise 11: Changing the font size, typeface, and attributes of display text

To change the current font size, typeface, and attributes of display text in the File Manager window, perform the following steps:

1. Choose Options from the File Manager menu bar.
2. Choose Font.

   The Font dialog box appears (see Figure 4-23).

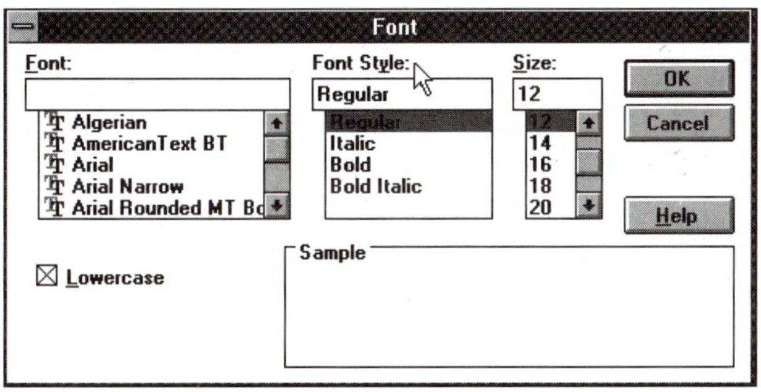

Figure 4-23 The Font dialog box

3. Select a font from the Font box.
4. Select a style from the Font Style box.
5. Select a font size from the Size box.

   The resulting type style will be displayed in the Sample box.
6. Deselect Lowercase to specify that all file names will appear in uppercase letters.
7. Choose OK.

   The File Manager Windows displays all file names in uppercase.
8. Reset the options in the Font dialog box to their original settings.

Toggling the status bar

The display of the File Manager status bar can be turned on or off. When the status bar is displayed, the Status Bar option on the Options pull-down menu has a checkmark next to it. When the status bar is not displayed, the Status Bar option on the Options pull-down menu does not have a checkmark next to it.

Exercise 12: Changing the status bar display

To turn the display of the status bar on and off, do the following:

1. Choose Options from the File Manager menu bar.
2. Choose Status Bar.

   You are returned to the display windows, and the status bar disappears.
3. Choose Options from the File Manager menu bar.
4. Choose Status Bar.

   You are returned to the display windows, and the status bar appears.

Displaying the File Manager as an icon

There may be times when you want the File Manager to be available but don't want it to fill the screen. By activating the Minimize on Use option from the Options menu on the File Manager menu bar, you can reduce the File Manager to an icon. This enables you to work in other applications and access the File Manager whenever you need to. The Minimize on Use option operates as a toggle switch.

Exercise 13: Reducing File Manager to an icon

To reduce the File Manager to an icon, do the following:

1. Choose Options from the File Manager menu bar.
2. Choose Minimize on Use.

   A checkmark appears next to the option, indicating it is activated.

3. Choose the Windows directory from the Directory Tree window of the File Manager, if it is not already selected.

   The Windows directory appears as an open folder.

4. Choose the View option from the File Manager menu bar.
5. Choose By File Type.

   The By File Type dialog box appears.

6. Deselect all options in the By File Type dialog box except Programs.
7. Choose OK.

   The Directory Contents List displays only files from the Windows directory that end in .exe, .pif, .bat, and .com.

8. Scroll through the Directory Contents List until you find the write.exe file.
9. Double-click the write.exe file to load it into main memory.

   The Write document window is displayed on the screen, and the File Manager is reduced to an icon on the desktop (see Figure 4-24).

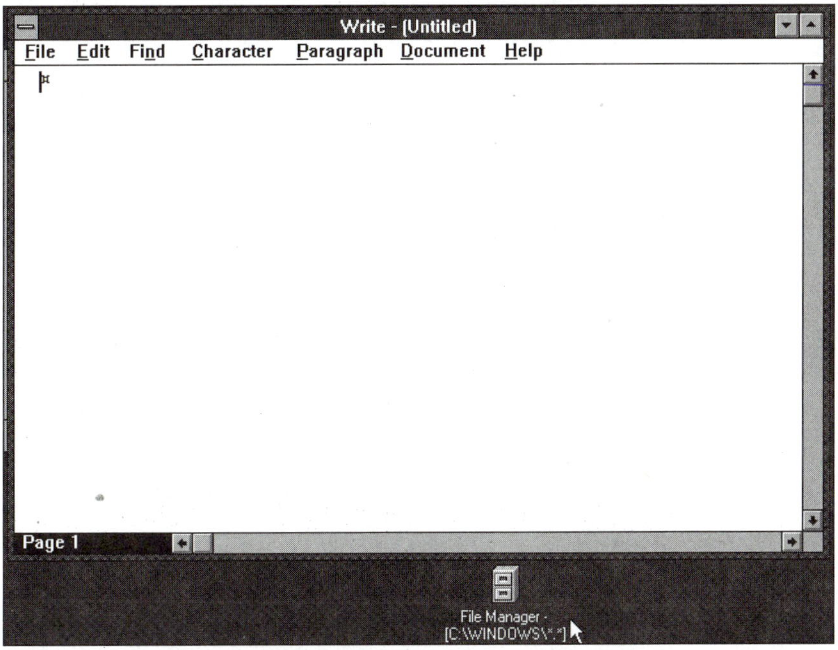

Figure 4-24 The File Manager window reduced to an icon on the desktop

10. Close the Write document window.
11. Double-click the File Manager icon  to restore the File Manager window to its previous size.

12. Deselect the Minimize on Use option so that the File Manager window does not reduce to an icon.
13. In the By File Type dialog box, select all options.

Using the Save Settings on Exit option

The Save Settings on Exit option in the Options pull-down menu enables you to return to the same display of File Manager windows that was displayed when you last exited Windows. This option operates as a toggle switch.

Exercise 14: Saving File Manager window display

To save the current File Manager window display, perform the following steps:

1. Choose Options from the File Manager menu bar.
2. Choose Save Settings on Exit, if it is not already selected.
3. Exit Windows.
4. Restart Windows.
5. Start the File Manager from the Main window.

   The screen displays the File Manager windows as they were when you exited Windows.
6. Choose Options from the File Manager menu bar.
7. Choose Save Settings on Exit to deselect it.

Chapter Summary

In this chapter, you gained a better understanding of how DOS organizes files and directories. More important, you learned how the Windows File Manager makes the DOS data structuring system much easier to work with by enabling you to expand and collapse directories and subdirectories in a graphical environment. You learned how to change the look of the File Manager window by changing font sizes, typefaces, and font attributes and displaying only the portions of a file that you want to view.

Review Questions

True/False Questions

_____ 1. The File Manager handles many of the same tasks as DOS.

_____ 2. All computer systems have the same number of disk drives.

_____ 3. You can use a single click to expand or collapse directory levels.

_____ 4. The Split command splits the display of File Manager windows horizontally.

_____ 5. The Sort by Type option sorts file names by their extensions.

Multiple-Choice Questions

_____ 6. To choose certain types of detailed information you want displayed in the Directory Contents List window, you would choose

A. View, All File Details.

B. Tree, Expand One Level.

C. Options, Confirmation.

D. View, Partial Details.

E. none of the above

_____ 7. To display plus and minus signs in the icons in the Directory Tree window, you would choose

A. View, Tree and Directory.

B. Options, Expand Branch.

C. Tree, Indicate Expandable Branches.

D. View, By File Type.

_____ 8. All the options located in the View pull-down menu are toggle switches except

A. Name.

B. Split.

C. By File Type.

D. Partial Details.

E. B and C only

_____ 9. It's a good idea to select the following Confirmation check box:

A. Directory Delete.

B. File Replace.

C. Disk Commands.

D. Mouse Action.

_____ 10. Program files may have the following extension:

A. .exe

B. .pif

C. .com

D. A and B only

E. all of the above

Fill-in-the-Blank Questions

11. The File Manager ______________ represents files and directories on a disk area.
12. A filing cabinet drawer could be compared to a ______________.
13. An arrow followed by an ellipsis at the top of the Directory Contents List can be used to move to the ______________ level directory.
14. The ______________ ______________ option can be used to view all the lower-level subdirectories found in the current drive area in the Directory Tree.
15. To have a file sorted by its size, choose the ______________ ______________ ______________ option in the View pull-down menu.

Acumen-Building Activities

Quick Projects

1. Using File Manager

1. Start the Windows program and display the File Manager window.
2. Change from the hard disk drive to drive A. Remember the rule you must follow to do this.
3. In the File Manager window, display the contents of the disk in drive A.
4. Return to the hard disk drive and display its contents in the File Manager window.
5. Identify the various parts of the File Manager window.

2. Using the Directory Tree

1. Using the File Manager, click the hard disk icon in the Directory Tree.
2. Open a directory of your choice that resides directly under the root directory of the hard disk.
3. Expand the level to include any subdirectories and files found under the open directory.

4. Issue the command that will inform you of directories that can be expanded or collapsed.
5. Issue the command to display only the extensions of the files in the Directory Contents List.

3. Working with File Manager

1. Using the File Manager, issue the command to display all file details in the Directory Contents List.
2. Collapse the directory.
3. Issue the command to expand all the directories found under the root directory.
4. Resize the Directory Tree so that it is 1 inch wide and 1 inch long.

4. Working further with File Manager

1. Using the File Manager, issue the command to display only the Directory Tree.
2. Issue the command to display only the Directory Contents List.
3. In the Directory Contents List, display the names of document files in uppercase letters.
4. Resize the File Manager, Accessories , and Games windows.
5. Tile the displayed windows.
6. Move the Games window to the bottom, right corner of the screen. Move the Accessories window to the top, left corner of the screen. Move the File Manager window to the center of the screen. Resize all three windows, if necessary.
7. Close the Games and Accessories windows.

In-Depth Projects

1. Working with the Directory Tree

1. Start Windows.
2. Open the File Manager window.
3. Expand all branches of the directories in the Directory Tree.
4. Change the font type of file names in the Directory Contents List to Century Schoolbook. Apply the Bold attribute, increase the size of the font to 16 points, and specify that file names will appear in all lowercase letters.
5. Sort the file names by size.

2. Using Windows

1. Open the following windows: File Manager, Main, and Accessories.
2. Issue the commands to reduce the File Manager to an icon on the desktop whenever an application is launched.
3. Start the following programs so that a document window for each appears on the screen: Write, Calendar, and Cardfile. Cascade the document windows.
4. Open the File Manager window and remove the status bar.
5. Make the Write document window the active window; then close it. Do the same with the Calendar and Cardfile document windows.
6. Change the setting used to reduce the File Manager to an icon back to its original setting. Undo any changes you made to the File Manager window. Close the File Manager and exit Windows.

3. Using File Manager

1. Launch Windows and open the File Manager window.
2. Use the Help option to look up the term *current directory*.
3. In the File Manager window, display only the Directory Tree.
4. Change the font type of file names in the Directory Tree to Times Roman. Apply the Italics Bold attribute and change the size of the font to 10 points.
5. Display the Directory Tree and Directory Contents List. Change the font back to its previous display.
6. Select a directory and display only its file names and file modification dates in the Directory Contents List.
7. Sort the files by date.
8. Issue the command to display only program files.
9. Issue the command to save the current display of the File Manager windows.
10. Exit Windows.
11. Restart Windows and display the File Manager windows.

Acumen Fundamentals Milestone

Individual Project:

Preparing Your Work Environment and Data Disk

You have been hired by Premier Systems Consulting (PSC), a firm that specializes in setting up computer systems for a variety of small businesses. Your first day on the job, your supervisor assigns you the following tasks:

1. Configure your computer with SmartMon, Vsafe Manager, and MSOffice in the Startup Group and minimize the group window.
2. Enlarge the Program Manager window so that it fills the screen and minimize the Game and Accessories group windows. Tile the Main window and the group windows that contain your word processing, database, and spreadsheet software. If your computer has the MSOffice program group, these program icons will be in the MSOffice window. Minimize any other groups and arrange the icons so that each is visible.
3. Format a floppy disk that you will use to store all your data files.
4. Create the following directories on your data disk: memos, database, workshts, myinfo, cardfile, and shows.
5. Copy all files with the extension .wri from the C:\windows directory to the floppy-disk directory A:\myinfo.
6. Store the disk in a safe place.

Team Project:

Preparing a Group Filing System

As part of a newly designed disaster-recovery plan, PSC has mandated that each work group maintain a team data disk that stores all the data files for each team member. Working with the other members of your team, use the following steps to create your team disk:

1. Format a high-density disk.

2. In the root directory of the team disk, create a directory for each member of the team using the team member's last name.
3. Each team member is responsible for copying all directories and files from his or her data disk to his or her directory on the team disk.
4. Use the Expand All selection on the Tree menu in the File Manager to verify that the team disk contains all the directories and files for each team member.
5. Store the disk in a safe place.

Part 2

Critical Thinking

Chapter 5

Managing Files and Disks with the File Manager

Objectives

- Using the Disk Menu
- Arranging Multiple Windows
- Naming a File
- Using the File Menu
- Organizing a File
- Applying File Attributes
- Using the Search Option
- Using the Delete Option

Key Terms

TERM	DEFINITION
Attribute	a characteristic—such as read only, archive, hidden, and system—that can be applied to a file
Disk-Level Command	a command that applies to an entire disk rather than a portion of a disk (such as a file or directory)
Format	to erase all information from a disk and prepare it for use on a particular computer platform (such as Macintosh or PC)
Source Drive	the disk drive from which information is currently being copied
Destination Drive	the disk drive to which information is currently being copied
Primary Name	the mandatory first part of a file name, which is one to eight characters in length

TERM	DEFINITION
Extension	the optional second part of a file name, which begins with a period that is followed by one to three characters
File-Level Command	a command that applies to a portion of a disk (such as a file or directory) rather than an entire disk
Selecting	choosing, or highlighting, an element (such as text, a graphic, an icon, a file, or a directory) in order to apply a command to that element
Bootable System Disk	a disk from which a computer can boot up—that is, launch its operating system

In this chapter, you will learn more about the File Manager and how to manipulate files and subdirectories on a disk. You will learn how to move, copy, delete, rename, search for, and apply attributes to files. Creating and removing subdirectories is also covered. Finally, you will practice arranging on the screen sets of windows that refer to different disk areas.

Objective 1: Using the Disk Menu

disk-level command

format

bootable system disk

The Disk menu in the File Manager menu bar enables you to perform a variety of disk-level commands on your floppy disks. A *disk-level command* is a command that applies to an entire disk rather than a portion of a disk (such as a file or directory). With these commands, you can copy information from one floppy disk to another, format a floppy disk, assign a volume label to a floppy disk to identify it, make a floppy disk a bootable system disk, and select a different disk drive from the Disk menu. *Format* means to erase all information from a disk and prepare it for use on a particular computer platform (such as Macintosh or PC). A *bootable system disk* is a disk from which a computer can boot up—that is, launch its operating system.

For the exercises in this chapter, you will need to have one 3.5-inch or 5.25-inch double density or high density floppy disk. Make sure this disk does not contain data you want to save. The density of a disk determines the amount of storage that is available on the disk. The floppy disk drives on different computers can read disks of different densities. Your instructor will tell you whether your computer can read only double-density disks or both double density and high density disks.

Formatting a disk

Before you can use a disk, it must be formatted. Unformatted disks are unreadable to a computer. The formatting process sets up tracks and sectors on the disk where information will be stored. If you try to access an unformatted disk, the File Manager will display an error message that reads `The disk in Drive` *`X`* `is not formatted. Do you want to format it now?` Table 5-1 describes various types of floppy disks.

When you format a disk, you also have the option of assigning a volume label to the disk. Label names are used to help identify the contents of a disk. Label names can include up to eleven characters and are displayed at the top of the Directory Tree and in the title bar of a window when the disk drive is active.

Table 5-1 Types of floppy disks

DISK TYPE	AVAILABLE STORAGE (in Bytes)	DENSITY	DRIVE USED
3.5"	1.44MB	HD	HD only
3.5"	720K	DD	HD or DD
5.25"	1.2MB	HD	HD
5.25"	360K	DD	HD or DD

HD = High Density K = Kilobytes
DD = Double Density MB = Megabytes

Exercise 1: Using the Format and Label options

In this exercise, you will format a blank disk and assign a label name to it.

1. Start Windows.
2. Open the File Manager window.
3. Place a blank diskette in drive A.
4. Choose Disk from the File Manager menu bar.

   The Disk pull-down menu appears.
5. Choose Format Disk.

   The Format Disk dialog box appears (see Figure 5-1).

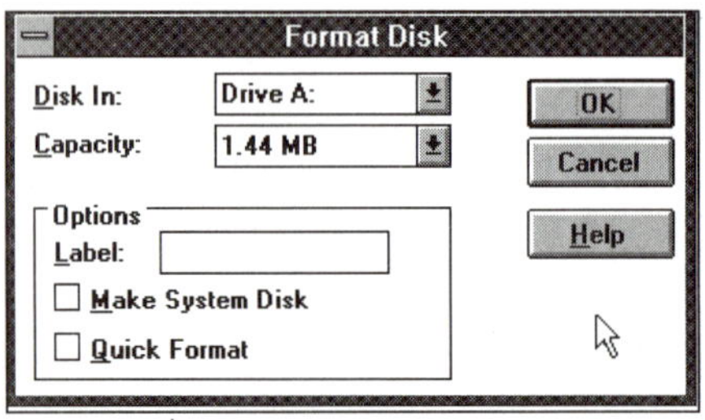

Figure 5-1 The Format Disk dialog box

Table 5.2 lists the options in the Format Disk dialog box.

Table 5-2 Options in the Format Disk dialog box

Label	Use this option to assign or change a volume label on a disk.
Make System Disk	Use this option to create a floppy disk and include the DOS system files on it. The floppy disk can then be used to boot up a system that uses the MS-DOS operating system.
Quick Format	Use this option to reformat a disk that has been formatted previously and that contains information you no longer need.

6. Make sure the Disk In text box displays `Drive A:`. You can click the arrow to the right of the text box to display other available choices (see Figure 5-2). The drop-down list shows the floppy disk drive areas with which your system is equipped.

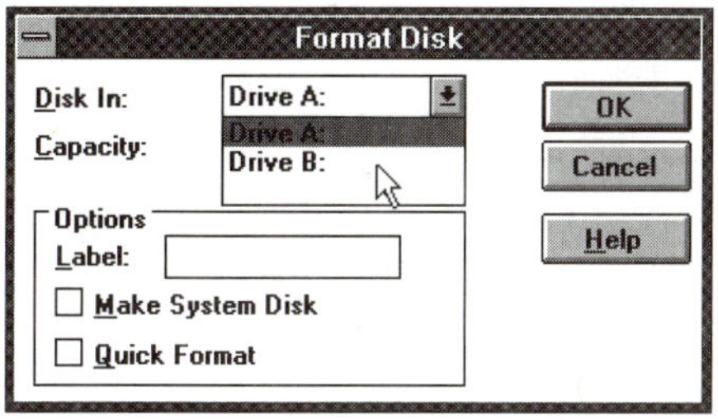

Figure 5-2 The drop-down list of available floppy disk drive areas

7. Make sure that the correct amount of floppy disk storage space is displayed in the Capacity text box. Click the arrow to the right of the text box to choose from a list of available choices.

WARNING If you try to format a disk with the incorrect capacity amount entered in the Capacity text box, an error message may appear, halting the process. If the formatting is completed with the incorrect capacity setting, information on the disk may be difficult or impossible to access.

8. In the Label text box, type DISK1.

   When you choose file names and label names, do not include any spaces, and make sure the name does not exceed 11 characters.

9. Choose OK to begin formatting.

   The Confirm Format Disk message box appears, alerting you that all data will be erased from the disk (see Figure 5-3).

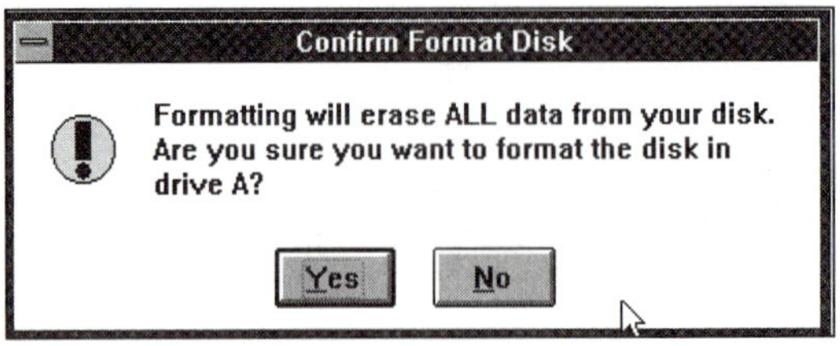

Figure 5-3 The Confirm Format Disk message box

10. Choose Yes to continue formatting.

    The Formatting Disk message box appears showing how much of the formatting process is complete (see Figure 5-4).

Figure 5-4 The Formatting Disk message box

When formatting is complete, the Format Complete message box appears, asking if you want to format another disk (see Figure 5-5).

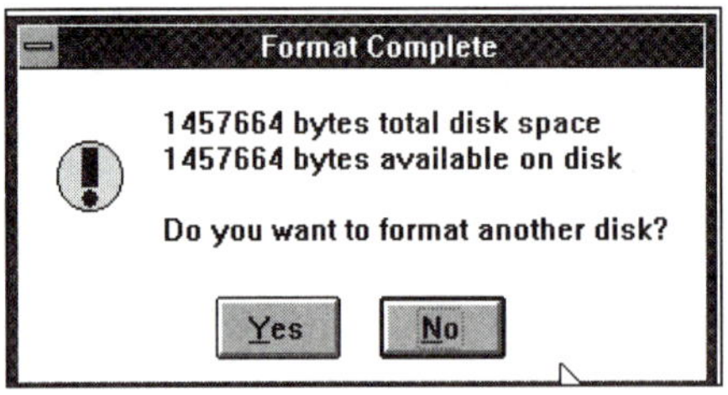

Figure 5-5 The Format Complete message box

11. Choose No.

    You are returned to the File Manager window.

12. Choose the drive A icon from the drive icon bar.

    The File Manager window displays the newly formatted floppy disk in the window (see Figure 5-6). The volume label name appears in the title bar of the window.

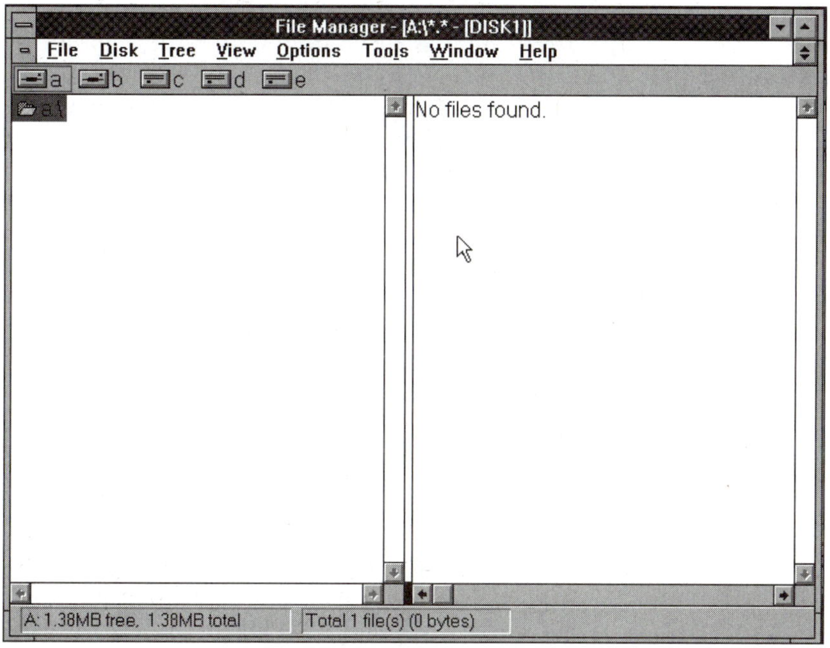

Figure 5-6 The formatted disk, including the volume label name DISK1, is displayed in the File Manager window

TIP You may find it more convenient to format many disks at once so that you will have a formatted disk on hand whenever you need it. To do this, choose Yes in the Format Complete message box, and you will be prompted to insert a new disk for formatting. Continue the formatting process until all the disks are formatted.

The Quick Format command

You may find, over time, that you accumulate disks containing information you no longer need. It is useful to recycle these disks by erasing the information they contain. The Quick Format command can be used to reformat a disk that has been formatted previously and that contains information you no longer need. The Quick Format command should *not* be used to format a brand-new disk because the Quick Format command—unlike the Format command—will not search for corrupted areas on the disk.

Copying a disk

The Copy Disk command on the Disk menu enables you to copy all the information on one floppy disk to another. The two disks used in this process must be the same size and have the same density. For example, to make a copy of the information on a 3.5-inch high density disk, the disk that you are copying to must also be a 3.5-inch high density disk.

source drive; destination drive

When you copy a disk to another disk, you will need to designate the *source drive* (the disk drive from which information is to be copied) and the *destination drive* (the disk drive to which information is to be copied) in the Copy Disk dialog box. The Copy Disk command will format an unformatted destination disk, thereby erasing any data that was stored on it.

The Copy Disk option can be used to make backups of documents and programs. It is a good idea to get in the habit of making backups on a regular basis. As any experienced computer user will attest, there is nothing worse than losing information and not being able to replace it with a recent backup of the original.

FEATURE

Recording Macros in Windows

The Recorder is a Windows accessory that you can use to record and play a macro. A macro is a set of commands that performs a specific task or tasks. The Recorder operates in the same fashion as a DOS batch file: When a macro is played back, the commands it contains are carried out, one by one, until the task is completed. A commonly used macro is one that makes a backup of a file, directory, or disk.

Exercise 2: Making disk copies

To make a copy of a disk, perform the following steps:

1. Insert the disk you want to copy into the source drive.
2. Insert the disk to which you want to copy information into the destination drive.
3. Choose Disk from the File Manager menu bar; then choose Copy Disk.

   The Confirm Copy Disk dialog box appears, informing you that the operation will erase all data from the destination disk and asking if you want to continue (see Figure 5-7).

Figure 5-7 The Confirm Copy Disk dialog box

4. Choose Yes.
5. Insert the disk that contains the information that you want copied, and then choose OK.

   The information on the source disk is copied into main memory. When the process is complete, the Copy Disk dialog box instructs you to insert the destination disk.
6. Insert the disk that you want the information to be copied to, and then choose OK.

TIP If your computer has only one floppy disk drive, you can designate that drive as both the source drive and destination drive. Windows will prompt you to insert first one disk and then the other into the floppy disk drive until all the information is copied from one disk to the other.

Objective 2: Arranging Multiple Windows

As you learned in previous chapters, Windows allows you to open several windows in the File Manager at once. You can arrange these windows so you can view the contents of each using the Window option on the File Manager menu bar.

Exercise 3: Arranging and viewing multiple windows

To view several windows in the File Manager at once, do the following:

1. Insert a formatted floppy disk in drive A.
2. Open the File Manager, if it is not already open.
3. Open the Windows directory on your hard disk and display the Directory Tree and Directory List Contents windows.
4. Choose Window.

   The Window pull-down menu appears.
5. Choose New Window.

   A duplicate of the Windows directory window is displayed (see Figure 5-8). Notice the *2* that appears in the title bar of the new window. This number indicates that this is the second window displayed for the current directory. The last window opened has a highlighted title bar, indicating that it is the active window.
6. Choose Window, and then choose Tile.

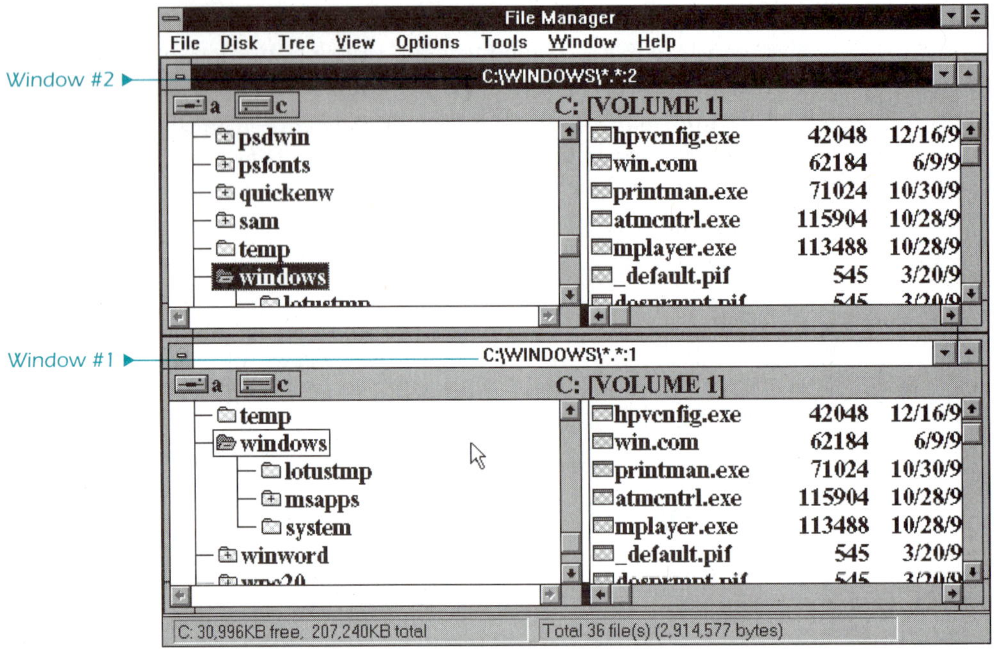

Figure 5-8 Duplicate windows

7. With the new window active, click the drive A icon from the drive icon bar.

   The new window displays the contents of the disk in drive A (see Figure 5-9).

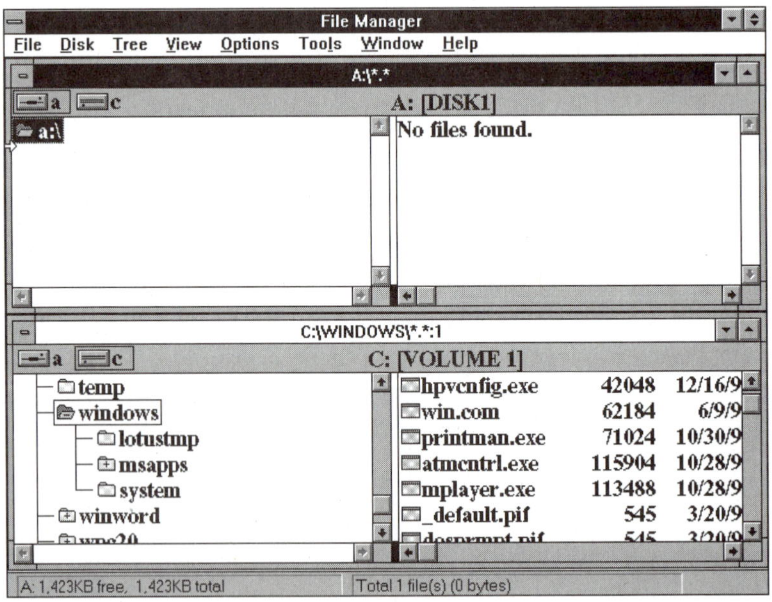

Figure 5-9 The new window displaying the contents of drive A

8. Choose Window, and then choose New Window.

   A duplicate window of drive A appears.

9. With the new window active, click the drive icon of the hard drive from the drive icon bar.

   The Windows directory is displayed in the new window.

10. Open the system subdirectory of the Windows directory.

    The contents of the system subdirectory are displayed in the new window. You can arrange the windows by using either the Tile or Cascade option on the Window pull-down menu.

11. Choose Window, and then choose Tile.

    The windows are arranged tiled on top of one another.

12. Close all the windows except for the C:\Windows window.
13. Maximize the C:\Windows window.

Objective 3: Naming a File

To maintain your files and directories, you need to understand the rules and conventions required by DOS to name files and directories. If you don't know and abide by these rules, you will have little success maintaining your files and directories.

All information on your computer is contained in files. Each file on your computer has a unique name. Two files may contain exactly the same information, but each must have its own file name.

primary name
extension

There are two parts to a file name: a *primary name* and an *extension*. A primary name is the mandatory first part of a file name, which is one to eight characters in length. An extension is the optional second part of a file name, which begins with a period that is followed by one to three characters. The period separates the primary name from the extension. Primary names and extensions must conform to the rules shown in Table 5-3. Table 5-4 gives examples of valid and invalid file names.

Table 5-3 Rules used to name files

Cannot include spaces.
Can include both uppercase and lowercase letters (A–Z).
Can include numbers (0–9).
Can include special characters, such as ~ ! @ # $ ^ & ( ) - _ { } '
Cannot include the following characters: . " / \ [ ] : * < > + = ;, ?

Table 5-4 Examples of valid and invalid file names

VALID FILE NAMES	INVALID FILE NAMES	REASON
1995.tax	abcdefghi.123	nine characters in primary name
Phone#s.lst	"my work.doc	quotation mark and space in file name
customer.dat	Jan.Report	six characters in the extension
homework.rpt		
$99^#!8?.000		
quiz1		
1.1		
a.123		
a		

When naming a file, you should name it according to its contents. For example, a letter to your mother could be given the name lettrma.doc. The primary name is lettrma, which tells you what the file contain. The extension .doc tells you that this is a document file.

Certain extensions should not be used to name your files because they are reserved by DOS for program and system files. Table 5-5 lists some of the file extensions that are reserved for DOS use.

TIP Don't create silly file names—chances are you won't remember the contents of the file if it's one you haven't used for awhile.

Table 5-5 File extensions reserved for use by DOS

FILE EXTENSION	USED FOR
.com	command files
.exe	executable files
.bat	batch files
.sys	system files
.hlp	help files
.ini	initialization files

Objective 4: Using the File Menu

file-level command

The File option in the File Manager menu bar offers file-level commands that enable you to maintain the files and directories on your hard and floppy disks. A *file-level command* is used to control individual files as well as sets of files in directories or subdirectories located on a hard or floppy disk. The File menu includes commands to open, print, search, rename, delete, move, and copy files and directories. You can also change the properties of a particular file, select a specific file, and create a directory. Many of these File menu commands can be activated using the mouse.

Using the Open option

You can launch an application, open a directory window, or open a document that is associated with an application by choosing the File option from the File Manager menu bar and then choosing the Open option.

Exercise 4: Starting an application using the Open option

To start the Write application using the Open option, do the following:

1. Open the File Manager window, if it is not already open.
2. Open the Windows directory that is located on your hard disk.
3. Find and select the write.exe file in the Directory Contents List window.

   The write.exe file is highlighted (see Figure 5-10).

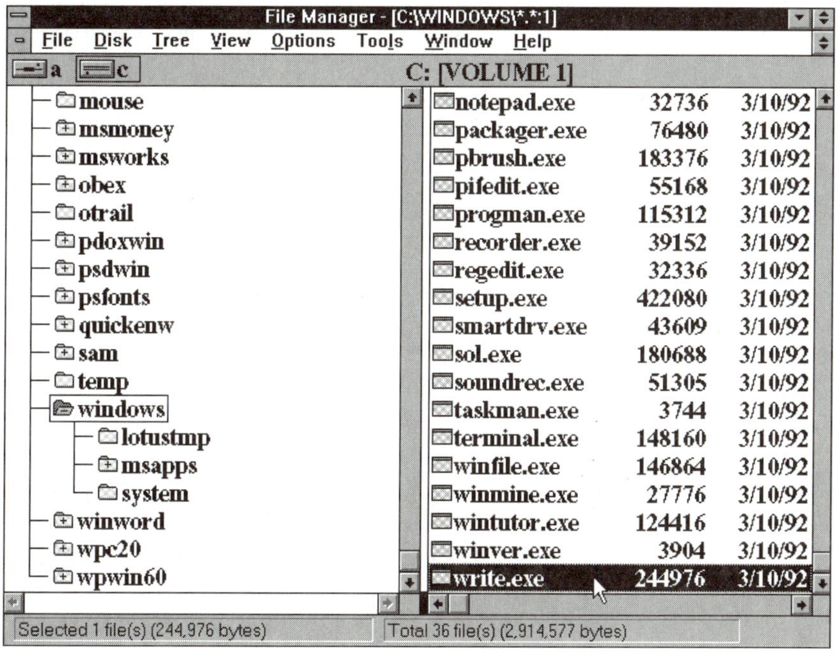

Figure 5-10 The write.exe file is highlighted

4. Choose the File option from the File Manager menu bar.
5. Choose Open.

   The Write program is started, and a Write document window appears on the screen.
6. Close the Write document window to return to the File Manager window.

Selecting files and directories from a listing

selecting

In the Windows environment, you must select an element before you can apply a command to it. *Selecting* an element means choosing, or highlighting, the element (such as text, a graphic, an icon, a file, or a directory) in order to apply a command to that element.

You can perform disk maintenance on several files and directories at one time; simply select all the files or directories before applying a command. You can use the mouse, keyboard, or Select Files menu to make selections. Table 5-6 lists different ways you can select files from a list using the mouse.

Table 5-6 Methods of selecting files in a list

TO SELECT A SINGLE FILE	CLICK THE FILE ONCE
To select several adjacent files	Click the first file, press and hold down Shift, and click the last file
To select several nonadjacent files	Click the first file, hold down Control, and click each file.
To cancel a single file	Click a different file or directory
To cancel the selection of one file in a list of selected files	Press Control and then click the file you no longer want selected.

Using the Select Files option

You can request a selected listing of files from a directory by specifying the extension of the files you want in the Select Files dialog box.

Exercise 5: Selecting files from a directory

To select all files from the Windows directory with the extension .bmp, do the following:

1. In the Directory Contents List, show the contents of the Windows directory.
2. Choose View from the File Manager menu bar, and then choose By File Type.
3. Make sure all boxes are selected, and then choose OK.
4. Type *.bmp in the Name text box.

   Only files with the .bmp extension are displayed.
5. Choose File, and then Select Files.

   The Select Files dialog box appears (see Figure 5-11).

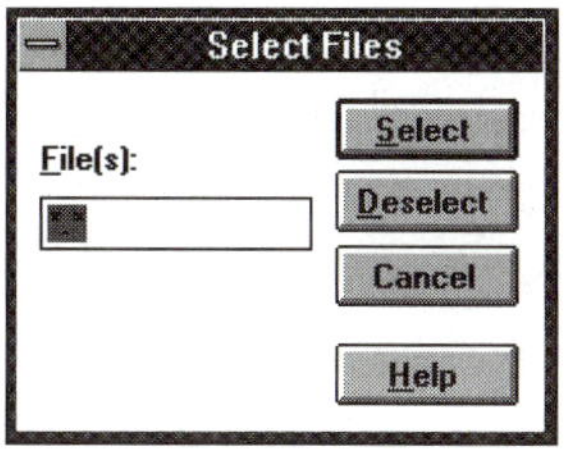

Figure 5-11 The Select Files dialog box

6. In the File(s) text box, type *.bmp to select only files with the .bmp extension.
7. Choose Select, and then choose Close.

   You are returned to the directory listing. Note that all files with the .bmp extension are highlighted, indicating that they are selected (see Figure 5-12).

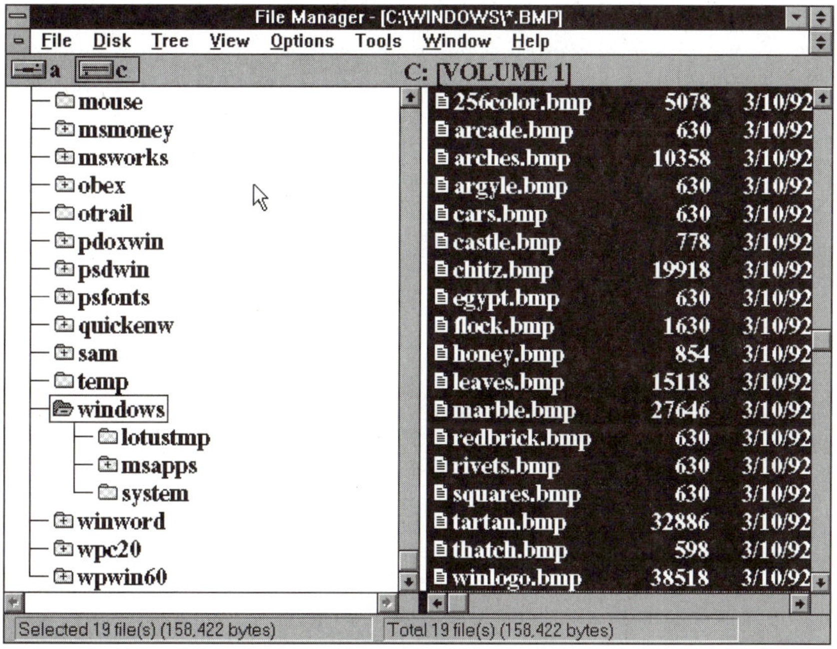

Figure 5-12 Files with the .bmp extension selected in the Directory Contents List

Exercise 6: Canceling a selection of files

To cancel a selection made to a group of files using the Select Files dialog box, perform the following steps:

1. Choose the File menu, and then choose Select Files.

   The Select Files dialog box appears.
2. Choose Deselect, and then choose Close.

   You are returned to the Directory Contents List, and the files are deselected.
3. Choose View, and then choose By File Type.

   The By File Type dialog box appears.
4. Type *.* in the Name text box.
5. Choose OK.

   You are returned to the Directory Contents List, and all files are listed.

Copying files and directories

You can copy files and directories from one location to another using the mouse or the Copy option from the File menu on the File Manager menu bar. This is a useful operation for making backups of important files. Before copying a file or group of files, make sure that the destination drive to which you are copying has enough available space to store the copied files. To check this, compare the size of the source area to the amount of free space on the destination drive.

Exercise 7: Using the mouse to copy a file

To make a copy of a file using the mouse, perform the following steps:

1. Insert a formatted floppy disk into your computer's floppy disk drive.
2. Open the File Manager window and display the contents of the Windows directory in the Directory Contents List.
3. Choose Window from the File Manager menu bar, and then choose New Window.
4. Select the drive A icon from the drive icon bar.
5. Choose Window, and then Tile.

   Two windows appear tiled; one shows the contents of the hard disk and the other shows the contents of the floppy disk (see Figure 5-13).

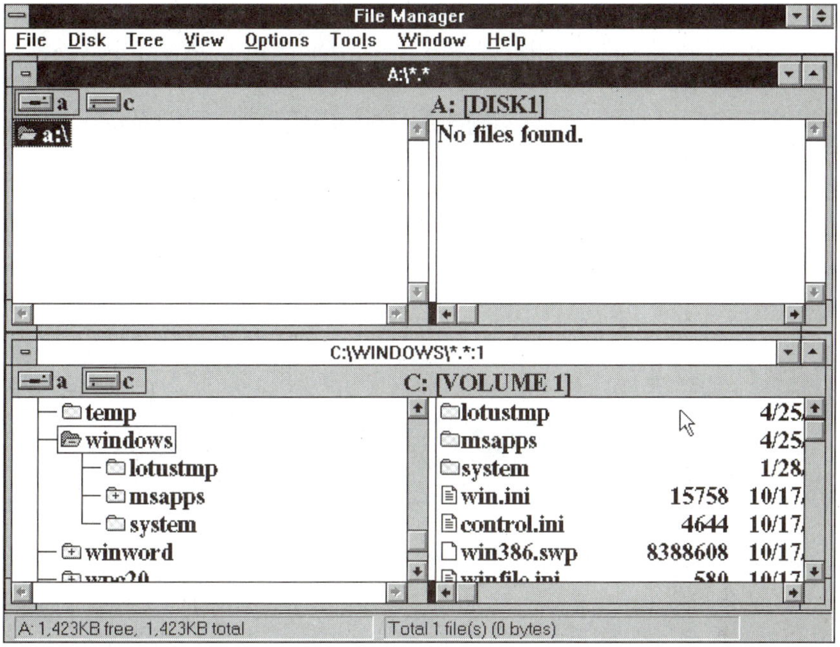

Figure 5-13 The Contents Directory List for the hard disk and the floppy disk

6. Activate the hard disk window.
7. Choose View, and then choose Sort by Name.
8. Select the file clipbrd.hlp from the Directory Contents List for the Windows directory. You may have to scroll through the window to locate it.
9. Drag clipbrd.hlp to the drive A window.

   As you drag the mouse, a document icon with a plus sign appears and the status bar indicates that you are copying the clipbrd.hlp file to drive A, which is the floppy disk drive.
10. Release the mouse button.

    The Confirm Mouse Operation message box appears, asking you if you want to copy the file to drive A (see Figure 5-14).

Figure 5-14 The Confirm Mouse Operation message box

11. Choose Yes.

    The clipbrd.hlp file appears in both windows (see Figure 5-15).

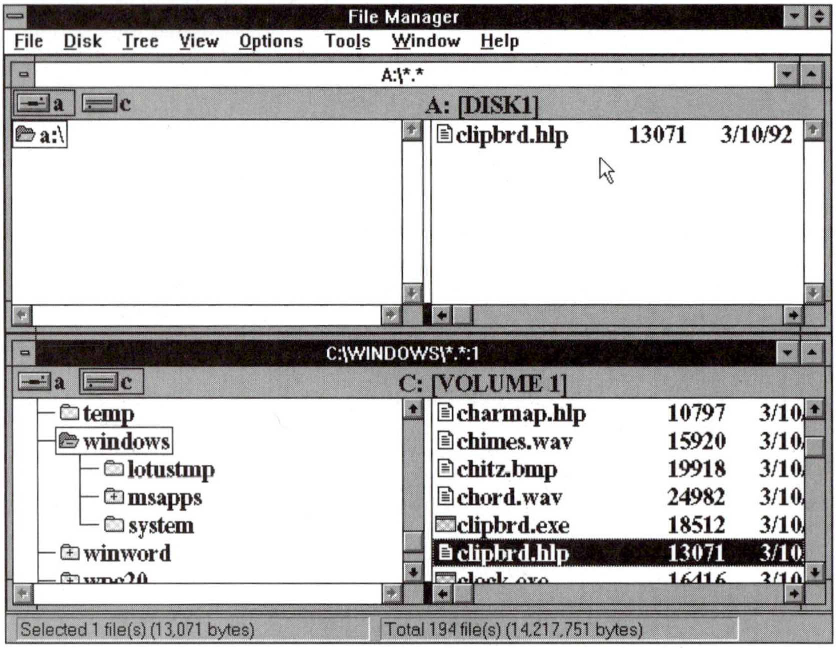

Figure 5-15 The clipbrd.hlp file copied to both disk drives

TIP You can copy source files from one location on a disk to a different location on the same disk: Hold down CTRL as you drag the mouse to the destination area.

Exercise 8: Copying multiple files

You can copy several source files at one time. To copy more than one file at a time to a destination area, perform the following steps:

1. Make sure the Windows directory is the active window.
2. Select the apps.hlp file.
3. Hold down CTRL and select calc.hlp and calendar.hlp.

   All three files are highlighted (see Figure 5-16). (You may be able to see only two of the selected files at one time. You can scroll through the listing to see the other selected file.)

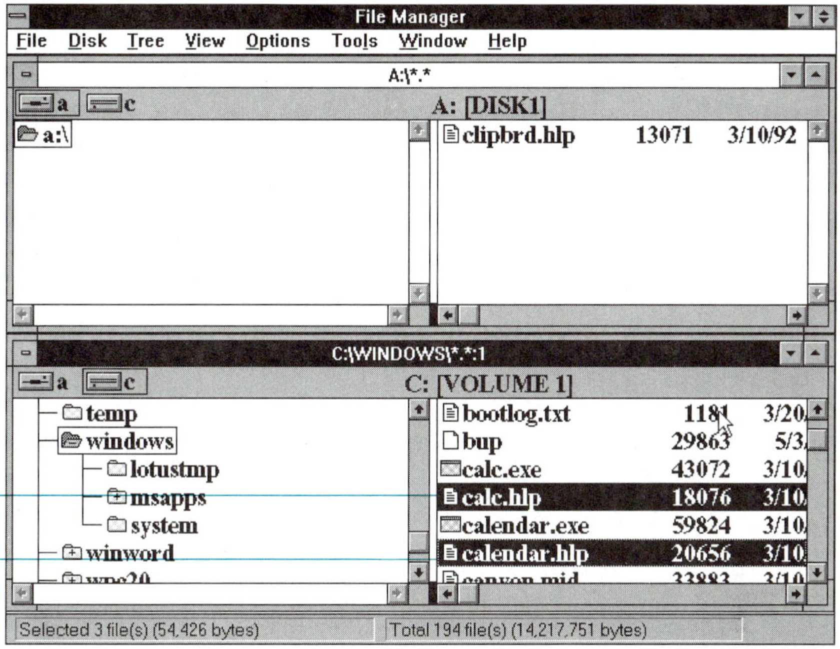

Non-adjacent files ▶

Figure 5-16 Three files selected for copying in the Windows directory listing

4. Drag the selected files to the drive A window.

   As you drag the mouse, an icon representing multiple files (each with a plus sign) appears.

5. Release the mouse button.

6. Select Yes when prompted by the message box.

   All three files are copied to the drive A destination area.

Exercise 9: Using the File option to copy a file

To use the Copy option from the File menu, perform the following steps:

1. Select charmap.hlp from the Windows directory listing.

2. Choose the File option from the File Manager menu bar, and then choose Copy.

   The Copy dialog box appears (see Figure 5-17).

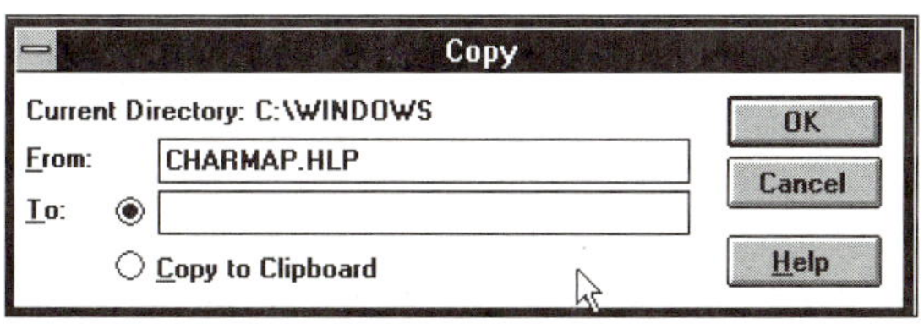

Figure 5-17 The Copy dialog box

The currently selected file name appears in the From text box. If the file name you want to copy is not listed in the From text box, you can type it in. For this exercise, you will use the currently selected file.

3. In the To text box, type A:. Drive A is the destination area for the file to be copied.
4. Select OK.

   Once the file is copied, the file name is displayed in the drive A window.

Renaming a file or directory

You can rename a file or directory using the Rename option on the File menu. When you rename a file or directory, you replace the original name with a new name.

Exercise 10: Giving a file a new name

To rename the apps.hlp file found on the floppy disk in drive A, perform the following steps:

1. Make sure the drive A directory window is active.
2. Maximize the window.
3. Select the apps.hlp file.
4. Choose File from the File Manager menu bar, and then choose Rename.

   The Rename dialog box appears (see Figure 5-18). The From text box displays the currently selected file.

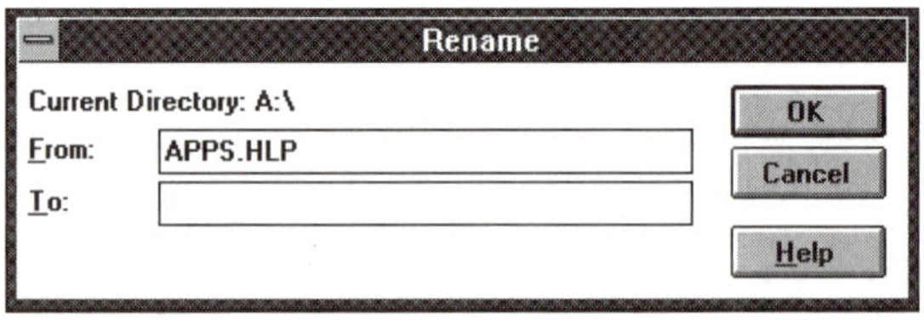

Figure 5-18 The Rename dialog box

5. In the To text box type newname.doc, and then choose OK.

   The drive A window displays the newname.doc file (see Figure 5-19).

On-line Abuse Help Available

Some electronic bulletin board services are joining the fight against domestic violence by offering support services that victims and abusers can access from their homes. Those involved in domestic violence are often reluctant to seek support and therefore never get help that might change their lives.

On-line support services don't claim to be a panacea for abuse problems, but they do act as a forum where people from all over the country can send and receive messages to one another. Messages range from pleas for moral support to financial strategies for single parents. A major advantage to the electronic approach is that callers are able to protect their anonymity.

While professionals in the field of domestic violence remain skeptical of the new wave of on-line counseling, they do agree that when people open up and share their feelings with others it is usually a positive experience.

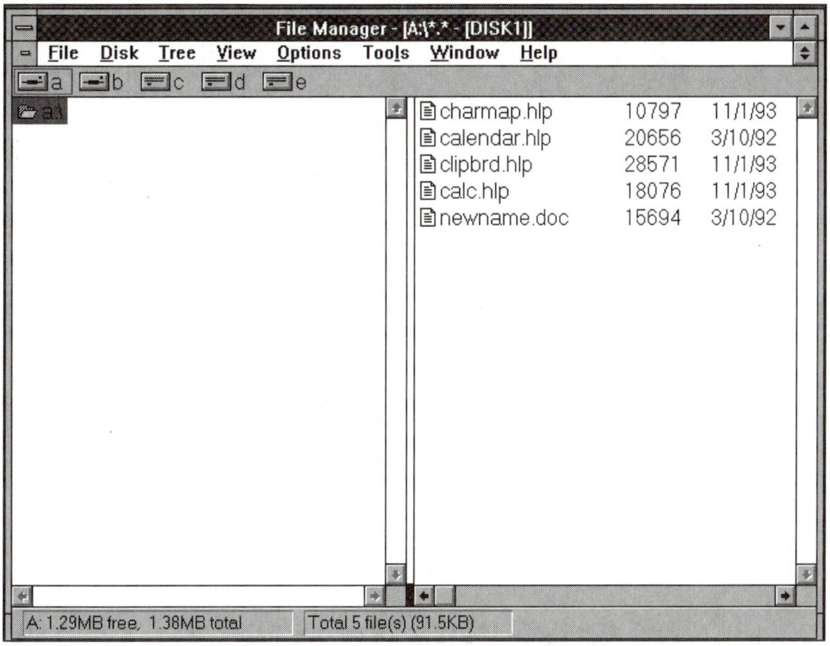

Figure 5-19 The newname.doc file in the Contents Directory List

Objective 5: Organizing Your Files

You can organize your files by placing them in directories. Think again of the filing cabinet analogy discussed in Chapter 4: Just as you can place sets of documents in a single drawer of a filing cabinet to organize them, you can place electronic files in a single directory to organize them.

Exercise 11: Creating a directory

You can create a directory to store your files by using the Create Directory option in the Disk pull-down menu. In the following exercise, you will create a new directory on the disk in drive A.

1. Insert the floppy disk in drive A, if it is not already inserted.
2. Activate the disk in drive A in the File Manager window.
3. Maximize the window.
4. Choose File from the File Manager menu bar, and then choose Create Directory.

   The Create Directory dialog box appears (see Figure 5-20).

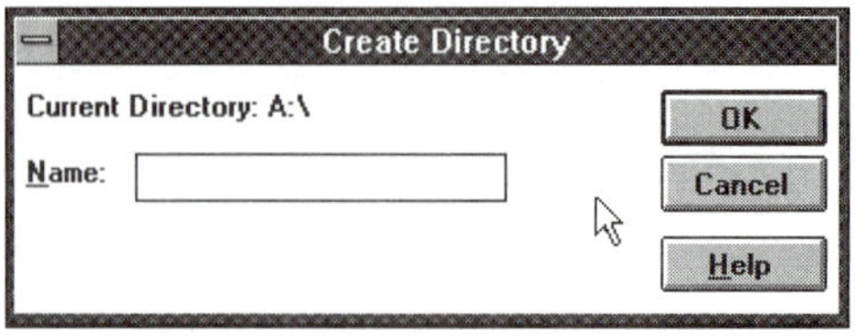

Figure 5-20 The Create Directory dialog box

5. In the Name text box, type Data, and choose OK.

   The Directory Tree and the Directory Contents List display the newly created Data directory (see Figure 5-21).

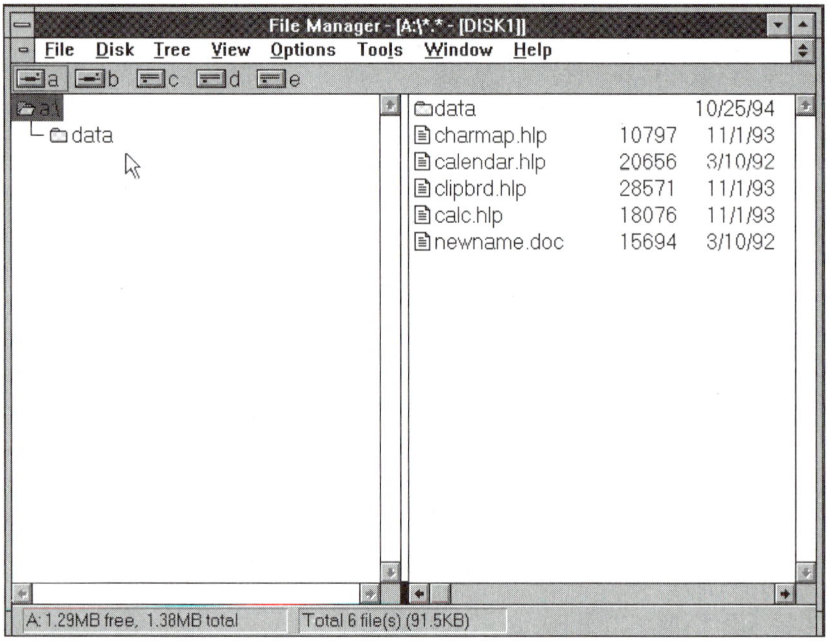

Figure 5-21 The Data directory in the Directory Tree and Directory Contents List

Moving files and directories

You can move files and directories by dragging their icons or using the Move option on the File menu on the File Manager menu bar. When you move a file or directory icon, it is removed from the source area and relocated to the destination area.

Exercise 12: Moving files into a directory

To move two files from the floppy disk in drive A to the Data directory you just created, perform the following steps:

1. Drag calendar.hlp and place it on top of the Data directory icon in the drive A window. You will see a blank document icon  as you move the file.

   The mouse confirmation message box appears asking if you want to move the selected file (see Figure 5-22).

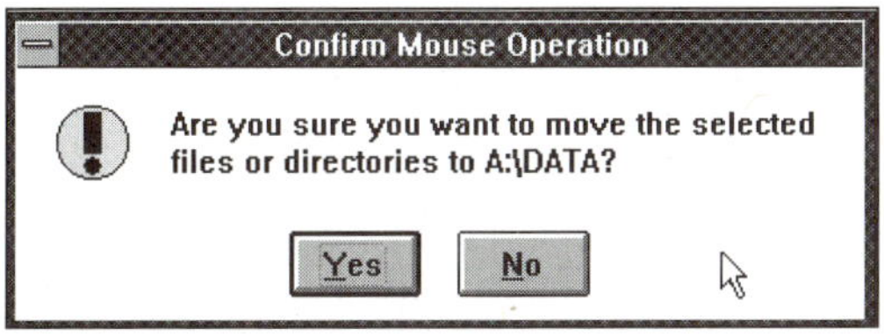

Figure 5-22 The Mouse Confirmation message box

2. Choose Yes.

   The calendar.hlp file is located in the Data subdirectory, not in the root directory of drive A (see Figure 5-23).

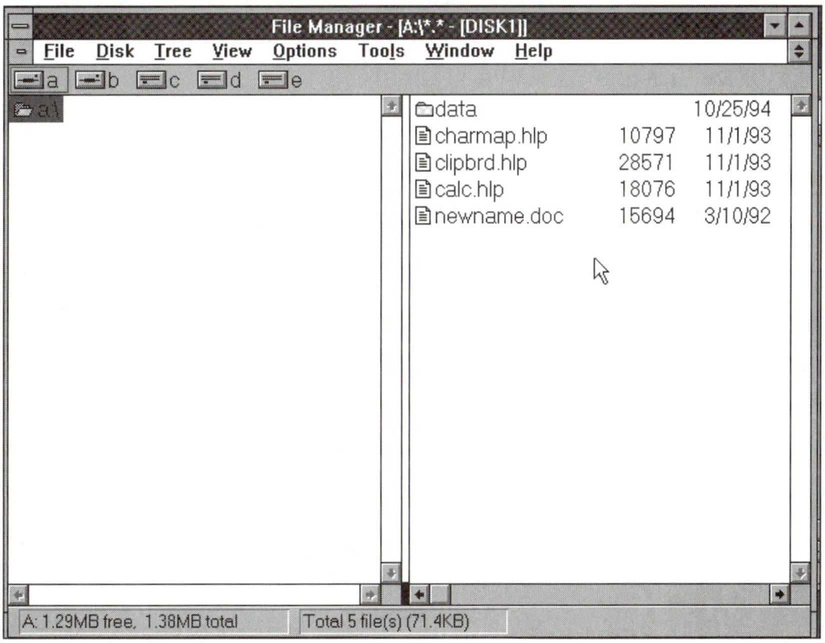

Figure 5-23 The Data directory in its new location on the drive A

3. Repeat Steps 1 and 2 to move the clipbrd.hlp file to the Data directory.
4. Open the Data directory to display its contents.

   The clipbrd.hlp and calendar.hlp files are displayed in the Directory Contents List for the Data directory (see Figure 5-24).

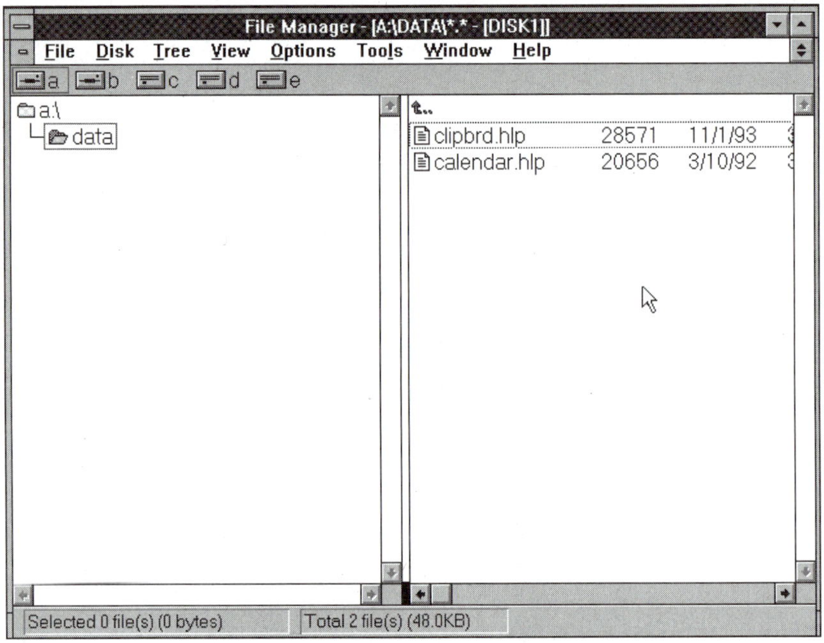

Figure 5-24 The Directory Contents List of the Data directory displaying clipbrd.hlp and calendar.hlp

5. Double-click the arrow followed by an ellipsis at the top of the Directory Contents List to return to the root directory of drive A.

Objective 6: Applying File Attributes

attribute

You can indicate certain characteristics of a file by applying attributes to the file. An *attribute* is a characteristic—such as read only, archive, hidden, and system—that can be applied to a file. File attributes are applied using the Properties option on the File menu. Table 5-7 defines each type of attribute.

Table 5-7 File attributes

Read Only (R)	Changes the property of a file so that it will not accept new data and allows only data to be read from the file. This attribute protects files from being changed or deleted.
Archive (A)	Alerts DOS to designate whether a file has been changed since the Backup command was last issued. Those archive files that have been changed since the last backup procedure are included in the current backup

continued

Table 5-7 continued

	procedure. Those archive files that have not been changed since the last backup procedure are ignored during the current backup procedure. The archive attribute acts as a flag for DOS and is reset each time the file is backed up.
Hidden (H)	Prevents a file from being displayed in a file listing.
System (S)	Identifies a file as an MS-DOS system file. The file will not appear in an MS-DOS directory listing.

Exercise 13: Making a read-only file

To apply the read-only attribute to a file, perform the following steps:

1. Select newname.doc from the A drive directory listing.
2. Choose File, and then choose Properties.

   The Properties for NEWNAME.DOC dialog box appears (see Figure 5-25). Note that the dialog box displays the date and time that the file was last changed.

Figure 5-25 The Properties for NEWNAME.DOC dialog box

3. In the Attributes section, select Read Only.
4. Make sure Archive is selected.
5. Select OK.
6. Choose View from the File Manager menu bar, and then choose Partial Details.
7. Deselect all options except File Attributes, and then choose OK.

   The Directory Contents List appears, displaying the newname.doc file with *ra* next to the file name (see Figure 5-26). The *r* indicates that newname.doc is a read-only file. The *a* indicates that the newname.doc is an archive file.

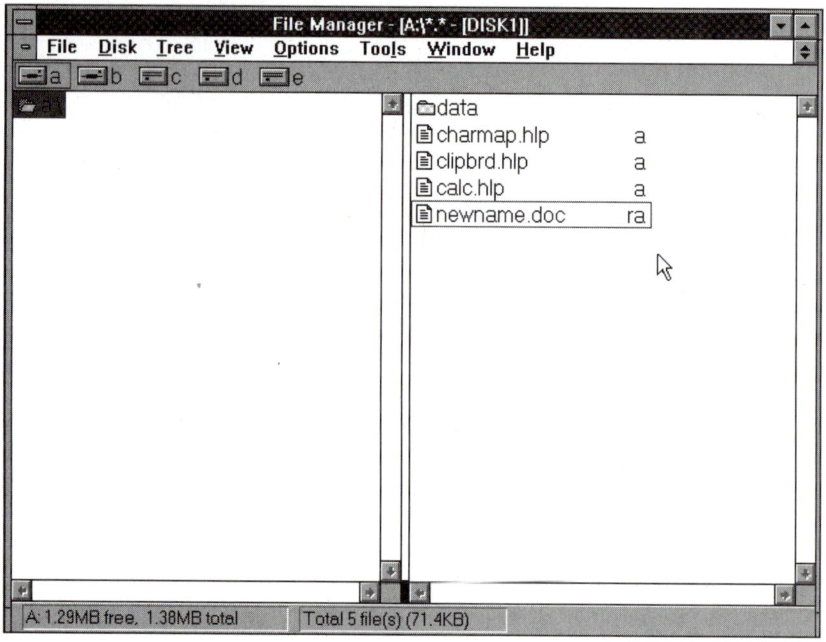

Figure 5-26 **The Directory Contents List displaying newname.doc and its read-only and archive designations**

Objective 7: Using the Search Option

Using the Search option on the File menu of the File Manager menu bar, you can search quickly and easily for specific files or directories. Wildcard characters can be used if you do not remember the exact name of a file or directory or if you want to find a group of similarly named files and directories. You can begin a search within a specific directory if you know the name of the directory where the file is found. If you have no idea where the file is located, you can search an entire disk area.

Exercise 14: Searching a disk for files

To search for a file in the Windows directory of your hard disk, perform the following steps:

1. Choose Window.

   A menu appears, displaying the opened windows.
2. Choose C:\Windows.
3. Choose File from the File Manager menu bar, and then choose Search.

   The Search dialog box appears (see Figure 5-27).

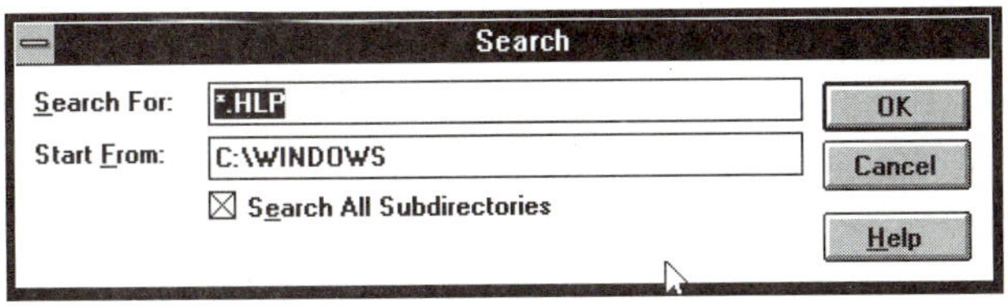

Figure 5-27 The Search dialog box

4. In the Search For text box, type w*.exe.

   This command indicates that you want to find all file names that have a primary name that begins with *w* and the extension .exe. In the Start From text box, the current hard drive and subdirectory are listed.

5. Choose OK to begin the search.

   The Search Results window appears displaying a list of file names that match the criteria you designated in the Search For text box (see Figure 5-28).

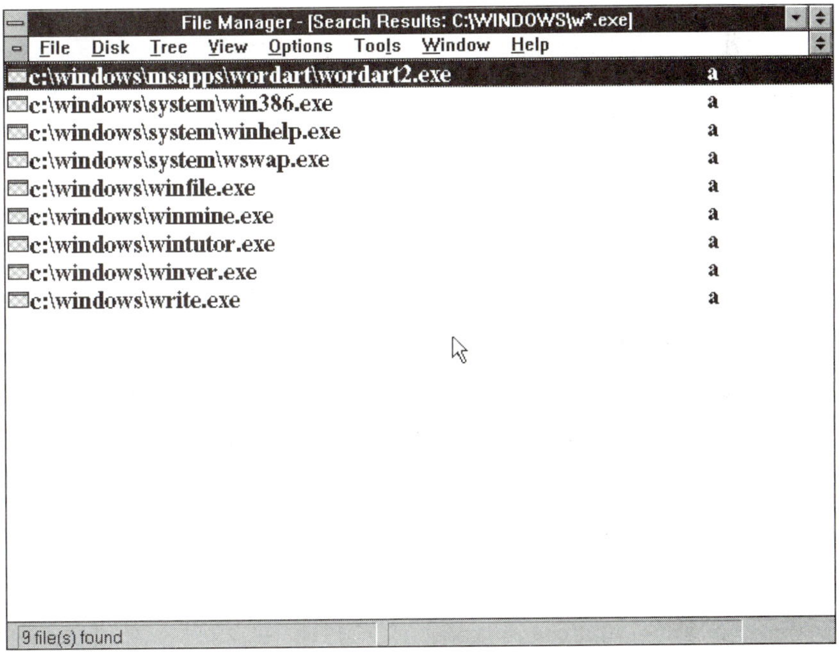

Figure 5-28 The Search Results window

6. Choose the control menu box in the Search Results window, and then choose Close.

   You are returned to the File Manager window.

TIP To search an entire disk, begin the search from the root directory. To limit your search to the current directory, make sure that the Search All Subdirectories check-box is not selected.

Objective 8: Using the Delete Option

To free up space on hard and floppy disks you can delete files and directories you no longer need. The Delete command is useful but dangerous. You must be careful when deleting files and directories because you cannot recover deleted information. As we discussed in Chapter 4, it is a good idea to keep the File Delete and Directory Delete options in the Confirmation dialog box turned on at all times because they give you an added opportunity to make sure you want to make a specified deletion. You can access the Confirmation dialog box from the File Manager menu bar (choose Options, choose Confirmation). Remember: If you delete a directory, all files residing in that directory are deleted as well.

Exercise 15: Deleting a directory and files from a disk

To delete the Data directory and newname.doc file from the floppy disk in drive A, perform the following steps:

1. Display the File Manager window for the floppy disk in drive A.
2. Maximize the window.
3. Select the Data directory from the Directory Contents List.

   The Data directory is highlighted.
4. Choose File from the menu bar, and then choose Delete.

   The Delete dialog box appears displaying the selected disk drive (see Figure 5-29).

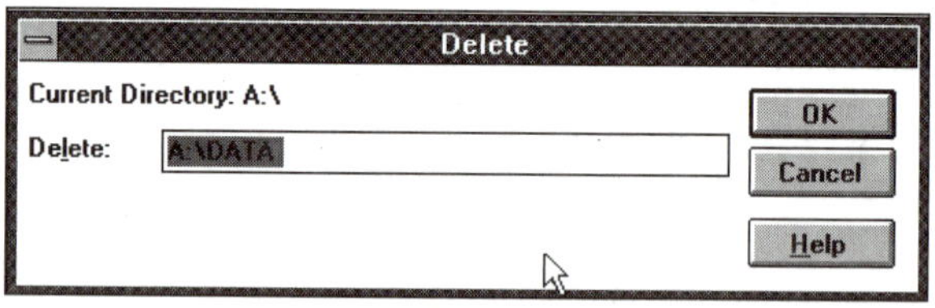

Figure 5-29 The Delete dialog box

5. Choose OK.

   The Confirm Directory Delete message box appears, asking you if you want to delete the Data directory.
6. Choose Yes.

   The Data directory is deleted from the Directory Contents List.
7. Select newname.doc and charmap.hlp from the drive A listing.
8. Choose File, and then choose Delete.

   The Delete dialog box appears, displaying the names of the selected files in the Delete text box (see Figure 5-30).

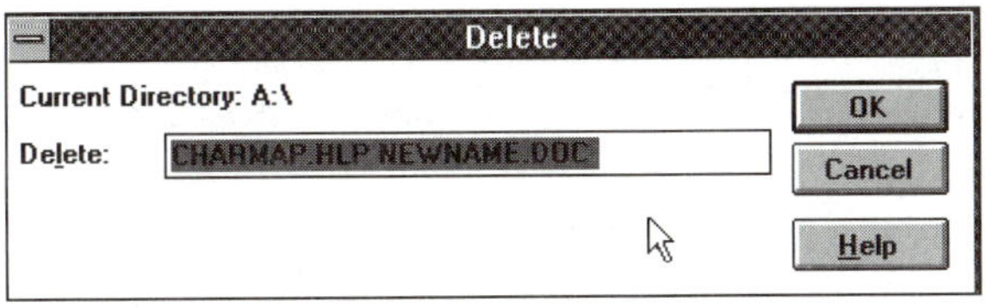

Figure 5-30 The Delete dialog box displaying more than one file name

9. Choose OK.

   The Confirm File Delete message box appears, asking if you want the charmap.hlp file deleted.

10. Choose Yes.

    The Confirm File Delete message box appears, indicating that the newname.doc file is a system, hidden, or read-only file (see Figure 5-31). (Remember that you added the read-only attribute to this file in Exercise 13).

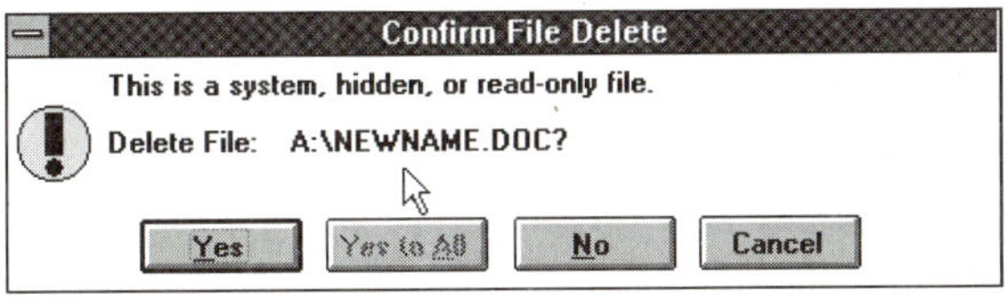

Figure 5-31 The Confirm File Delete message box

11. Choose Yes.

    Newname.doc and charmap.hlp are removed from the disk in drive A.

Chapter Summary

In this chapter, you learned how to use the commands that are contained in the File Manager menu. You saw how the Windows environment makes file managing easy by providing pull-down menus, as well as a visual display of files. You learned the rules of file-naming and learned the disk organization techniques used by the File Manager. You should now be able to search for files, apply attributes to them, and delete them using the methods covered in this chapter.

Review Questions

True/False Questions

_____ 1. The only difference between the Format command and the Quick Format command is that the latter works more rapidly.

_____ 2. You can have several files or directories opened in different windows within the File Manager window.

_____ 3. A file's primary name must be eight characters in length.

_____ 4. You can copy files from a disk to a different location on the same disk.

_____ 5. When you use the Rename command, you end up with the same file with two different names.

Multiple-Choice Questions

_____ 6. Which of the following procedures would you use to select several nonadjacent file names in a list?

A. Click the first file, hold down Ctrl, and click remaining files.

B. Hold down Shift and drag across the files you want to select.

C. Click the first file, hold down Shift, and then click the last file.

D. none of the above

_____ 7. Which of the following options would you use to apply the read-only attribute to a file?

A. Format

B. Associate

C. Properties

D. Make System Disk

_____ 8. To display several different directory windows on the screen at one time, you would choose

A. File, Open.

B. Disk, Select Drive.

C. Window, New Window.

D. View, Tree and Directory.

____ 9. When making a copy the contents of one disk onto another disk, you must make sure that

A. the source area is smaller than the destination area.

B. the source and destination disks are the same density.

C. the destination area has enough room for the information stored in the source area.

D. the source and destination disks are the same size.

E. B and C only

____ 10. The File option includes all the following options except

A. Open.

B. Move.

C. Label.

D. Search.

Fill-in-the-Blank Questions

11. The Format command will find any ____________ ____________ on a disk and alert you to them.
12. The ____________ ____________ option will format a ____________ disk if it is not already formatted.
13. Duplicate displays of windows for a directory appear with ____________ on the title bar.
14. The Open option can be used to ____________ ____________ ____________.
15. When you delete a directory, all the ____________ within it are also deleted.

Acumen-Building Activities

Quick Projects

You will need a new, unformatted floppy disk for the following Quick Projects.

1. Managing files

1. Format the floppy disk and give it the volume label DISK2.
2. Create a directory and name it Practice.
3. Copy the following files from the Windows directory to the Practice directory on the floppy disk.

   accessor.grp
   applicat.grp
   games.grp
   main.grp
   startup.grp

2. Renaming files

1. In the Directory Contents List, select the five files in the Practice directory, using the Select Files dialog box.
2. Issue the command to make a copy of these files to the root directory of the floppy disk.
3. Once the files are in the root directory, rename games.grp, main.grp, and startup.grp by adding *1* to the end of each file's primary name. For example, change games.grp to games1.grp.

3. Applying attributes

1. Move the three renamed files to the Practice directory.
2. Apply the archive attribute to the three renamed files in the Practice directory.
3. Apply the read-only attribute to applicat.grp.
4. Display the windows for each of the following:
   the floppy disk in the drive A
   the Windows directory on your hard disk
   the System directory, which is a subdirectory of Windows
   the Msapps directory, which is a subdirectory of Windows
5. Tile these four windows on your screen.
6. Search for all files with the extension .dll in the Msapps directory.

4. Using File Manager

1. Begin this exercise at the DOS prompt.
2. Launch Windows and open the Main and Accessories windows.
3. Start the File Manager from the Main window.
4. Minimize the Accessories window to a program-group icon.
5. Insert DISK2 in the floppy disk drive and display its window in the File Manager window.
6. Display the contents of the Msapps directory, which is located on the hard disk drive.
7. Search the Windows directory for files with the extension .exe.
8. Launch Cardfile from the appropriate .exe file in the File Manager window.
9. Display the resulting Cardfile document window, the Program Manager window, and the File Manager window on the desktop at the same time.
10. Close the Cardfile document.
11. Delete the files in the root directory of the floppy disk in drive A.
12. Leave the Practice directory on the floppy disk in drive A.

In-Depth Projects

1. Working with File Manager

1. Start Windows and open the Main and Accessories windows.
2. Create a new program group and call it Disk Organization.
3. Choose an available icon, name it Manager, and place it in the new program group's window.
4. Make a copy of the File Manager icon from the Main window and place it in your new Disk Organization group window.
5. Tile the opened windows.
6. Start the File Manager from your new group window.
7. Create a directory on a floppy disk in drive A and name it lpex1.
8. Move the files from the Practice directory to the lpex1 directory.

2. Managing files

1. Make a copy of all the files in the Windows directory with the extension .hlp and move them to the root directory of your floppy disk.
2. Minimize the Main and Accessories windows.
3. In the Directory Contents List, display only the names and dates of the files in the lpex1 directory.
4. Sort the files in the lpex1 directory by extension.
5. Issue the command to have the File Manager reduced to an icon whenever Windows is started.
6. Save the Windows settings and exit the Windows program.

3. Reviewing File Manager techniques

1. Start the Windows program and change the name of the Disk Organization window to Disk Files.
2. Assign a shortcut key to the File Manager icon you created in the Disk Files group window.
3. Issue the commands to have the Solitaire program displayed on the screen whenever you launch Windows.
4. Start the Write and Calendar programs and use their control menu boxes to switch between the applications.
5. Change the font size and typeface of the display for drive A window.
6. Delete the Disk Files group window and all items in it.
7. Return all settings to their original values.

Chapter 6

The Control Panel

Objectives

- Using the Control Panel
- Changing Colors
- Using Desktop Options
- Changing Mouse and Keyboard Actions
- Setting the Date and Time
- Using Printer Options
- Installing Sound
- Changing International Settings
- Adding Fonts

Key Terms

TERM	DEFINITION
Printer Driver	a file containing information that is supplied to a program to identify a specific type of printer
Configure	to choose settings in a program or a computer system to meet individual needs
Font	the weight, size, and form of a set of characters
Pixel	a dot on the computer screen that, when combined with other dots, makes up a display screen
WYSIWYG	an acronym for What-You-See-Is-What-You-Get; a mode in which on-screen characters appear as they will when printed out
Screen Saver	a program that conserves a monitor's life by displaying a moving graphic on the screen when the computer is turned on but not in use
Sizing Grid	an invisible set of specifications used to align windows and icons on the desktop

The Windows control panel enables you to customize your system by providing tools to adjust the hardware and software settings of your computer. For example, you can change the colors and design of the desktop, adjust mouse and keyboard functions, set the time and date for your system, and configure ports and printers to new settings—all accomplished using the icons in the Control Panel window.

Objective 1: Using the Control Panel

The control panel is included with the Windows program; it contains a Settings menu and a variety of descriptive icons that represent applications that can be used to change various aspects of your Windows program. The options listed on the menu correspond to the icons found in the control panel window. You can select from the menu options or you can double-click an icon to begin an application to customize your Windows settings.

Exercise 1: Starting the control panel

To start the control panel, do the following:

1. Launch Windows, if it is not already launched.
2. Open the Main group window.
3. Double-click the Control Panel icon 

.

   The Control Panel window appears (see Figure 6-1).

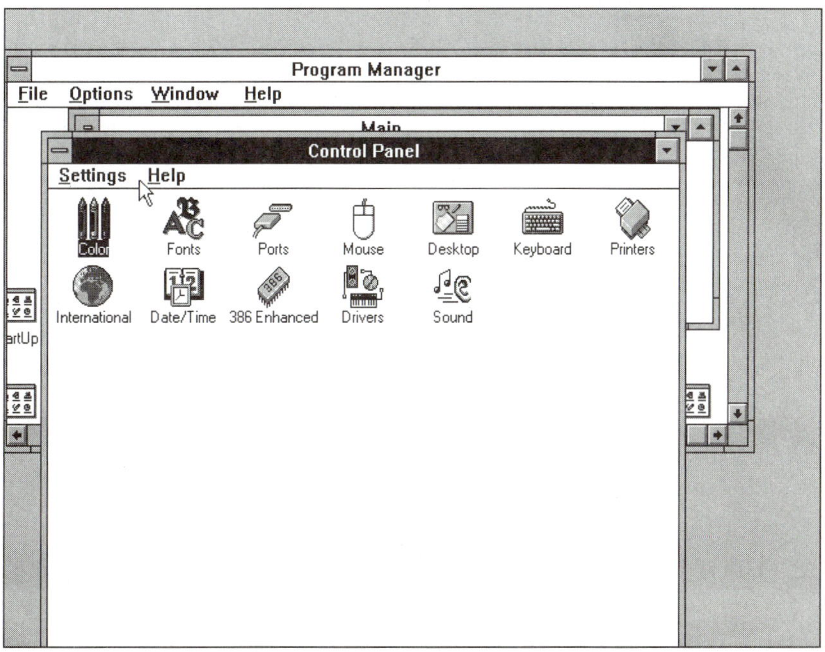

Figure 6-1 The Control Panel window

Table 6-1 lists the icons found in the Control Panel window and defines each icon's function.

Table 6-1 Functions of the Control Panel icons

ICON	DESCRIPTION
Color	Sets the colors for the screen display.
Fonts	Adds or removes fonts available for printing.
Ports	Describes the parameters for serial ports.
Mouse	Customizes the speed of mouse operations, such as clicking and moving.
Desktop	Changes the design of the desktop patterns and the arrangement of icons.
Keyboard	Sets the keyboard repeat rate.
Printers	Adds and removes printers; changes the configuration of existing printers.
International	Changes the international settings for formatting numbers, currency, dates, and times; changes the default language and system of measurements.
Date/Time	Sets the system date and time.
Drivers	Configures drivers for optional hardware devices that you can add to your computer, such as sound and video equipment.
Sound	Enables or disables the warning beep that signals an error.

Objective 2: Changing Colors

You can change the colors displayed on the Windows desktop by selecting a predefined color scheme or creating your own color scheme.

Exercise 2: Using a predefined color scheme

To change the current color scheme displayed on your desktop using a predefined color scheme, perform the following steps:

1. Double-click the Color icon in the Control Panel window.

   The Color dialog box appears (see Figure 6-2). The name of the currently displayed color scheme is displayed in the Color Schemes text box.

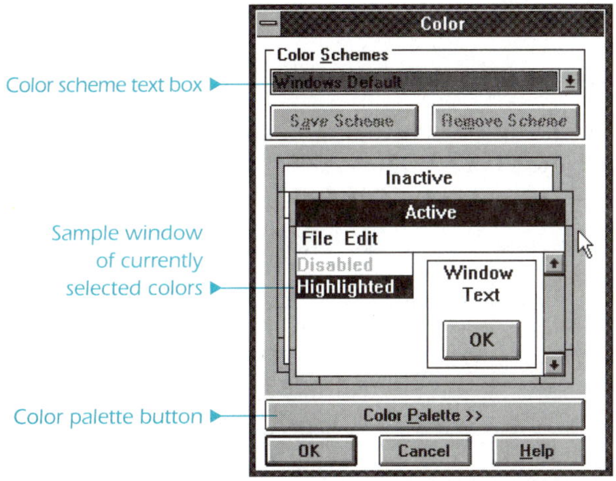

Figure 6-2 The Color dialog box

2. Click the down arrow next to the Color Schemes text box.

   A drop-down list of available predefined color schemes appears (see Figure 6-3).

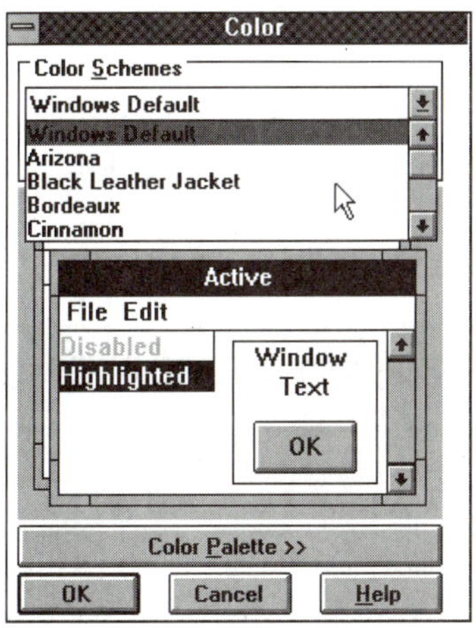

Figure 6-3 A drop-down list of predefined color schemes

3. Choose any color scheme from the list.

   The sample window displays the color scheme you select.

4. Continue to change the color scheme to display different sample windows.
5. Return to Windows default color scheme.

Exercise 3: Creating your own color scheme

You can customize the desktop by creating a color scheme of your own. You will first choose an existing color scheme and then change it using the Color Palette button.

1. Double-click the Color icon, click the Color Scheme down arrow, and choose any scheme.
2. Choose the Color Palette button in the Color dialog box.

   The window enlarges to include additional options for creating your own color scheme (see Figure 6-4).

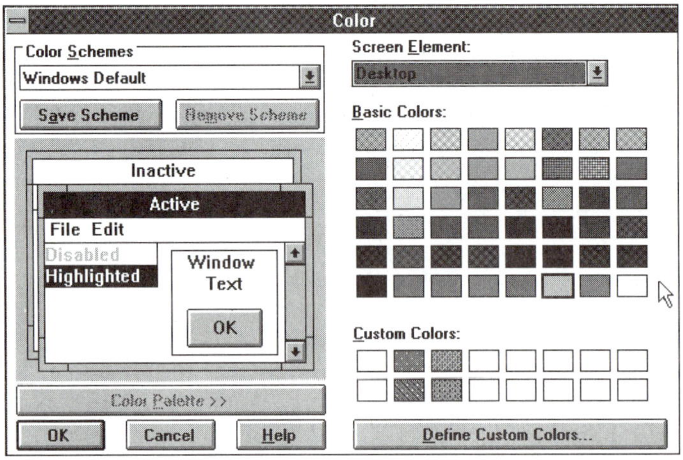

Figure 6-4 **The enlarged Color dialog box displaying additional options**

3. Choose a color from the Basic Colors group.

   The desktop portion of the sample window reflects the color change.
4. Click the down arrow to the right of the Screen Element text box.

   A drop-down list of screen element names appears (see Figure 6-5).

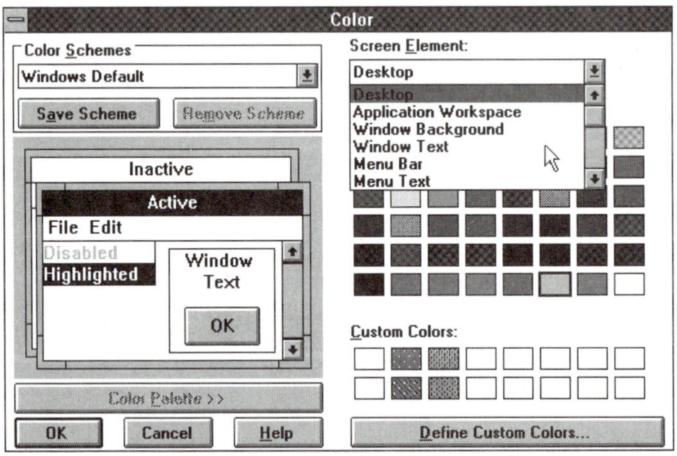

Figure 6-5 **The Screen Element drop-down list**

5. Click any screen element and then choose a color from the Basic Colors group to apply to the selected screen element. Continue this process until you have chosen a color for all the screen elements.
6. Choose the Save Scheme button.

   The Save Scheme dialog box appears (see Figure 6-6).

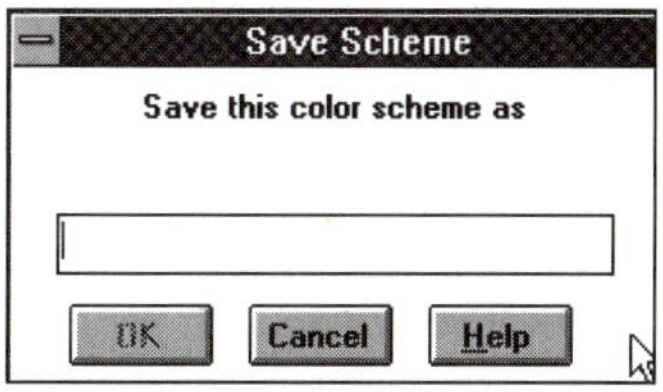

Figure 6-6 The Save Scheme dialog box

7. Type *your name* to name the color scheme.
8. Choose OK to save the scheme and return to the Color dialog box.
9. Choose OK to return to the Control Panel window.

   Your new color scheme is displayed on the screen.

Exercise 4: Removing a color scheme

To remove an existing color scheme, perform the following steps:

1. Activate the Color dialog box from the Control Panel window.
2. Activate the drop-down listing of color schemes.
3. Choose the *your name* color scheme you created in Exercise 3.
4. Choose the Remove Scheme button.

   The Control Panel message box appears, asking you if you want to remove the *your name* color scheme.
5. Choose Yes.

   The *your name* color scheme disappears from the drop-down list in the Color dialog box.

Objective 3: Using Desktop Options

Activating the Desktop icon in the Control Panel window opens the Desktop dialog box where you can customize and control the display of desktop components. Table 6-2 describes the options available in the Desktop dialog box.

Table 6-2 Options in the Desktop dialog box

OPTION	DESCRIPTION
Pattern	Changes the surface of the desktop by providing predefined patterns and enabling you to create patterns of your own.
Applications	Switches quickly from one running application to another using Alt+Tab.
Screen Saver	Offers available Screen Saver programs and sets the amount of time you want to delay the screen saver program before it is displayed.
Wallpaper	Offers available designs to decorate the background of the desktop.
Icons	Sets the spacing between icons in a window.
Sizing Grid	Sets up invisible gridlines on the screen to which windows will automatically snap; changes the width of the border around windows.
Cursor Blink Rate	Increases or decreases the blink rate of the cursor.

Exercise 5: Using the Pattern option

You can add a background pattern to your desktop—or change the current one—using the Pattern option in the Desktop dialog box. To add or edit a pattern, perform the following steps:

1. Double-click the Desktop icon  in the Control Panel window.

   The Desktop dialog box appears (see Figure 6-7).

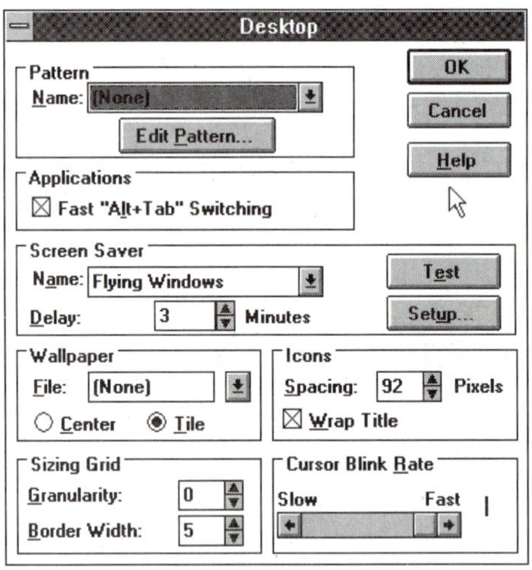

Figure 6-7 The Desktop dialog box

2. Click the down arrow to the right of the Name text box in the Pattern portion of the Desktop dialog box.

   A drop-down listing of predefined patterns appears (see Figure 6-8).

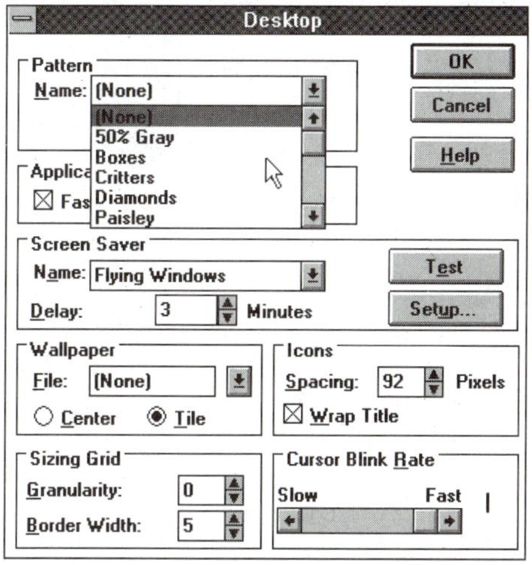

Figure 6-8 A drop-down listing of predefined patterns

3. Choose Scottie.
4. Choose the Edit Pattern button.

   The Desktop – Edit Pattern dialog box appears, displaying the currently selected pattern (see Figure 6-9).

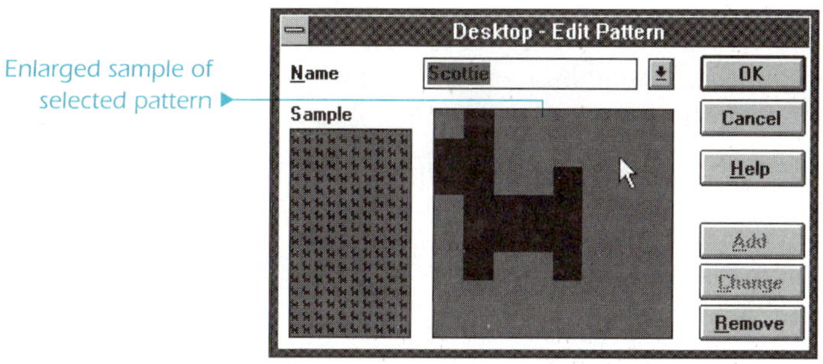

Figure 6-9 The Desktop—Edit Pattern dialog box

5. Choose OK to return to the Pattern dialog box.
6. Choose OK to return to the Windows desktop to see the result of your changes (see Figure 6-10).

Windows desktop

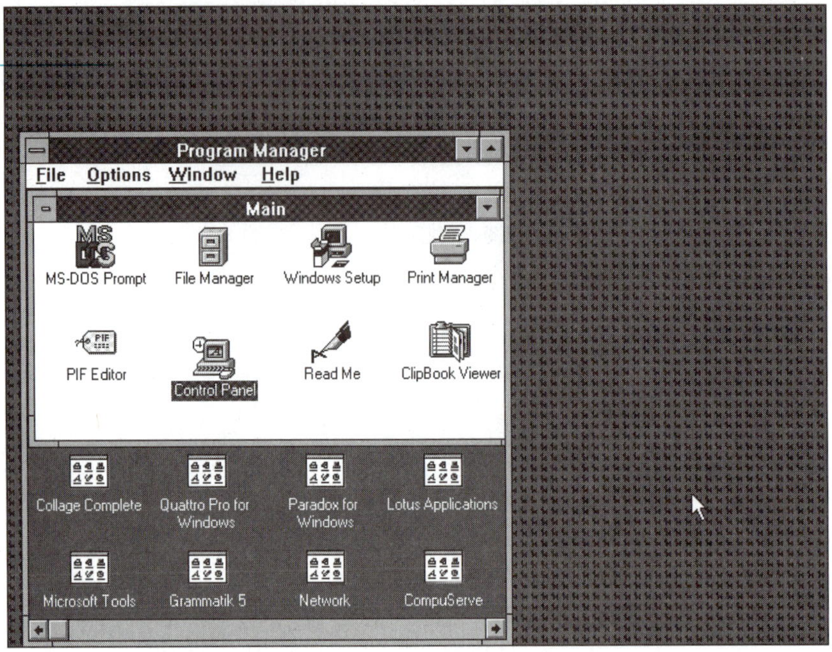

Figure 6-10 The Windows desktop displaying the Scottie pattern

7. Return the desktop to its original pattern.

Exercise 6: Using the Applications option

The Applications option, located in the Desktop dialog box, is activated when Windows is first installed. It enables you to switch quickly from one running application to another by pressing Alt+Tab. You can deactivate this option by toggling off the Fast Alt+Tab Switching option in the Desktop dialog box. To demonstrate how this option works, perform the following steps:

1. Start the following applications and display each in a window on the screen: Write, Calculator, Cardfile, and Minesweeper.
2. Close the Accessories, Games, and Control Panel windows.
3. Arrange the remaining windows on the desktop so that you can view all of them.
4. Display the Desktop dialog box and make sure the Fast Alt+Tab Switching option is activated.
5. Close the Desktop dialog box.
6. Minimize the Program Manager window.
7. Press and hold down ALT. At the same time, press TAB several times to display all your running applications in a message box, one by one.
8. When the Cardfile program appears in the message box (see Figure 6-11), release ALT to activate the Cardfile window.

   The Cardfile window is the active window on your screen (see Figure 6-12).

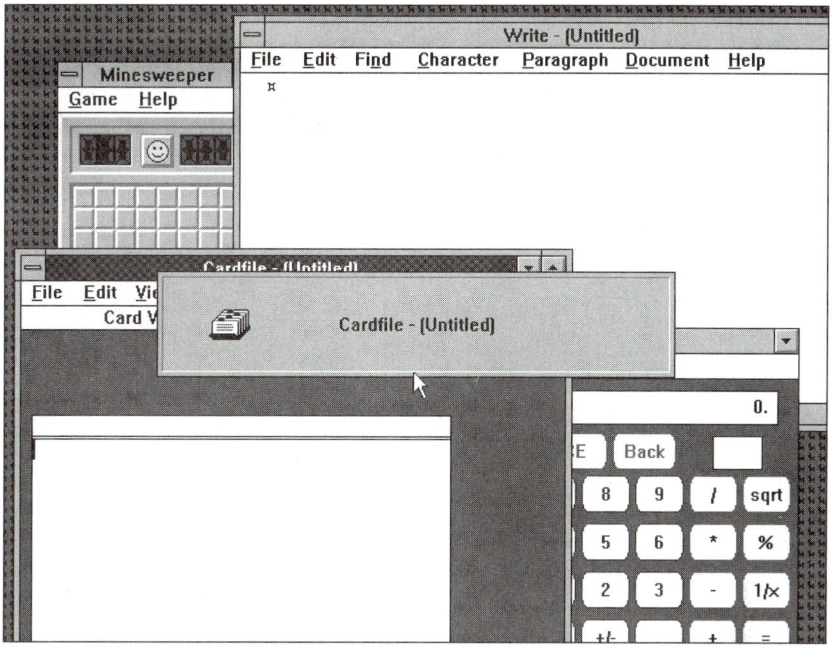

Figure 6-11 The Cardfile message box

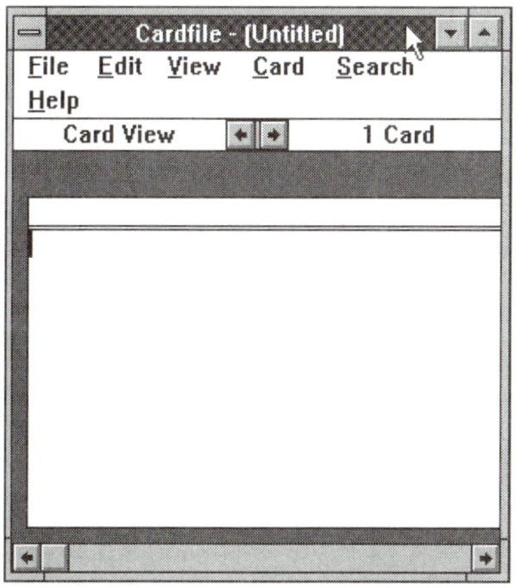

Figure 6-12 The Cardfile window as the active window

Understanding screen savers

screen saver A *screen saver* is a program that conserves a monitor's life by displaying a moving graphic on the screen when the computer is turned on but not in use. Screens that display nonmoving images for long periods of time can permanently burn an image onto the screen and thus damage your monitor. A screen saver temporarily replaces the image on your screen with some type of moving image. If you press a key or move the mouse, your original screen image returns.

Exercise 7: Choosing a screen saver

The Screen Saver option in the Desktop dialog box enables you to choose a screen saver from a variety of choices and to determine how long a nonmoving image remains on your screen before the screen saver of your choice is launched. To choose a screen saver and determine its delay time, perform the following steps:

1. Display the Desktop dialog box.
2. Click the arrow to the right of the Name text box in the Screen Saver portion of the Desktop dialog box.

   A drop-down list of screen savers appears (see Figure 6-13).

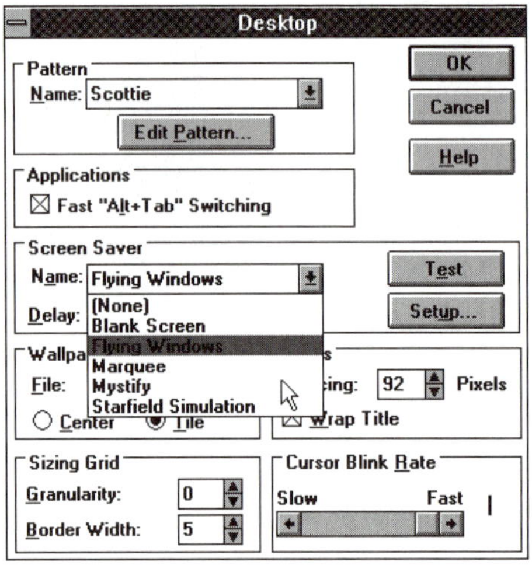

Figure 6-13 The Screen Saver drop-down list of names

3. Choose Flying Windows.
4. In the Delay text box, type 1.

   This sets the delay time for one minute.
5. Choose the Test command button.

   The currently selected screen saver appears on the screen (see Figure 6-14).

Figure 6-14 The Flying Windows screen saver

6. Return the Delay text box to its original setting.

Exercise 8: Spacing icons across a window

You can specify the amount of space between icons and whether the title of an icon will wrap to the next line by using the Icon option in the Desktop dialog box. Icon spacing is measured by the number of pixels that exist between each icon. A *pixel* is a dot on the computer screen that, when combined with other pixels, makes up a display screen. The maximum number of pixels that can be entered in the Desktop dialog box is 512. To change the spacing of an icon, perform the following steps:

pixel

1. Type 200 in the Spacing text box in the Icons portion of the Desktop dialog box.
2. Deselect the Wrap Title check box, and then choose OK.

   You are returned to the Windows screen display.
3. Open the Main window and maximize it.
4. Choose Window, and then choose Arrange icons.

   Notice how the icons in the Main window are spaced far apart from each other and that each icon title appears on a single line (see Figure 6-15).

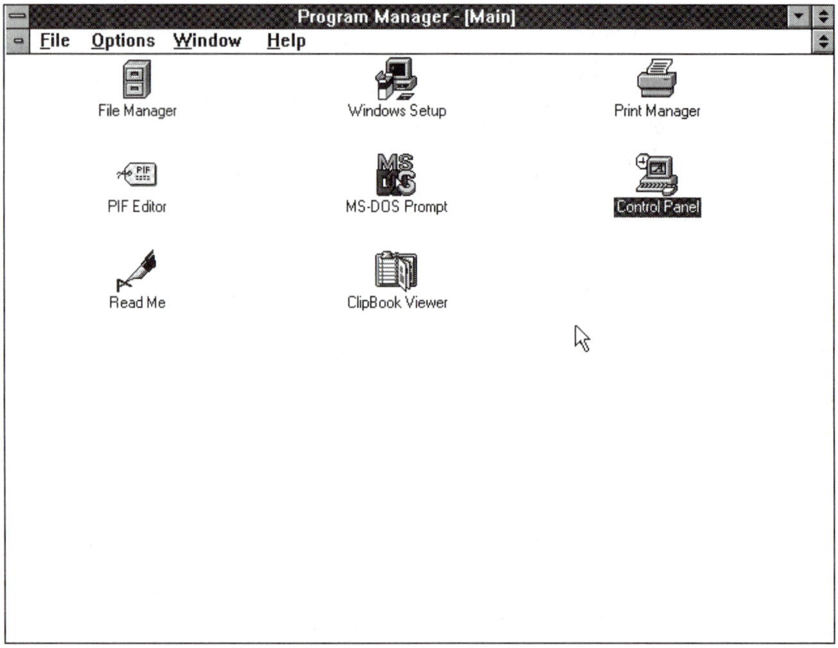

Figure 6-15 Icons spaced 200 pixels apart in the Main window

5. Open the Control Panel window and display the Desktop dialog box.
6. Reset the icon spacing to its original number and select the Wrap Title option.
7. Choose OK.

   You are returned to the Windows screen display, and the icons display their original format.

Understanding the Granularity and Border Width options

sizing grid

A *sizing grid* is an invisible set of specifications used to align windows and icons on the desktop. You can change the sizing grid that Windows uses by adjusting its granularity level with the Sizing Grid option in the Desktop dialog box. The granularity factor of the sizing grid affects the number of pixels between each window or icon on the desktop. As you increase the granularity factor, the distance between each window or icon becomes larger. In addition, borders around application and document windows can be increased or decreased by adjusting their border widths with the Sizing Grid option of the Desktop dialog box.

Exercise 9: Adjusting the sizing grid and border widths

You can make adjustments to the sizing grid and border widths using the Sizing grid option located in the Desktop dialog box. A value between 0–49 can be specified for the granularity setting, and a value of 1–50 can be used for the border-width setting.

1. Display the Desktop dialog box.
2. In the Granularity text box in the Sizing Grid portion of the Desktop dialog box, type 15.

WARNING Setting the granularity too high can cause problems when you try to arrange windows and icons on the screen.

3. In the Border Width text box in the Sizing Grid portion of the Desktop dialog box, type 15.
4. Choose OK to return to the Windows screen display.

   The border around the Control Panel window is much wider (see Figure 6-16).

Control panel border ▶

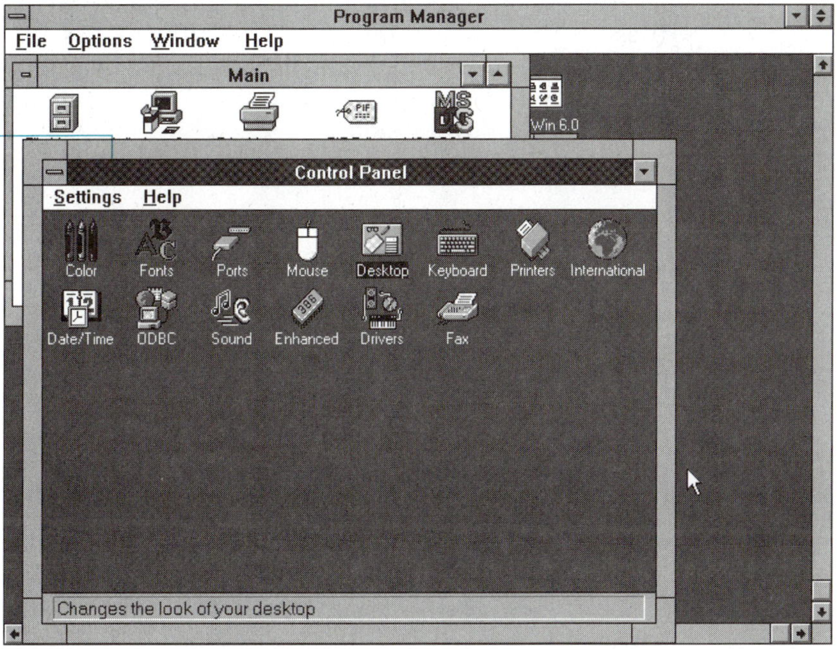

Figure 6-16 The Control Panel window with a widened border

WARNING Setting border widths too low can cause problems when you try to use the mouse to resize a window.

5. Drag the title bar of the Control Panel window to move the window to another location on the desktop.

   As you drag the window to a different location, the window snaps to the nearest gridline. Notice that you have very little flexibility when moving the window around on the screen.
6. Drag the widened border of the Control Panel to resize it.
7. Return the Sizing Grid option to its original settings.

Exercise 10: Setting the cursor blink rate

To make the blink rate of the cursor slower or faster to suit your own preference, perform the following steps:

1. Display the Desktop dialog box.
2. In the Cursor Blink Rate portion of the Desktop dialog box, drag the scroll box to the right or left to increase or decrease the blink rate of the cursor.

   A sample of the currently chosen cursor blink rate is displayed as you make the changes.

Exercise 11: Placing wallpaper on the desktop

Wallpaper designs that come with Windows can be placed on the desktop, or you can use the Paintbrush program to create a design of your own. Wallpaper files are graphic bitmapped files with the extension .bmp and usually require a lot of computer memory and hard disk space. For this reason, many people choose not to use them. To place wallpaper on the desktop, perform the following steps:

1. Display the Desktop dialog box.
2. In the Wallpaper portion of the Desktop dialog box, click the arrow to the right of the File text box.

   A drop-down list of wallpaper files appears (see Figure 6-17).

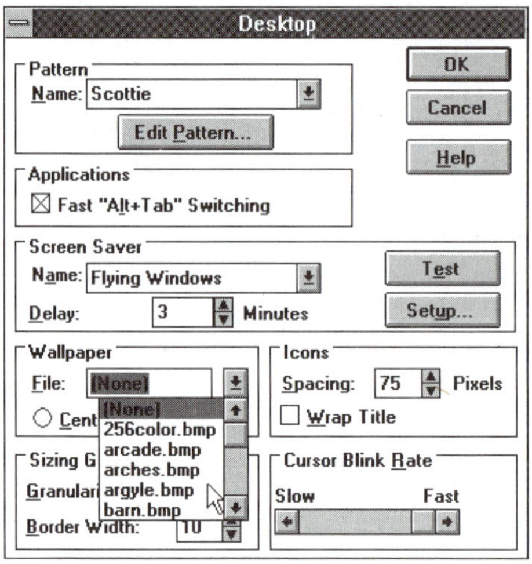

Figure 6-17 A drop-down listing of wallpaper files

3. Select a wallpaper design from the listing.
4. Choose Tile.

   The Tile option causes the wallpaper design to repeat itself until the desktop is completely covered.

Pain in the Neck

More and more people are using computers on the job, and more and more of them are complaining of physical aches and pains. Sitting, typing, and staring at a computer all day can produce ailments that range from shoulder, neck, leg, and arm pain to visual disturbances. Some of the following suggestions may help to correct these physical stresses:

Maintain correct posture.

Use ergonomically structured furniture.

Take a 10–15 minute each hour to stretch and relax muscles and refocus eyes on long-distance objects.

Consult an occupational therapist to determine where individual problems are most likely occur.

TIP Choosing the Center option places the selected wallpaper in the center of the screen. You may not be able to see it unless you minimize all the windows on your desktop.

5. Choose OK.

   The wallpaper design is displayed on the desktop.

Objective 4: Changing Mouse and Keyboard Actions

There are many ways to change the way your mouse and keyboard behave in the Windows environment. You can rearrange the functions of the mouse buttons (which is especially useful if you are left-handed). You can increase the double-clicking speed of the mouse button or increase the movement of the mouse as you move it across the screen. You can even have the mouse leave a trail across the screen as you drag it. And you can adjust the keyboard so that it repeats a character at various speeds when that character's key is depressed.

Exercise 12: Controlling the behavior of the mouse

To change the way the mouse operates, perform the following steps:

1. Double-click the Mouse icon in the Control Panel window.

   The Mouse dialog box appears (see Figure 6-18).

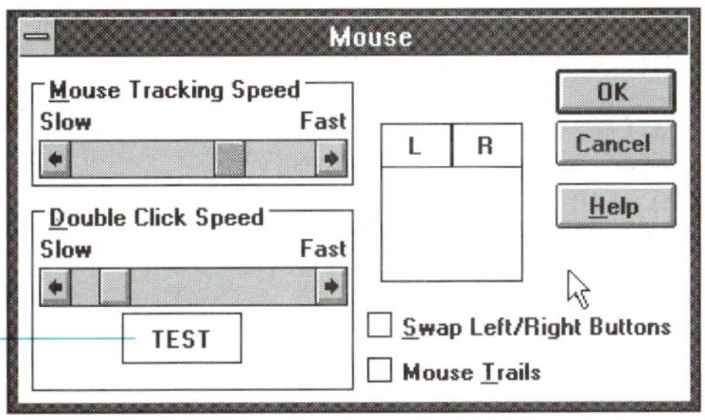

Figure 6-18 The Mouse dialog box

2. On the Mouse Tracking Speed scroll bar, drag the scroll box to the left or right; this decreases or increases the movement of the pointer as it moves across the screen, respectively.
3. On the Double Click Speed scroll bar, drag the scroll box to the left or right; this decreases or increases the reaction of the mouse to a double-click, respectively.

4. Double-click the Test button to see the change in the mouse's reaction speed.

   The Test button becomes highlighted when you double-click correctly.

5. Activate the Mouse Trails check box.

TIP Certain systems will not support the visual display of mouse trails.

6. Choose OK.

   You are returned to the Windows display screen.

7. Move the mouse pointer across the desktop to see the change in pointer speed and the mouse trails.
8. Reset all options in the Mouse dialog box to their original settings.

TIP The Swap Left/Right Buttons option in the Mouse dialog box can be activated to reverse the actions of the left and right mouse buttons. This option can be especially useful to left-handed users.

Exercise 13: Changing the speed and delay time of repeating keys

To control the repeat rate of a key and set the delay time once a key has been pressed, perform the following steps:

1. Double-click the Keyboard icon located in the Control Panel.

   The Keyboard dialog box appears (see Figure 6-19).

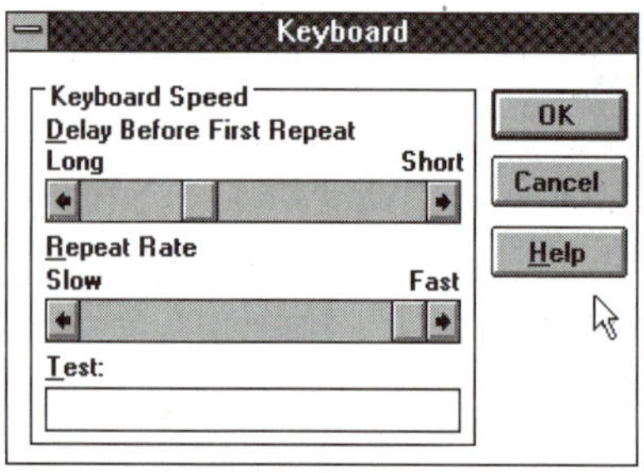

Figure 6-19 The Keyboard dialog box

2. On the Delay Before First Repeat scroll bar, drag the scroll box to the left or right to cause a long or short delay time. This delay time determines how long you must hold down a key before it will repeat its character a second time on the screen.
3. On the Repeat Rate scroll bar, drag the scroll box to the left or right to decrease or increase the rate of speed that a key repeats.
4. Position the pointer in the Test text box and press and hold down any letter on the keyboard to display the speed of the new delay and repeat rates.
5. Reset all options in the Keyboard dialog box to their original settings.

Objective 5: Setting the Date and Time

Setting the date and time for your computer system is easy when you use the Date/Time icon in the Control Panel window. In the Date & Time dialog box, you can change the current time, day, month, and year.

Exercise 14: Changing your system's date and time

To change your system's date and time, perform the following steps:

1. Double-click the Date/Time icon  located in the Control Panel window.

   The Date & Time dialog box appears (see Figure 6-20).

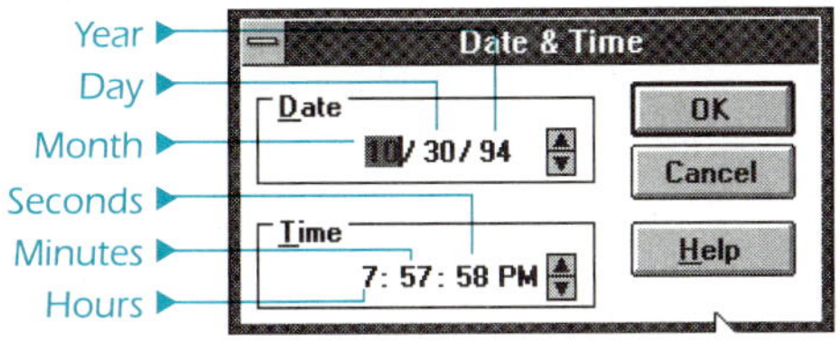

Figure 6-20 The Date & Time dialog box

2. In the Date option box, select each number (month, date, and year) in turn and type the current date or use the scroll arrows to set the current date.
3. In the Time option box, select each number (hour, minute, and second) in turn and type the current time or use the scroll arrows to set the current time.
4. Choose OK.

Objective 6: Using Printer Options

The Printers icon in the Control Panel window can be used to activate, install, change, or remove printers that work with the Windows environment. When you install a new printer to work with your computer system,

configure

you must *configure* it to work with the Windows environment. To configure means to choose settings in a program or a computer system to meet individual needs. During the installation process, a printer driver is installed.

printer driver

A *printer driver* is a file containing information that is supplied to a program, such as Windows, to identify a specific type of printer. Windows provides some printer drivers; others are often included with the printer that you purchase.

The Printers dialog box enables you to select a default printer when you have more than one printer from which to choose. The default printer is the printer to which documents are automatically sent.

TIP The Use Print Manager option that appears in the Printers dialog box can be enabled to automatically route files you choose to print. Chapter 9 describes this option in greater detail.

Exercise 15: Installing a new printer driver

To add a new printer driver to the Windows environment, perform the following steps:

1. Double-click the Printers icon in the Control Panel window.

   The Printers dialog box appears (see Figure 6-21).

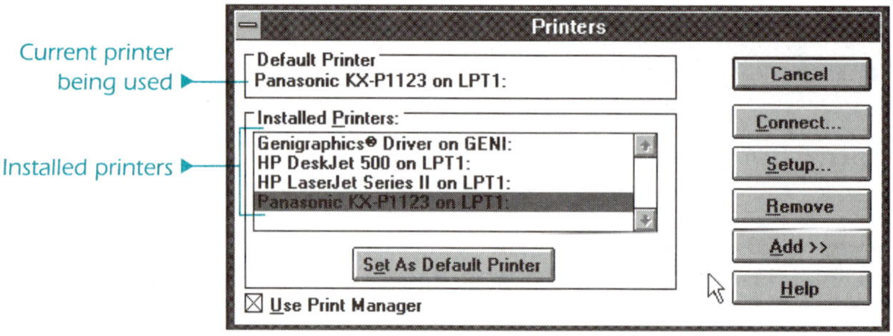

Figure 6-21 The Printers dialog box

   The name of the current default printer appears in the Default Printer box and is highlighted in the Installed Printers box.

2. Choose Add>>.

   A list of available printers is displayed at the bottom of the window (see Figure 6-22).

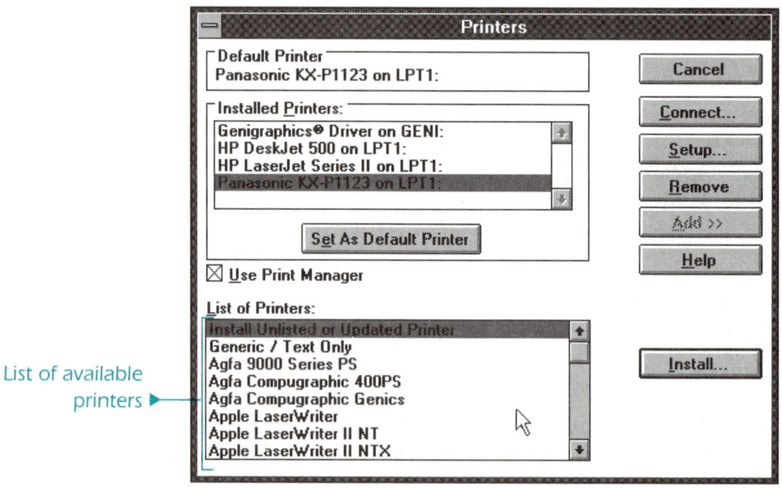

Figure 6-22 The List of Printers display box

> **FEATURE**
>
> **COM ports**
> Communications ports can be set up to work with the Windows program by activating the Ports icon in the Control Panel window. COM ports (also called serial ports) can be used with a modem and certain printers. The COM Ports dialog box sets options for baud rate, data bits, parity, stop bits, and flow control. These settings must be configured properly to establish communication between computers.

3. Choose the name of the printer you want to add to the Windows environment.
4. Choose Install.

   The printer appears in the Installed Printers list.
5. Insert the floppy disk that contains the needed printer driver. This disk is either one of the Windows installation disks or a disk that came with the printer you are installing.
6. Choose OK.

   The new printer appears in the Installed Printers list.

Exercise 16: Selecting the default printer

To select the default printer, perform the following steps:

1. Display the Printers dialog box.
2. Choose a different printer name in the Installed Printers box.
3. Choose the Set As Default Printer button.
4. Choose Close to accept the new default printer.
5. Reset the default printer in the Printers dialog box to its original setting.

Objective 7: Installing Sound

The Sound icon can be used to assign sounds to various application events and turn a system's error warning beep on or off. You must have a sound card installed in your computer to assign sounds. You will notice that the items in the Sound dialog box are dimmed (indicating that they are unavailable) if Windows does not detect a sound card.

Exercise 17: Disabling the error warning beep

Any time you cause an error while using your computer, the system notifies you with a warning beep. To silence the beep on your system, perform the following steps:

1. Double-click the Sound icon  located in the Control Panel window.

   The Sound dialog box appears (see Figure 6-23).

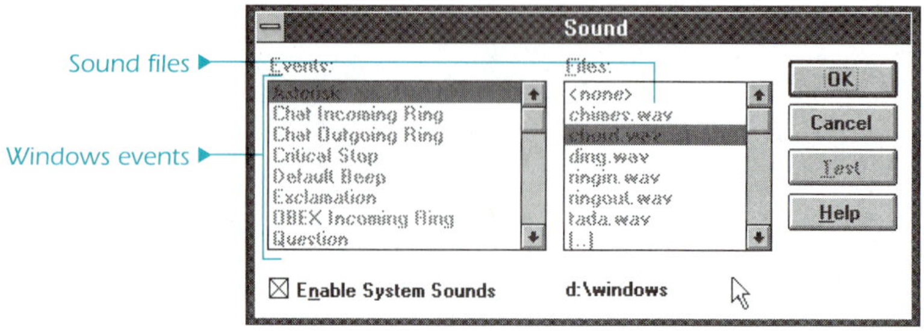

Figure 6-23 The Sound dialog box

2. Deactivate the Enable System Sounds check box, and then choose OK. When an error is made, the warning beep will not sound.
3. Reset this option to its original setting.

Objective 8: Changing International Settings

The International icon in the Control Panel enables you to change various character sets—such as date, currency, time, and numbers—to conform to the conventions of countries outside the United States. The settings that you choose in the International dialog box affect any Windows-based application on your computer.

Exercise 18: Defining an international setting

To change the country, language, keyboard, and measurements options in the International dialog box, perform the following steps:

1. Double-click the International icon in the Control Panel window. The International dialog box appears (see Figure 6-24).

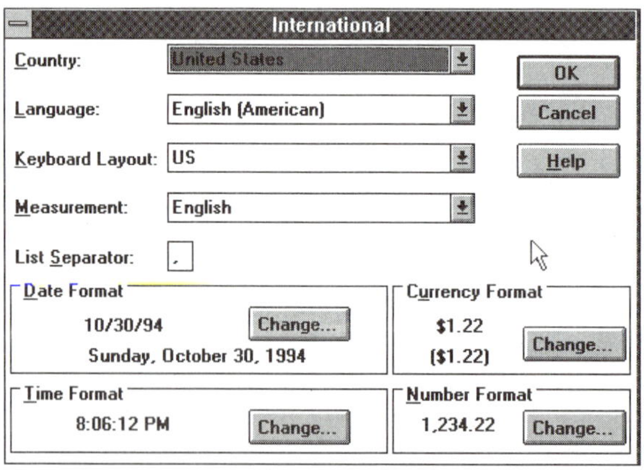

Figure 6-24 The International dialog box

2. Click the arrow to the right of the Country text box.

   A drop-down list of countries appears (see Figure 6-25).

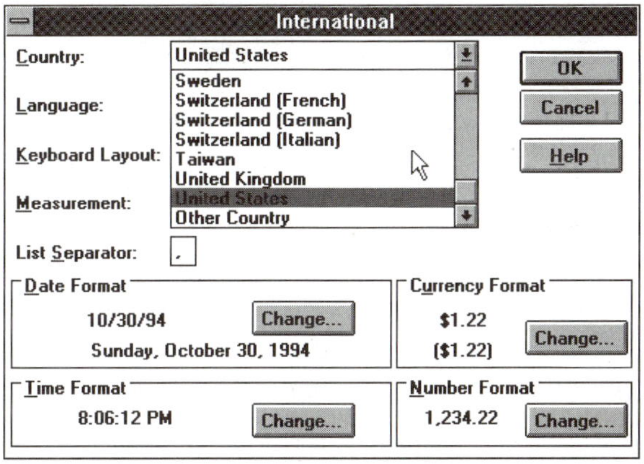

Figure 6-25 The drop-down list of countries in the International dialog box

3. Choose Sweden.

   Notice that the information in the Date Format, Currency Format, Time Format, and Number Format boxes reflects the change you made in the Country text box.
4. Click the arrow to the right of the Language text box.

   A drop-down list of languages appears.
5. Choose Swedish.
6. Click the arrow to the right of the Keyboard Layout text box.

   A drop-down list of keyboard layouts appears.
7. Choose Swedish.
8. Click the arrow to the right of the Measurement text box.

   A drop-down list of measurements appears.
9. Choose Metric.
10. Choose OK to return to the Windows screen.
11. Reset all options in the International dialog box to their original settings.

Exercise 19: Changing an international number format

To change the Number Format option, perform the following steps.

1. Display the International dialog box.
2. Choose the Change button in the Number Format portion of the International dialog box.

   The International—Number Format dialog box appears (see Figure 6-26).

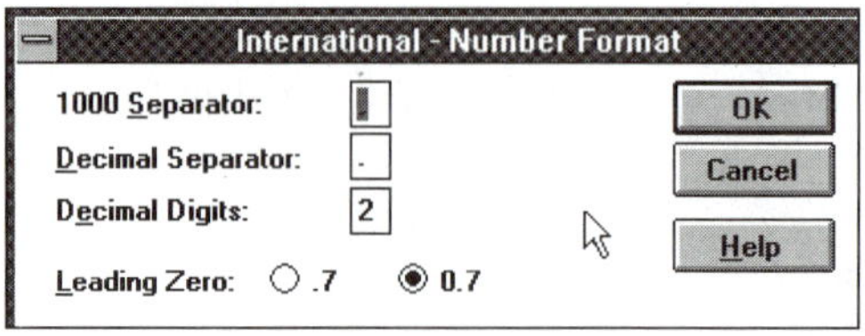

Figure 6-26 The International—Number Format dialog box

3. In the Decimal Digits box, type 3. This option indicates the number of digits you want to appear to the right of the decimal separator.
4. Select .7 for the Leading Zero option. This indicates that you do not want to display a leading zero in front of the decimal separator.

TIP The 1000 Separator box enables you to type the character you want to separate thousands. The Decimal Separator box enables you to type the character you want to separate decimal digits from whole numbers.

5. Choose OK.

   The International dialog box appears.
6. Choose OK.
7. Reset all options in the International dialog box to their original settings.

Table 6-3 describes other options in the International dialog box.

Table 6-3 International dialog box options.

OPTION	DESCRIPTION
List Separator	Use this text box to enter the list separator or your choice to separate elements in a list.
Date Format	Use this option to change the format of a short or long date. You can change the order of elements in a date (for example, month/date/year or date/month/year), change the separator used between items in a date (for example, / or –), or add leading zeroes before single-digit months and days.
Currency Format	Use this option to change the way number symbols are placed, to select the way a negative number appears, to specify the currency symbol you want to use, and to specify the number of decimal digits you want to include.
Time Format	Use this option to display the time in a format of your choice. You can display the time in 12- or 24-hour settings, select the separator to use between time elements, and choose to display leading zeroes.

Objective 9: Adding Fonts

The Fonts icon in the Control Panel window is used to activate the Fonts dialog box. From the Fonts dialog box, you can install new fonts, delete existing fonts, and select TrueType fonts that come with the Windows pro-
font gram. A *font* is a specific character typeface, such as Courier or Times New Roman, in a particular weight and size. Fonts fall in two categories: screen fonts (those you view on the screen) and printer fonts (those that appear on a printed document). Screen fonts often look different than their corresponding printer fonts.

The Windows program provides a number of TrueType fonts. TrueType fonts are scaleable fonts that operate in What-You-See-Is-What-You-Get
WYSIWYG (WYSIWYG) mode. WYSIWYG means that on-screen characters appear as they will when they are printed out. A scaleable font is displayed in the size you assign, no matter how large that size may be.

Exercise 20: Adding fonts to the Windows program

If you decide to purchase additional fonts for your printer or purchase a new printer that comes equipped with additional fonts, you will have to add them to the Windows program so that Windows will recognize them. Fonts that accompany a new printer can be added to the Windows directory when you install the printer. To add fonts to the Windows program, perform the following steps:

1. Double-click the Fonts icon  in the Control Panel window.

   The Fonts dialog box appears, displaying the currently installed fonts (see Figure 6-27).

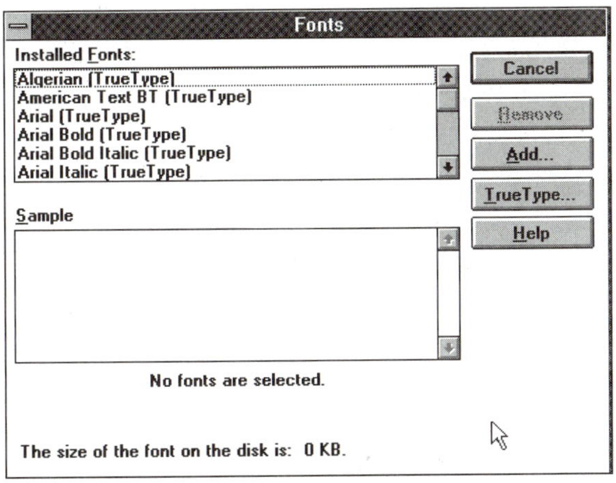

Figure 6-27 The Fonts dialog box

2. Choose Add.

   The Add Fonts dialog box appears (see Figure 6-28).

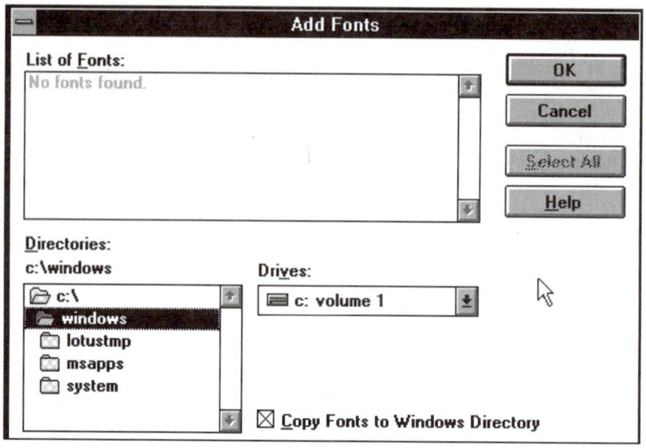

Figure 6-28 The Add Fonts dialog box

3. Select the type of fonts that you want to add from the List of Fonts box.

WARNING If the fonts you want to add were not previously copied to the Windows directory, they will not appear in the List of Fonts box. Deselect the Copy Fonts To Windows Directory check box, and then specify the drive that holds the disk containing the font files you want to add.

4. Choose OK.

   The fonts are added to the Windows program.

Exercise 21: Enabling TrueType fonts

To enable TrueType fonts in the Windows program, perform the following steps:

1. Display the Fonts dialog box.
2. Choose TrueType.

   The TrueType dialog box appears (see Figure 6-29).

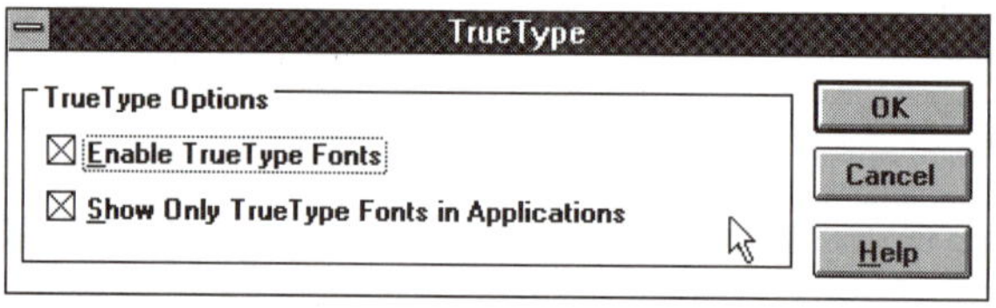

Figure 6-29 The TrueType dialog box

3. Activate the Enable TrueType Fonts option.
4. Choose OK.

   Your Windows applications display TrueType screen fonts in WYSIWYG mode.

WARNING TrueType fonts require large amounts of computer memory. Check with your instructor to make sure that the system you are using is not limited in memory. If your system has memory constraints, you may need to deselect the Enable TrueType Fonts option.

TIP The Show Only TrueType Fonts in Applications option restricts any nonTrueType fonts from being displayed.

Chapter Summary

In this chapter, you learned how to customize your system using the various icons in the Control Panel window. You now know how to change a variety of options, including the screen color scheme, screen saver, icon and window spacing, cursor blink rate, mouse operations, and date and time settings. You learned how to place wallpaper on the desktop, and you know how to add fonts and configure new printers to the Windows environment.

Review Questions

True/False Questions

_____ 1. You can customize various system settings by activating icons in the Accessories window or by using the Settings menu.

_____ 2. The Desktop icon enables you to set the keyboard repeat rate.

_____ 3. To create a color scheme of your own for the Desktop, you must choose the Color Palette button.

_____ 4. The Applications option enables you to switch quickly from one group window to another.

_____ 5. Icon spacing is measured by the number of pixels that exist between each icon.

Multiple-Choice Questions

_____ 6. Changing the granularity factor affects

A. the spacing between icons.

B. the arrangement of group windows on the desktop.

C. border widths.

D. all of the above

E. A and B only

_____ 7. The maximum amount of pixels that can be used to space icons is

A. 200.

B. 512.

C. 50.

D. none of the above

_____ 8. Wallpaper design files all have the extension

A. .dll.

B. .exe.

C. .bmp.

D. .cgm.

_____ 9. TrueType fonts are fonts that

A. are scaleable.

B. appear on-screen as they will when printed.

C. can be enabled or disabled.

D. all of the above

E. A and B only

_____ 10. All the following options are included in the International dialog box except

A. Date Format.

B. Currency Format.

C. Keyboard Format.

D. Country.

Fill-in-the Blank Questions

11. _______________ _______________ are used to increase the longevity of your monitor.

12. _______________ _______________ fonts use large amounts of computer memory.

13. The _______________ _______________ of the cursor can be increased or decreased.

14. You can disable the __________ __________ that sounds when an error is made.
15. Your system must have a __________ __________ in order to use some of the options in the Sounds dialog box.

Acumen-Building Activities

Quick Projects

1. Using the control panel

1. Start Windows and activate the appropriate icons.
2. Display the Pastel color scheme on the desktop.
3. Display the Waffle pattern on the desktop.
4. Activate the option to enable you to switch quickly from one running application to another.
5. Display the Flying Windows screen saver on the desktop. Set the delay time for 4 minutes. Test your changes.
6. Set the icon spacing to 25 pixels and disable the Wrap Title option.
7. Reset all options to their original settings.

2. Making changes in the control panel

1. Start Windows and activate the appropriate icons.
2. Set the granularity level to 30.
3. Set the border width to 15.
4. Set the cursor blink rate to the fastest possible speed.
5. Decrease the double-clicking speed of the mouse.
6. Select the option to display mouse trails.
7. Increase the movement of the mouse pointer as it moves across the screen.
8. Set the delay time of a key once it is pressed to the longest possible duration.
9. Increase the repeat rate of the key.
10. Change the system date and time to July 5, 1996, 11:20 p.m.
11. Reset all options to their original settings.

3. Using Windows

1. Start Windows.
2. Display the Accessories, Main, and Games group windows.
3. Overlap all three windows on the screen.

4. Activate the Accessories window and launch the Write program.
5. Minimize the Write program to an icon on the desktop.
6. Start the Calendar program and minimize it to an icon on the desktop.
7. Turn off your system's error warning beep.
8. Change the default printer.
9. Change your system's international settings to conform to Germany's standards.
10. Change the format of the date to year/month/date.
11. Enable the TrueType fonts option.
12. Close all open windows except the Control Panel window.
13. Reset all options to their original settings.

4. Working in Windows

1. Start Windows.
2. Open the Main, Accessories, and StartUp windows.
3. Resize all three windows so they appear tall and narrow.
4. Start the File Manager.
5. Display the contents of the floppy disk you created in Chapter 5.
6. Create a new directory on the floppy disk in drive A and name it chap6.
7. Copy all the files in the lpex1 directory to the chap6 directory.
8. Delete the lpex1 directory from the drive A disk.
9. Rename all the files in the chap6 directory so they all have the extension .six.
10. Create a color scheme for the Windows desktop and save it as mycolors.
11. Adjust the setting that spaces icons in group windows.
12. Turn off the screen saver.
13. Remove the mycolors color scheme.
14. Reset all options to their original settings.

In-Depth Projects

1. Exploring Windows

1. Start Windows.
2. Open the following group windows: Main, Accessories, Games, and StartUp.
3. Activate the Program Manager menu bar using the keyboard.
4. Using the keyboard method, move the Main window to the lower, right corner of the screen.

5. Using the keyboard method, resize the StartUp window so that it is very small.
6. Close all the open group windows.
7. Choose the command to arrange icons across the bottom of the Program Manager window.
8. Choose a screen saver and set its delay time to 2 minutes.
9. Set the amount of space between icons to 40 and disable the Titles Wrap option.
10. Set the cursor blink rate to the slowest possible speed.
11. Place a wallpaper design on the desktop and center it.
12. Reset all options to their original settings.

2. Exploring Windows further

1. Start Windows.
2. Place a bookmark on the help topic Options Menu Commands.
3. Print the help topic for Quitting Windows.
4. Copy the Cardfile and Calculator icons to the StartUp window.
5. Start the File Manager.
6. Using the floppy disk labeled DISK2, view the Directory Tree of that disk only in the File Manager window.
7. Create a subdirectory within the chap6 directory and name it subdir6.
8. Display the expandable branches of the disk in drive A.
9. Change the system date and time to 10/31/94 and 1:00 p.m.
10. Change the International settings to reflect the country of France and the Currency setting of F 1.
11. Reset all options to their original settings.

3. Checking your Windows skills

1. Start Windows.
2. Using the floppy disk labeled DISK2, view only the file names and dates of files located in the chap6 directory.
3. Choose the option that will cause confirmation warning messages not to display when copying or moving files with the mouse.
4. Change the name of the DISK2 disk to PROJECTS.
5. Make a disk copy of PROJECTS to DISK1.
6. Slow the mouse pointer movement across the screen.
7. Display mouse trails.
8. Display a sample of a TrueType font in the Fonts dialog box.
9. Adjust the setting of the key repeat rate to its slowest rate.
10. Reset all options to their original settings.

Chapter 7

Using Write

Objectives

- Creating a Document
- Moving around a Document
- Editing a Document
- Saving and Opening a Document
- Selecting Text
- Moving, Copying, and Deleting Text
- Formatting Text
- Using the Ruler
- Printing a Document

Key Terms

TERM	DEFINITION
Header	text that appears at the top of every page in a document; the header often includes the document title and author name
Footer	text that appears at the bottom of every page of a document; the footer often includes the current page number
Word Wrap	a feature in word processing programs where the program recognizes the right margin and automatically ends one line and continues text on the next line
End-of-File Marker	a character used to indicate the end of a document
Point	a unit of measurement used to describe the height of a character; one point equals $1/72$ of an inch

TERM	DEFINITION
Clipboard	a temporary storage area in RAM that holds text or graphics that have been copied from another location
Insertion Point	a flashing vertical bar within a document window that indicates where text that is typed will appear

Windows provides a number of programs that can be used to perform daily work tasks. In this chapter, you will investigate the capabilities of the Write program, which is part of your Windows package. With the Write program, you can create professional-looking documents.

Objective 1: Creating a Document

Write is a word processing program located in the Accessories group window. With Write, you can create, save, and print documents. The program includes options to enhance text, place headers and footers within a text document, and align paragraphs automatically. Write also provides a variety of fonts from which to choose. Write is located in the Accessories group window and is represented by a pen icon.

A document window in Write includes a title bar, a menu bar, scroll bars, minimize and maximize buttons, and a control menu box. The title bar displays the name of the program, along with the title of the document. When you create a new Write document, the title of the document is Untitled. Write also includes a page status area on the bottom of the Write document window.

FEATURE

Enhancing Documents with Images

The Write program enables you to place graphical objects in a document, which can enliven and enhance a document. Write does not include any graphics files of its own, but you can use bit-mapped files or scanned images created in other programs and place them in a Write document. The methods used to include a picture in a Write document are copying, pasting, and using Object Linking and Embedding (OLE) technology.

Exercise 1: Starting the Write program

To begin Write, perform the following steps:

1. Open the Accessories group window.
2. Double-click the Write icon.

   The Write document window appears (see Figure 7-1).

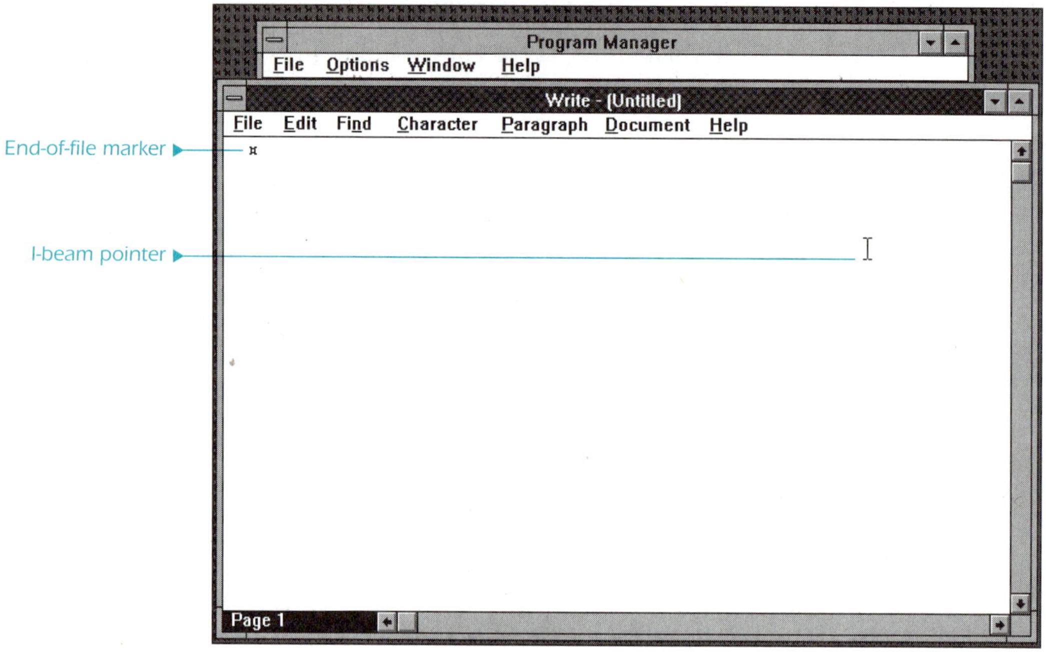

Figure 7-1 The Write document window

Entering text

insertion point

end-of-file marker

To enter text in a Write document, you simply start typing. As you type text, the insertion point and the end-of-file marker moves. The *insertion point* is the flashing vertical bar within the document window, indicating where text that is typed will appear. The *end-of-file marker* is the tiny box next to the insertion point, indicating the end of the document.

word wrap

When the text you type reaches the right edge of the document window, you do not have to press Enter to continue typing on the next line. Word processing programs use a feature called *word wrap* that causes the text you are typing to drop to a new line when the text reaches the program's automatic margin. Enter should be used only to end a short line, end a paragraph, or insert a blank line in a document.

Exercise 2: Typing text in a document

To enter text in the document, perform the following steps:

1. Type the following text. Include all spelling errors and don't worry if the lines of your document do not end up the same as the one in the figure. Do *not* press ↵ ENTER at the end of each line.

```
We would like to take theis opportunity to welcome
all of the new comitee members who have decided to
join the American Saddle Horse Association. We are
pleased to announce that as of July 5, 1994, four new
members were chosen to work with us to help us acheive
the goals set for the 1995 horse show season. The 1995
show season promises to be one of great compatition
among owners of American Saddlebred horses and we
hope that it will be a lucky season for all.
```

2. Press ↵ ENTER twice.

   Your document should resemble Figure 7-2.

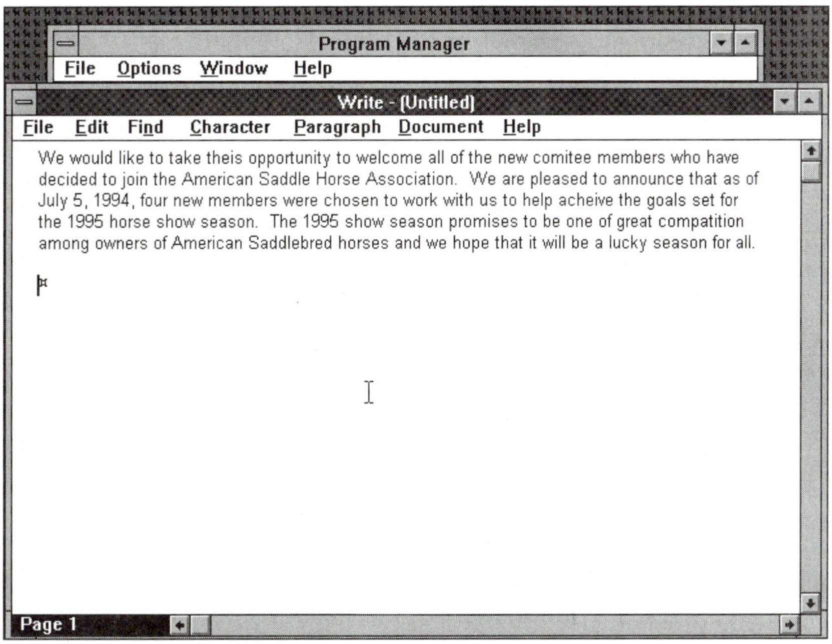

Figure 7-2 The document with text

Objective 2: Moving around the Document

You can reposition the insertion point in the document using the direction keys on the keyboard or the mouse. If you press Home, the insertion point moves to the beginning of the current line. If you press End, the insertion point moves to the end of the current line.

TIP You cannot position the insertion point in a blank text area.

Exercise 3: Using the mouse and keyboard to reposition the insertion point

To move around the document you created in Exercise 2, perform the following steps:

1. Press ↑ on the keyboard repeatedly until you reach the first sentence at the top of the document.

   The insertion point moves up one line each time you press the key.
2. Press ↓ repeatedly until you reach the last sentence at the bottom of the document.

   The insertion point moves down each time you press the key.
3. Use ← and → to move horizontally on the document screen.
4. Position the insertion point at the end of a line. Press HOME.

   The insertion point is repositioned at the beginning of the line.
5. Press END.

   The insertion point is repositioned at the end of the line.
6. Place your insertion point on the last line of the document.
7. Press ↓ twice.

   Your insertion point is repositioned before the end-of-file marker.
8. Press →.

   Your computer beeps, indicating that it cannot move the insertion point where there is no existing text.
9. Using the mouse, move the mouse pointer so that it is positioned before the word *Association*.

   The mouse pointer changes to an I-beam.
10. Click the left mouse button.

    The insertion point appears before the word *Association*.
11. Use the mouse to position the insertion point before the word *lucky*.

Objective 3: Editing a Document

To correct spelling errors in a document, you can use Backspace and Delete. Backspace deletes a character to the left of the insertion point; Delete deletes a character to the right of the insertion point.

Exercise 4: Using Backspace and Delete to edit text

To correct the spelling errors in the document you created in Exercise 2, perform the following steps:

1. Position the insertion point after the *h* in *theis* in the first sentence.
2. Press DELETE.

   The *e* is removed.
3. Reposition the insertion point in front of the *m* in *comitee* in the first sentence.
4. Type m.

   As you type, the existing characters move to the right to make room for the text you insert.
5. Place an additional *t* after the *t* in *comitee.*
6. Use the mouse to reposition the insertion point in front of the *v* in *acheive* in the second sentence.
7. Press ← BACKSPACE twice. Type ie.

   The corrected document should resemble Figure 7-3.

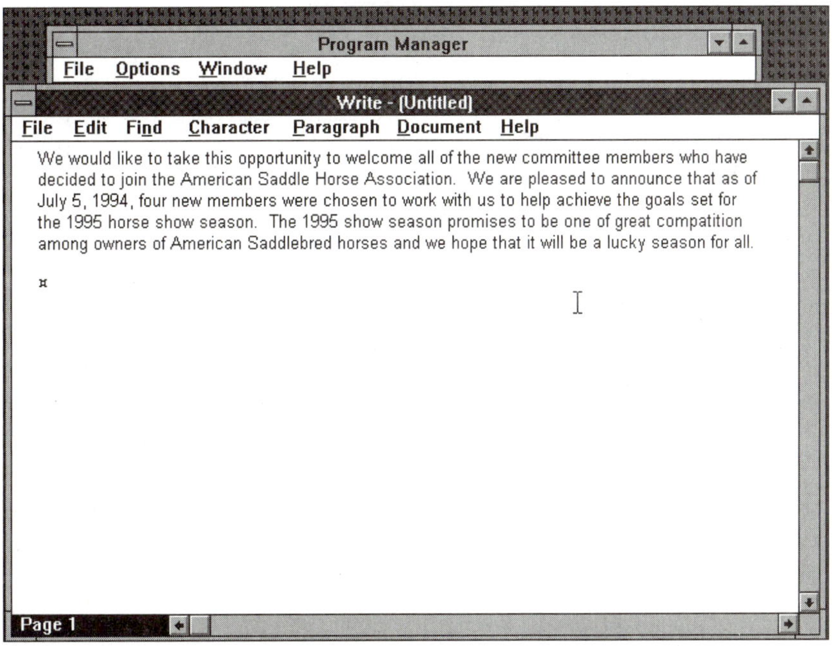

Figure 7-3 The corrected document

Objective 4: Saving and Opening a Document

The document you have been typing is currently stored in main memory. To store the document permanently so that you can retrieve it at a later time, you must save it to disk. The document does not have a name at this time. The Save As command is used to save a file for the first time or to rename a file. The Save command is used to save a file with the same name after it has been modified. As you type a document, remember to save your changes every 10 to 15 minutes so you won't lose your work.

Exercise 5: Saving a file

In the following exercise, you will save the document you typed to the floppy disk DISK1 in drive A. To name the Write file that you have created and save it to disk, perform the following steps:

1. Insert DISK 1 in drive A.
2. Choose File from the Write menu bar.

   The File menu appears.
3. Choose Save As.

   The Save As dialog box appears (see Figure 7-4).

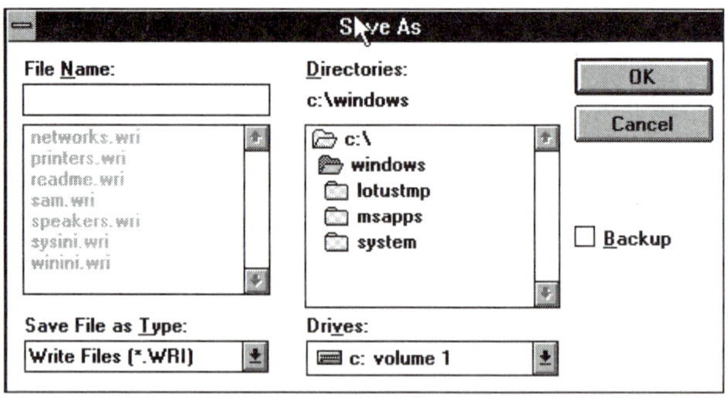

Figure 7-4 The Save As dialog box

4. Position the insertion point in the File Name text box.
5. Type horses.
6. Click the arrow to the right of the Drives box.

   A list of available drives for your system is displayed.
7. Click drive A so that the document will be saved to the floppy disk in drive A.

   Notice that when you switch the drive area, the information displayed in the Save As dialog box changes to reflect the drive area you have selected (see Figure 7-5).

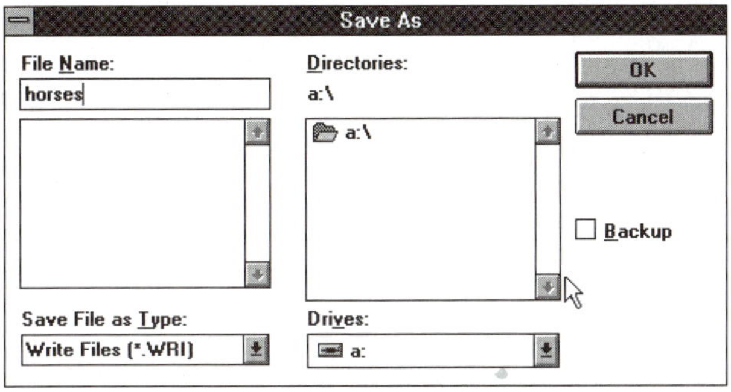

Figure 7-5 The Save As dialog box after switching drive areas

The Save File as Type box enables you to change the default file extension (.wri) to any valid extension of your choice.

8. Choose OK.

   You are returned to the Write document; the file name appears in the Write title bar (see Figure 7-6).

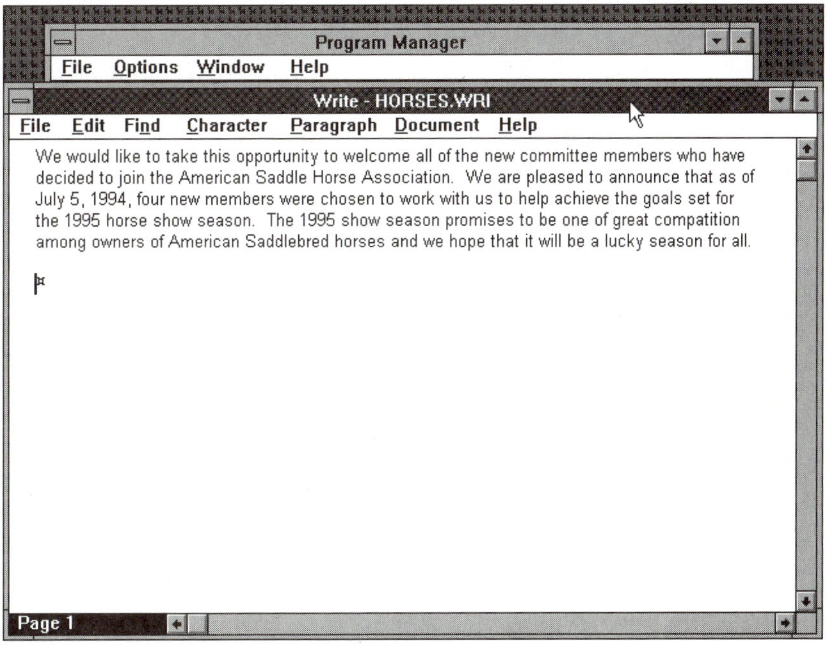

Figure 7-6 The file name in the Write title bar

9. Change the *a* in *compatition* to an *e*.
10. Choose File from the menu bar, and then choose Save.

    The file is saved with the same name. Note that a dialog box was not displayed when you selected Save.

Using the New command

To open a new document, choose the New command from the File menu. If you have another document displayed and you have saved all current changes to the document, Write automatically closes the displayed document and displays a new blank screen. If you have not saved the currently displayed document before selecting New, Write displays a message box asking if you want to save the changes before proceeding to the new document (see Figure 7-7).

Figure 7-7 The Write message box asking if you want to save current changes

Exercise 6: Opening and exiting a new document

In the following exercise, you will choose the New command. To open a new document, perform the following steps:

1. Choose File, and then choose New.

   Write closes the horses document and displays a new blank document on the screen.

2. Choose File, and then choose Open.

   The Open dialog box appears (see Figure 7-8).

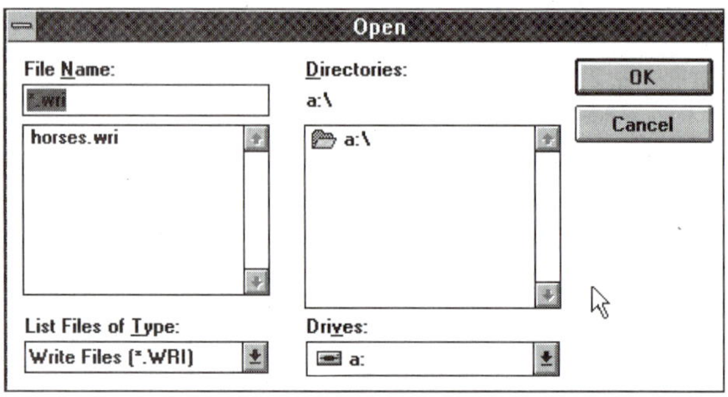

Figure 7-8 The Open dialog box

TIP Only those files with the .wri extension are shown in the File Name list box. To see all the files on drive A, click the arrow in the List Files of Type list box and choose All Files.

3. Select the horses.wri file.

4. Choose OK.

   The horses.wri file is displayed on the screen.

5. Add the following text to the horses.wri file exactly as it appears. Press ↵ ENTER to end each paragraph and insert a blank line above and below each heading.

```
Association Philosophy

It is the philosophy of the American Saddle Horse
Association to promote the Amercian Saddlebred horse
and improve the integrity of the breed. Members of the
association are committed to work towards refinement of
the breed and follow closely all guidelines regarding
breeding, competing, training, and owning an American
Saddlebred horse.

Opening Show Season Dinner

On May 10, 1995, the Saddle Horse Association is
planning a dinner and presentation for all members of
the Saddle Horse Association. Dinner will be served at
7:00 p.m. and will include a choice of sirloin tip beef
or chicken cordon bleu. An open bar will be provided
from 6:00-11:00 where refreshments will be served.

Ticket prices are $30.00 per person and can be pur-
chased from the secretary's office beginning the first
week of May.

Presentation Speakers

Presentation speakers at the dinner will include the
president of the American Horse Show Association,
Mr. James Kevin. Mr. Kevin will discuss the 1995
show season itinerary and present awards to last years
high point contestants. Dr. Mary Mark, author of the
book Treating Your Horses Lameness will be on hand to
discuss the controversy surrounding vitamin therapies
currently being used for treatment of lameness prob-
lems. Questions and comments are welcome during the
presentation sessions.

Scheduled Classes for May 1995 Class A Show
```

6. Save this document and type horses as its name.

TIP You can create a backup copy of a document by selecting the Backup check box in the Save As dialog box. When prompted to replace the exiting file, choose Yes. An additional copy of the file will be added to your disk with the extension .bak.

Objective 5: Selecting Text

Before you can issue commands that affect text, you must select the text you want to change. You can select text using the mouse or keyboard. Additionally, you can place the mouse pointer in the far left margin until it turns into a right-pointing arrow. You can then select the single line of text, a paragraph, multiple paragraphs, or the entire document. Text that is selected is highlighted.

To deselect text, you can click any part of the document window. Table 7-1 lists the methods used to select text with the mouse and with the keyboard.

Table 7-1 Methods used to select text

TEXT TO BE SELECTED	PROCEDURE
Using the mouse	
A single word	Double-click the word.
The current line	Move the cursor to the left margin until is becomes a right-pointing arrow; point to the line and click.
The current paragraph	Move the cursor to the left margin until it becomes a right-pointing arrow; point to the paragraph and double-click.
Any amount of text	Place your insertion point at the beginning of the text, and then drag the mouse until you reach the end of the text.
The entire document	Press CTRL and click.
More than one line	Move the cursor to the left margin until it becomes a right-pointing arrow; click the first line of text and drag the mouse down to select each line.
Using the keyboard	
Characters to the right	Press SHIFT+→.
Characters to the left	Press SHIFT+←.
A word to the right	Press SHIFT+CTRL+→.
Select a word to the left	Press SHIFT+CTRL+←.
Several lines	Press SHIFT+↑ or Press SHIFT+↓.

Exercise 7: Selecting text using the mouse and keyboard

To use the mouse and keyboard to select text from the document created previously, perform the following steps:

1. Point to the word *opportunity* in the first sentence and double-click. The word is selected.
2. Deselect the text by clicking anywhere within the document window but off the highlighted area.

3. Position the mouse pointer in the far left margin of the first sentence.

   The mouse pointer becomes a right-pointing arrow.

4. Click once.

   The first sentence of the paragraph is selected.

5. Place the mouse pointer anywhere in the left margin and press CTRL and click.

   The entire document is selected.

6. Deselect the text.

7. Place the insertion point at the beginning of *We* and drag the mouse diagonally down through the paragraph until the last word of the paragraph is highlighted.

   The first paragraph is selected.

8. Deselect the text.

9. Using the keyboard, place the insertion point before *opportunity* in the first sentence.

10. Press SHIFT+CTRL+→.

    The word is selected.

11. Deselect the text.

12. Place the insertion point after *welcome* in the first sentence.

13. Press SHIFT+CTRL+←.

    The word is selected.

14. Deselect the text.

15. Position the insertion point before *We*.

16. Hold down SHIFT as you repeatedly press the ↓ until the entire first paragraph is highlighted.

    The first paragraph is highlighted.

17. Deselect the text.

Objective 6: Moving, Copying, and Deleting Text

The Windows environment enables you to copy and move text from one location to another using the Cut, Copy, and Paste commands. Information that is cut or copied is automatically stored in a temporary storage area in RAM called the *Clipboard*; you can then retrieve that information using the Paste command. Before information can be cut or copied, it must be selected.

clipboard

Existing text can be deleted by selecting it and then pressing Delete. If you want to replace existing text with new text, you select the text you want to replace and then type the new text or choose the Paste command.

WARNING The Clipboard holds only one item at a time. If you cut or copy an item so that it is stored in the Clipboard and then cut or copy another item, the first item in the Clipboard is overwritten by the second item.

Exercise 8: Moving text in a document

You can move text from one area in a document to a different area in the same document using Cut from the Edit menu. When you cut text, the text is removed from its original location; it reappears when you paste it in its new location. You can also delete text using the Cut command. To delete and move text using the Cut command, perform the following steps:

1. Position the insertion point before *Opening* in the third paragraph.
2. Select *Opening Show Season Dinner* as well as the paragraph under it. Include the blank line under the paragraph (see Figure 7-9).

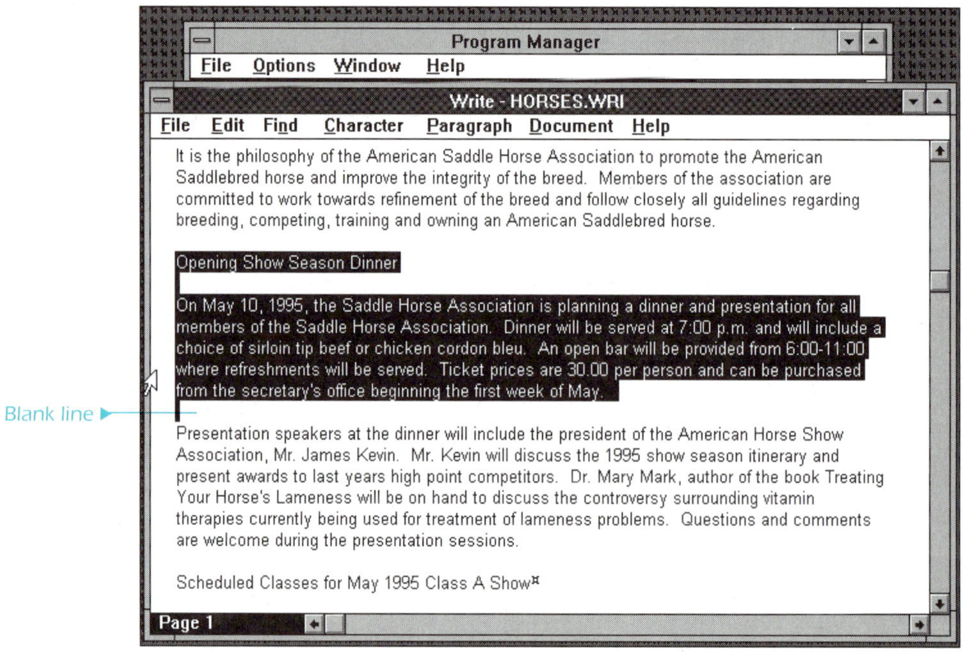

Figure 7-9 Selected text

3. Choose Edit, and then choose Cut.

   The selected text disappears.

4. Place the insertion point at the bottom of the document under *Scheduled Classes for May 1995 Class A Show.*

5. Choose Edit, and then choose Paste.

   The paragraph that you cut reappears at the end of the document (see Figure 7-10).

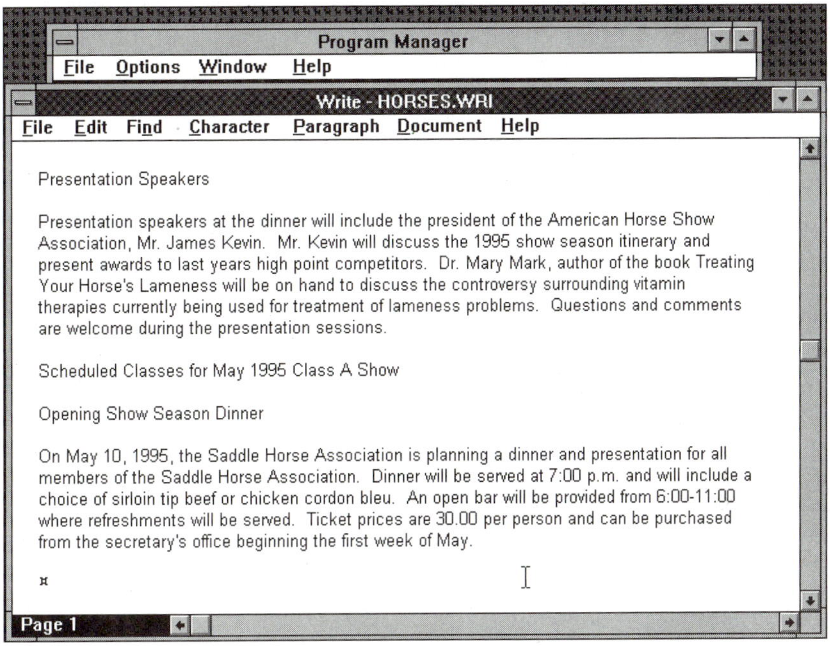

Figure 7-10 The cut-and-pasted text at the end of the document

Copying text in a document

Unlike the Cut command, which deletes selected text, the Copy command makes a duplicate copy of the selected text. After you paste the selected text, it appears in its original location as well as the new location.

Exercise 9: Copying text

To place an additional copy of a paragraph in the document you created earlier, perform the following steps:

1. Place your insertion point in the blank space above the heading *Presentation Speakers.*
2. Press ↵ ENTER.
3. Select the heading *Opening Show Season Dinner* and the following paragraph, which begins *On May 10, 1995....*
4. Choose Edit, and then choose Copy.
5. Place the insertion point on the blank line above the heading *Presentation Speakers.*
6. Choose Edit, and then choose Paste.

   A duplicate copy of the selected text appears at the beginning of the document (see Figure 7-11).

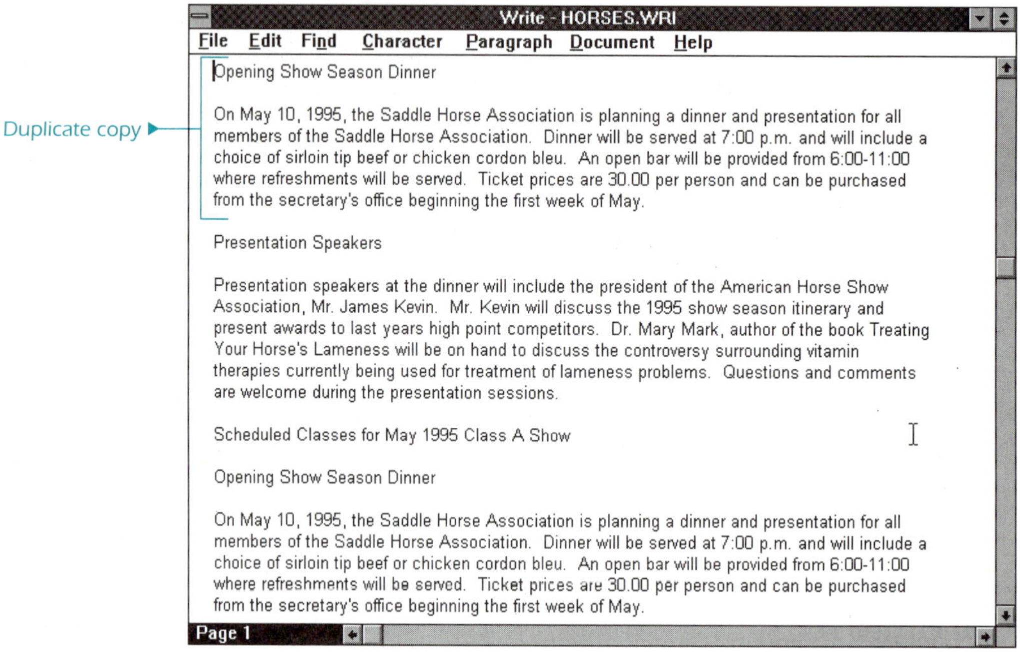

Figure 7-11 A duplicate copy of the heading and paragraph

7. If necessary, scroll through the document to see both copies of the text.

Exercise 10: Deleting text

You can delete blocks of text by selecting the text block, and then pressing Delete. To remove the original copy of the selected text in Exercise 9, perform the following steps:

1. Select the heading *Opening Show Season Dinner* and the following paragraph, which begins *On May 10, 1995...* that appear at the end of the document.
2. Press DELETE.

   The heading and paragraph are removed.

Exercise 11: Replacing text

To replace existing text with new text, you select the existing text, and then type the new text. To replace existing text, perform the following steps:

1. Select *Scheduled Classes for 1995 Class A Show.*
2. Type Class A Show Dates and Times.

   When you type the first letter of the new text, the selected text is removed. To complete the next exercise, *do not* save your document at this point.

The Undo command

Sometimes you want to reverse a change you have made to a document. The Undo command can reverse the last two changes made to a document; in other words, you can undo a change, and you can undo an undo. Changes that can be undone include editing, typing, and formatting. The Undo option on the Edit menu is displayed differently depending on the type of change that was last made.

Exercise 12: Using Undo

In Exercise 11, you replaced a heading at the end of the document. To reverse the action, perform the following steps:

1. Choose Edit.

   Notice that the menu displays the option Undo Typing (see Figure 7-12).

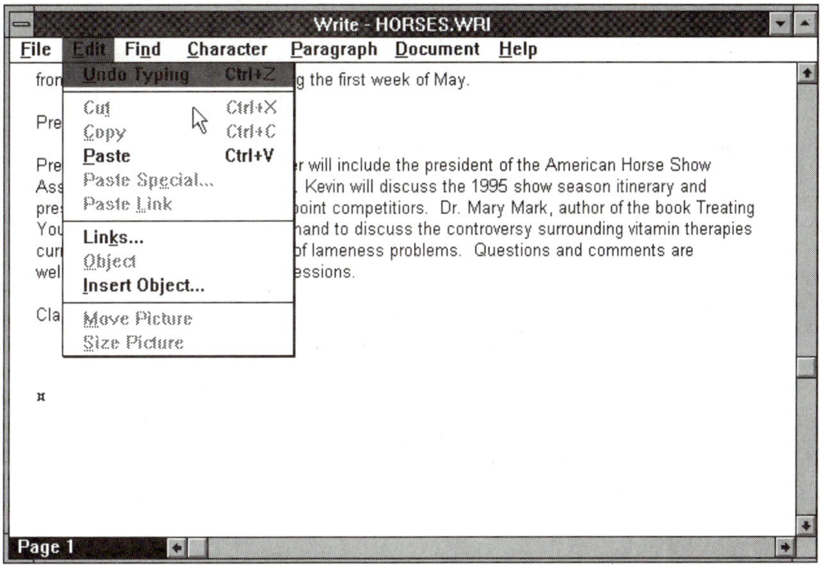

Figure 7-12 The menu reflects the type of undo that can be performed

2. Choose Undo Typing.

   The previous heading replaces the current heading.

Objective 7: Formatting Text

Formatting options in Write enable you to apply different fonts, font sizes, and attributes to text to change the printed appearance of your document. The type of font you use changes the way a character looks. Courier, Helvetica, and Times New Roman are examples of font types.

point You can increase or decrease the size of the font you are using by assigning a point size to the font. A *point* is a unit of measurement used to describe the height of a text character; one point equals $^{1}/_{72}$ of an inch. The most commonly used point sizes in books and periodicals are 10 and 12 points.

By applying attributes to text, you can make the text appear bold, italicized, or underlined. You can format text at three different levels: Character, Paragraph, and Document.

Character-level formatting

You can format individual characters, groups of characters, or an entire document using the Character menu. The Character menu enables you to apply attributes to text, change the size of text, apply a font type, or create superscripts and subscripts (see Figure 7-13).

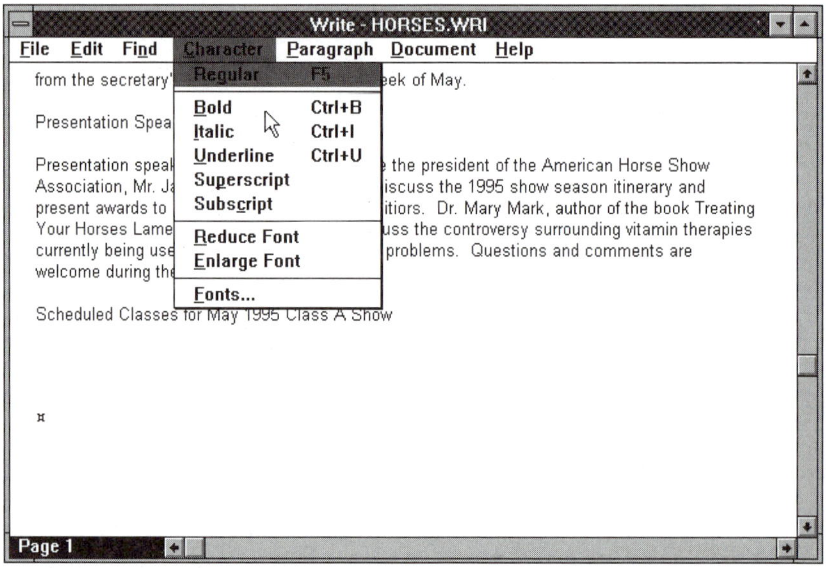

Figure 7-13 The Character menu

Exercise 13: Enhancing text at the character level

To enhance the text of the horses document using the Character menu options, perform the following steps:

1. Select *Association Philosophy*.
2. Choose Character, and then choose Bold.
3. Choose Character, and then choose Underline.
4. Choose Character, and then choose Enlarge Font.

   The font size increases by one point.

5. Choose Character, and then choose Enlarge Font.

   The font size increases again by one point.

   Each time you select the Enlarge Font option, the size of the selected text increases by one point.

6. Choose Character, and then choose Reduce Font.

   The font size decreases by one point.

7. Choose Character, and then choose Fonts.

   The Font dialog box appears (see Figure 7-14).

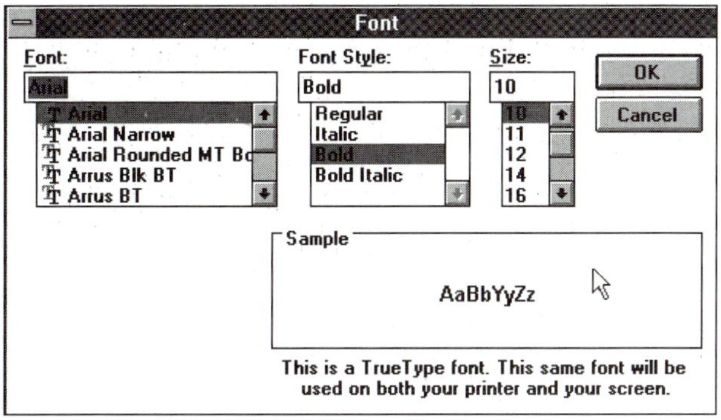

Figure 7-14 The Font dialog box

The name of the current font is displayed in the Font text box. A list of available font types appears in the Font list box.

8. Scroll through the Font list box and select a different font type. You can see a sample of the selected font in the Sample box. Notice how the information in the Font Style list box changes depending on the selected font.

9. In the Font list box, choose Arrus Blk BT.

   The double *T* that appears before the font name indicates that the font is a TrueType font. TrueType fonts print exactly as they appear on the computer screen.

10. Increase the point size to 14 in the Size list box, and then choose OK.

11. Deselect the text to see the enhancements you applied to the text.

TIP Try to avoid using too may fonts on a page. A general rule is to use no more than two fonts per page of text. When you apply more than two fonts for a page of text, the page looks cluttered and is distracting to read.

Paragraph-level formatting

A paragraph of text is defined by pressing Enter. Each time Enter is pressed, a paragraph mark (or hard return) is placed in the document. Formatting at the paragraph level enables you to align text, change the justification of text, indent lines of text, and adjust line spacing. The Paragraph menu displays the different options it offers (see Figure 7-15).

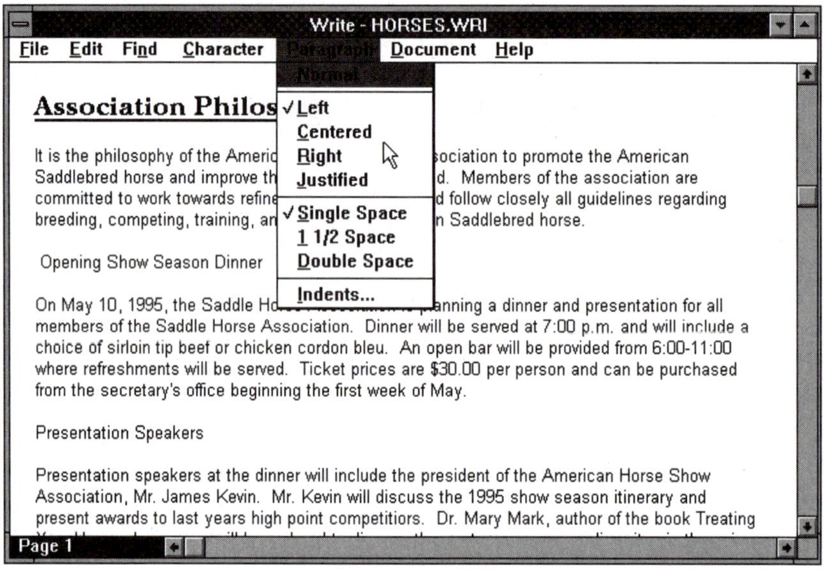

Figure 7-15 The Paragraph menu

Exercise 14: Indenting text

You can indent lines of text using the Indents option. To indent the information found under each heading, perform the following steps:

1. Select the paragraph that follows *Association Philosophy*.
2. Choose Paragraph from the menu bar, and then choose Indents.

   The Indents dialog box appears (see Figure 7-16).

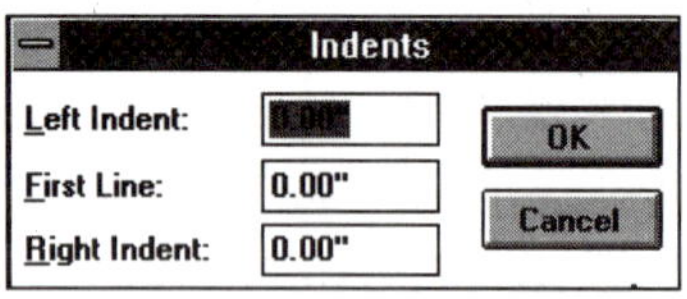

Figure 7-16 The Indents dialog box

3. In the First Line text box, type .5, and then choose OK.

   The first line of the paragraph indents 0.5" to the right of the left margin. The remaining lines of the paragraph align on the left margin.

4. Repeat Steps 1 and 2 to place a 0.5" first-line indent for each paragraph that follows a heading.

TIP To remove indents, choose Normal from the menu bar.

Table 7-2 defines other types of indents that can be created with the Indents dialog box.

Table 7-2 Indents created by the Indents dialog box

INDENTS	DESCRIPTION
Left Indent	Indents the left margin of a paragraph; applies to all lines in the paragraph.
Right Indent	Indents the right margin of a paragraph; applies to all lines in the paragraph.
Hanging Indent	Aligns only the first line of a paragraph on the left margin and places subsequent lines of the same paragraph farther to the right. To create a hanging indent, type a positive number in the Left Indent box and a negative number in the First Line indent box.

Text alignment

Write gives you four ways to align text. You can have text aligned on the right margin, the left margin, both right and left margins (justified), or centered (see Figure 7-17). Table 7-3 defines the alignment settings on the Paragraph menu.

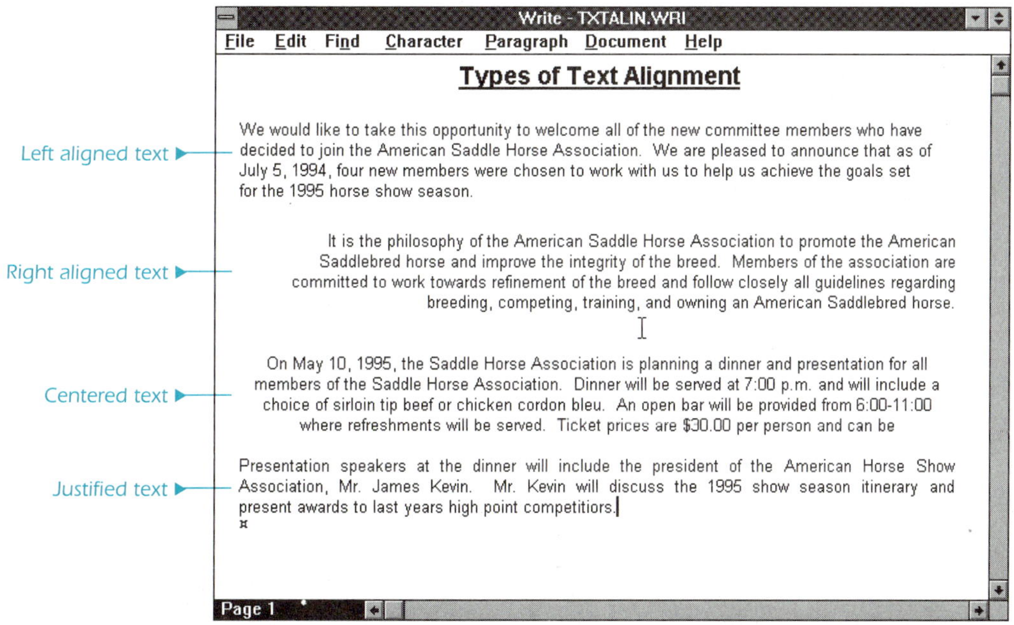

Figure 7-17 Paragraphs displaying left, right, centered, and justified alignment

Table 7-3 Alignment options in the Paragraph menu

OPTION	DESCRIPTION
Left	Each line aligns evenly at the left margin, leaving a ragged right side.
Right	Each line aligns evenly at the right margin, leaving a ragged left side.
Center	Each line is centered on the left and right margins, leaving ragged left and right sides.
Justified	Each line is aligned evenly on the left and right margins. Letters and words are spaced so that each line has the same length.

Exercise 15: Aligning the Text of a Document

In this exercise you will use center alignment to place a heading at the top of the horses.wri file. To place a heading for the horses.wri file and center it, perform the following steps:

1. Position the insertion point at the top of the document.
2. Press ENTER twice.
3. Position the cursor on the first blank line of the document.
4. Choose Paragraph, and then choose Centered.

   The insertion point jumps to the middle of the current line.
5. Type The American Saddle Horse Association and press ENTER.
6. Choose Paragraph, and then choose Left.

   The insertion point returns to the left margin.

Exercise 16: Adjusting line spacing

The Paragraph menu provides three different line-spacing options. You can choose to place a specific line spacing for an entire document or you can choose different line spacing amounts for each paragraph. Line spacing can be set to single, one-and-a-half, or double line spacing. To set the line spacing for the horses.wri file, perform the following steps:

1. Select the paragraph that begins *It is the philosophy of....*
2. Choose Paragraph, and then choose Double Space.

   The line spacing for the selected paragraph is double spaced.
3. Select the paragraph that begins *On May 10, 1995....*
4. Choose Paragraph, and then choose 1 1/2 Space.

   The line spacing for the selected paragraph is one-and-one-half spaced.
5. Reset the line spacing both paragraphs to single spaced.

Document-level formatting

The third level of formatting occurs at the document level. Document-level options affect the entire document; you cannot apply document-level formatting to selected characters or paragraphs. Options in the Document menu include adding headers and footers, turning on the Ruler, and setting tabs. Additionally, you can change margin settings and select page numbering with the Page Layout option.

Headers and footers

header

footer

A *header* is text that appears at the top of every page of a document. Headers are used most often to provide information such as the document's title or the current page number. A *footer* is text that appears at the bottom of every page of a document; footers usually display page numbers. You can prevent the printing of a header on the first page, as well as edit and format headers and footers just as you would regular text. When you choose the Header or Footer options, a Header or Footer window appears, which is where you enter text for the header or footer.

Exercise 17: Adding a header and footer

To add a header and footer to the horses.wri file, perform the following steps:

1. Choose Document, and then choose Header.

   The Page Header dialog box and Header window appear (see Figure 7-18).

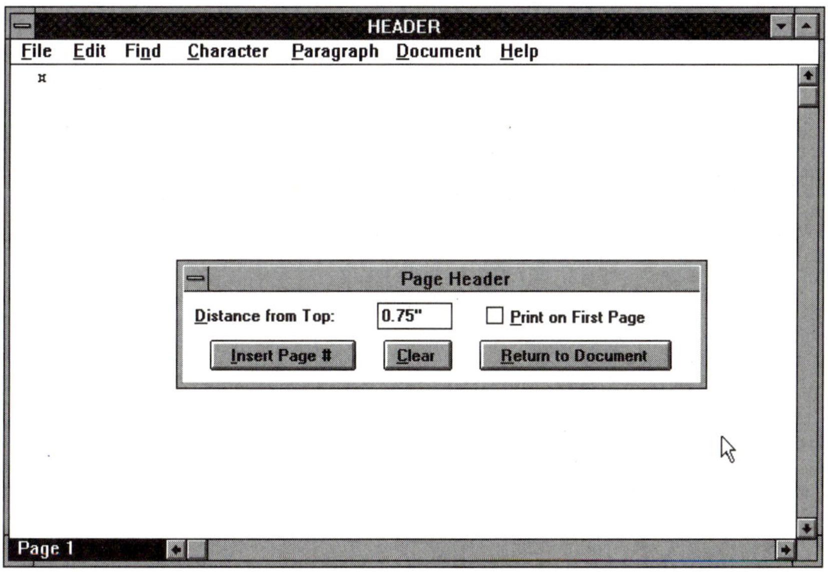

Figure 7-18 The Page Header dialog box and Header window

2. In the Header window, type your name, and then press ENTER.
3. Type today's date.

4. In the Page Header dialog box, in the Distance From Top text box, type .5. This places the header 0.5" from the top of the page.
5. In the Page Header dialog box, select Print on First Page, if it is not already selected.
6. Choose Return to Document.

   You are returned to the Write document window.
7. Choose Document, and then choose Footer.

   The Page Footer dialog box and Footer window appear (see Figure 7-19).

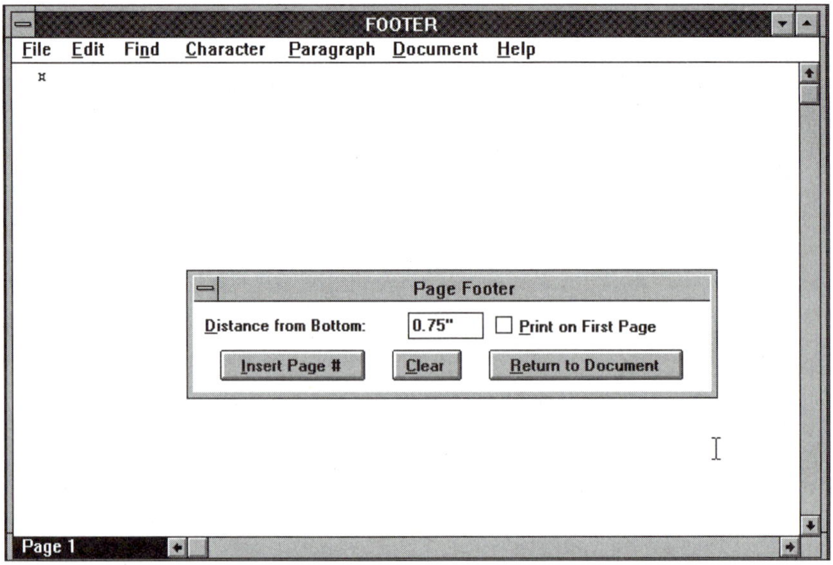

Figure 7-19 The Page Footer dialog box and Footer window

8. In the Page Footer dialog box, in the Distance From Bottom text box, type .5. This places the footer 0.5" from the bottom of the page.
9. Choose Insert Page #.

   A page number symbol appears at the insertion point in the Footer window indicating where page numbers will print.
10. Choose Return to Document.

    You are returned to the Write document window. Note that the header and footer you created do not appear in the document window. You must print the document to see them.

WARNING Make sure that you keep headers and footers within the margin settings you are using.

Choosing the Page Layout option

You can set margins, specify the first page number, and set measurements for the Write program using the Page Layout option on the Document menu. The default margins used by Write are 1 inch for the top and bottom margins and 1.25 inch for the right and left margins. Measurements can be set using inches or centimeters. You can specify the first page number of the document in the Start Page Numbers At text box.

Exercise 18: Setting margins and page numbering

To set margins and page numbering for the horses.wri file, perform the following steps:

1. Choose Document, and then choose Page Layout.

   The Page Layout dialog box appears (see Figure 7-20).

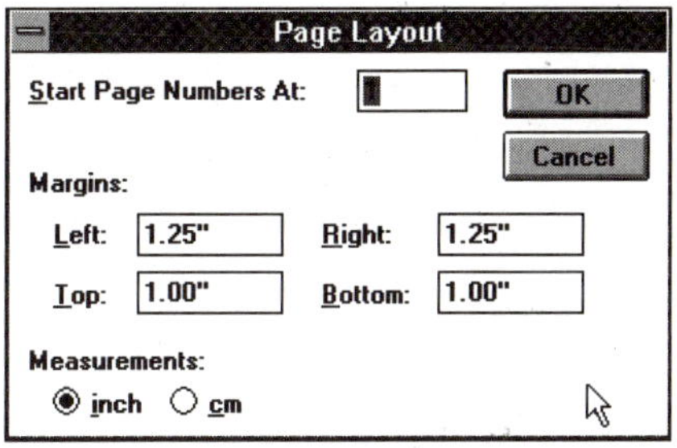

Figure 7-20 The Page Layout dialog box

2. In the Margins area, type 1 in the Left text box.
3. In the Margins area, type 1 in the Right text box.

   The left and right margins are reset to 1".
4. In the Start Page Numbering At text box, type 2.

   The first page is numbered 2. All subsequent pages are numbered consecutively. For example, the second page is numbered 3, and so on.
5. Choose OK to return to the document window.

Objective 8: Using the Ruler

The Ruler in Write enables you to use the mouse to set tabs, change margin settings, control line spacing, and change text alignment. The Ruler can be displayed or hidden. A tab can be repositioned on or removed from the Ruler by dragging it. Write places default left tabs every half inch across the Ruler. Figure 7-21 shows the components of the Ruler.

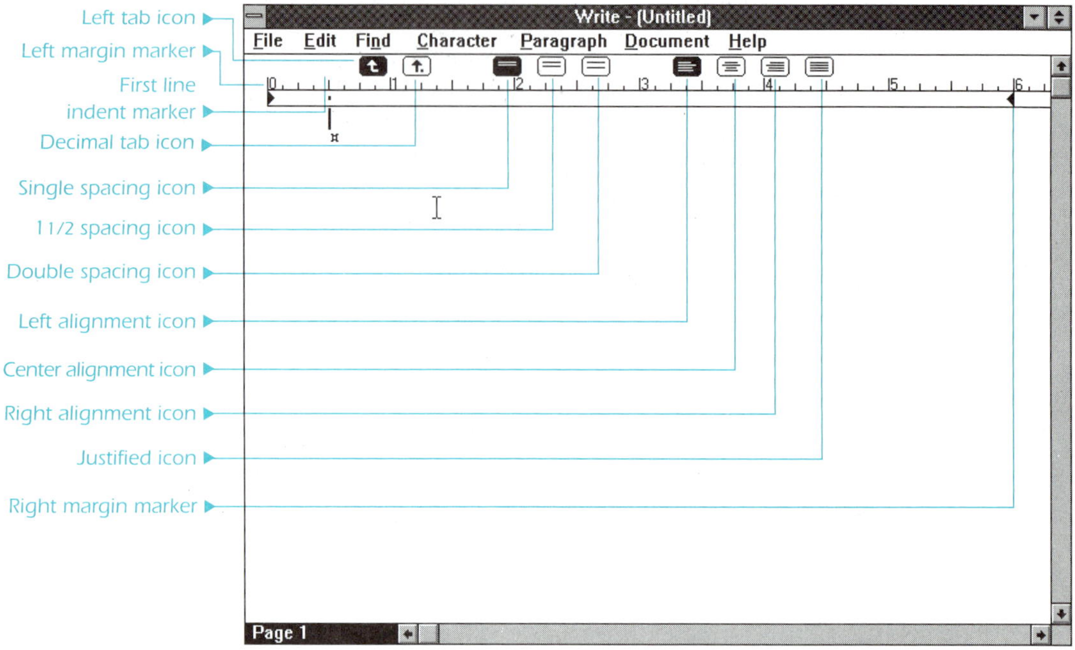

Figure 7-21 **The ruler**

Exercise 19: Using the Ruler to set tabs

To set tabs using the Ruler, perform the following steps:

1. Select the paragraph that begins *We would like....*
2. Choose Document, and then choose Ruler On.

   The ruler appears at the top of the document window. Notice the right-pointing triangle at the 0" mark on the Ruler. This is the left-margin marker.
3. With the mouse, drag the left-margin marker to the 0.5" mark on the ruler.

   The first line indent marker moves to indent the first line of the selected text at the 0.5" mark while the rest of the paragraph remains at the 0" mark (see Figure 7-22).

Need a Job? Ask your Computer

If you are looking for a job but afraid that your resume is not impressive enough, your computer can help. Computer software is now available to help you design and create a professional-looking resume. The programs offer a variety of resume templates from which to choose, including Chronological, Targeted, and Functional. The software automatically lays out areas such as job target, education, and work history. You can change the look of your resume using a variety of formatting options that include various fonts and bulleted lists. These programs even provide spell checkers and thesauruses. The software also will help track your job-search endeavors and write cover letters.

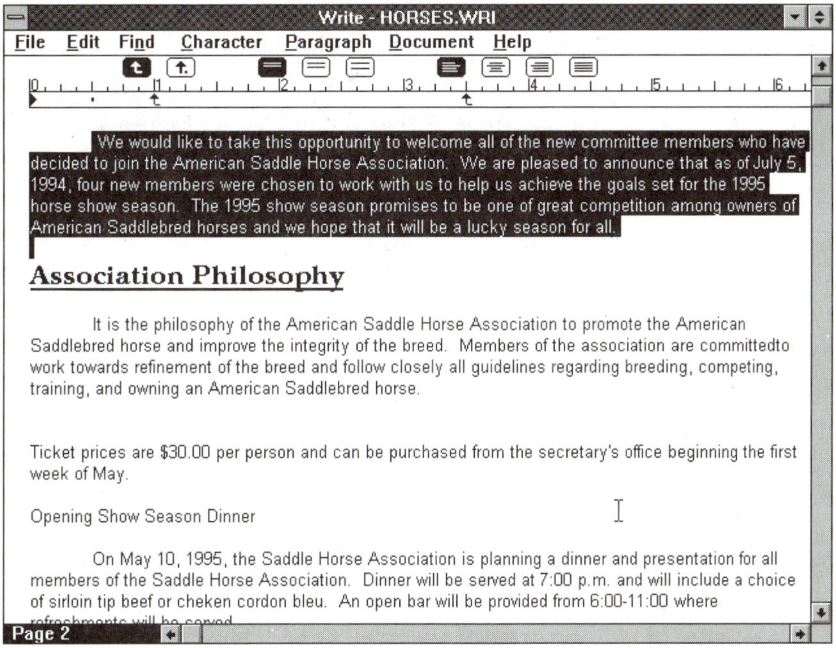

Figure 7-22 Selected paragraph with first line indented

4. Deselect the text.
5. Position the insertion point on a blank line two lines below the heading *Scheduled Classes for May 1995 Class A Show*.
6. On the ruler, click the left-tab icon to choose it.
7. Point to the 1" mark on the ruler and click.

   A left tab appears at the 1" mark.
8. On the Ruler, click the left-tab icon to choose it.
9. Point to the 3.5" mark on the Ruler and click.

   A left tab appears at the 3.5" mark.
10. Type the following information, pressing TAB and ENTER as indicated:

    ASB 3-Gaited Pleasure TAB 8:00A.M. ENTER ENTER
    ASB 5-Gaited Show TAB 8:45 A.M. ENTER ENTER
    ASB Country Pleasure TAB 9:30 A.M. ENTER ENTER
    ASB 3-Gaited AOTR TAB 10:15 A.M. ENTER ENTER
    ASB 3-Gaited Fine Harness TAB 11:00 A.M. ENTER ENTER
    Lunch Break ENTER ENTER
    ASB 5-Gaited Pony TAB 1:00 P.M. ENTER ENTER
    ASB 5-Gaited Ladies To Ride TAB 1:45 P.M. ENTER ENTER
    ASB 3-Gaited Equitation TAB 2:00 P.M. ENTER ENTER

ASB William Shatner Award TAB 2:45 P.M. ↵ ENTER ↵ ENTER
ASB Pleasure Driving TAB 3:30 P.M. ↵ ENTER ↵ ENTER

The text aligns in two columns: The first aligns at the 1" mark and the second aligns at the 3.5" mark (see Figure 7-23).

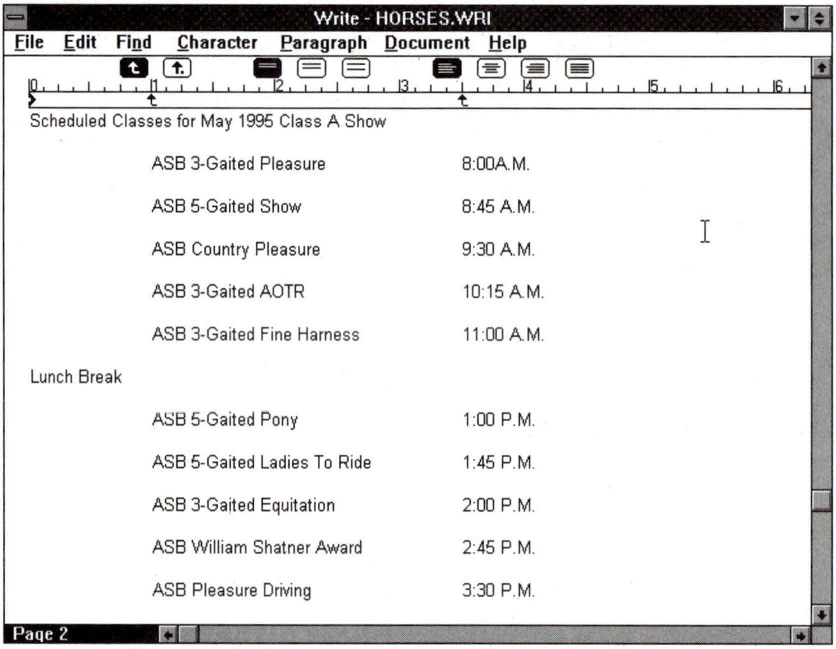

Figure 7-23 Text aligned at the 1" and 3.5" tab marks

11. Choose Document, and then choose Tabs.

    The Tabs dialog box appears (see Figure 7-24).

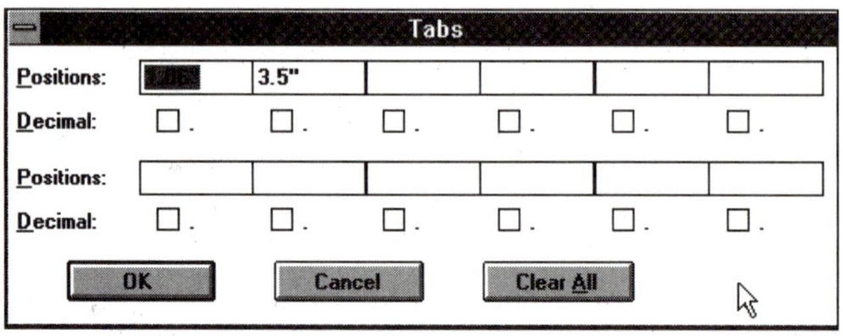

Figure 7-24 The Tabs dialog box

The Tabs dialog box lets you set new tabs and change or remove existing tabs.

12. Choose Cancel.
13. Save the horses.wri file.

Objective 9: Printing a Document

After creating a document, you usually want to print it. The Print dialog box enables you to print the entire document, a specified text selection, or you a range of pages. You can also specify the number of copies that you want to print in the Print dialog box.

Exercise 20: Printing a document

To print the horses.wri file, perform the following steps:

1. Choose File, and then choose Print.

   The Print dialog box appears (see Figure 7-25).

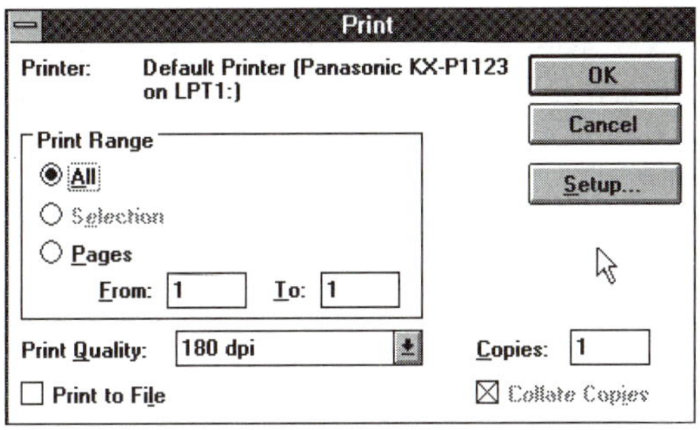

Figure 7-25 The Print dialog box

   The default for the Print Range option is All, which prints the entire document.

2. Choose OK.

   The Print message box appears, telling you that the document is being sent to the printer.

3. Choose File, and then Exit.

   You exit Write and are returned to the Program Manager window.

Chapter Summary

The Write program is a word processing program included with the Windows program that helps you create professional-looking documents. In this chapter, you learned to use the Write program to set margins, line spacing, and tabs. You learned how to enhance text by applying attributes—such as bold, italic, and underline—to text. You also learned that you can create headers and footers and align paragraphs of text.

Review Questions

True/False Questions

____ 1. The Write program is represented by an icon resembling a notepad.

____ 2. The Write program contains sophisticated features that include a spell checker and thesaurus.

____ 3. You can change tab settings using the Ruler or Tabs dialog box.

____ 4. The Undo command can be used to reverse only the last change made to a document.

____ 5. The insertion point can be repositioned using the mouse or keyboard.

Multiple-Choice Questions

____ 6. ↵ ENTER should be used to do all the following except

A. end short lines.

B. end a paragraph.

C. end a sentence.

D. insert a blank line.

____ 7. DELETE can be used to delete all the following except

A. selected text.

B. a character to the right of the insertion point.

C. a paragraph.

D. a file.

____ 8. To close an existing document and open a new blank document, you would choose

A. File, Close, File, Open.

B. File, Exit, File, Open.

C. File, Close, New.

D. File, Exit, File, New.

____ 9. Which menu option includes the header and footer option?

A. Edit

B. Character

C. Document

D. Paragraph

_____ 10. If you have a right-pointing arrow in the left margin and you double-click, you will select

A. a word.

B. a sentence.

C. the current line.

D. a paragraph.

Fill-in-the-Blank Questions

11. You must ____________ text before it can be cut or copied.
12. The Write program is located in the ____________ window.
13. The Paste command is located in the ____________ menu.
14. Seventy-two points equal ____________ ____________.
15. ____________ ____________ is the default alignment used by the Write program.

Acumen-Building Activities

Quick Projects

1. Creating a .wri document

1. Create a directory on your DISK1 floppy disk and name the directory wpfiles.
2. Start the Write program and enter the following text—exactly as it appears below—in a blank document window.

```
Dear Mary Mark:

Congratulations!

We have selected you as the new grand prise winner of
the Creative Short Story Contest Award for your chil-
dren's story "The Magical Forest". As a recipeint of
the award you are entitled to a variety of excoting
prizes and traveling opportunities that we hope you
and your family will enjoy durig the next year.

We would like to take this time to ask you if you are
interested in participating in the educational and
recreational seminars for children that will be offered
at the Hebron Public Library during the months of
January through March of 1996. Additionally we would
```

```
appreciate the opportunity to have you as a guest
speaker at a seminar held at our Child Readinge
Developemtn Center on January 25, 1996.

To claim your prizes, contact our office at the above
address at your convenience. Please let us know if
you will be able to attend the seminar that will be
held on January 25, 1996 as soon as possible so we
can start making arrangements for your appearance.
Once again, congratulations on your story!
```

3. Save the file as story.doc on your DISK1 floppy disk in the wpfiles directory.
4. Print the document.
5. Correct all spelling errors, and then save the file as correct.doc in the wpfiles directory on the DISK1 floppy disk.
6. Print the document.

2. Modifying the correct.wri document

Using the correct.doc file, do the following:

1. Set the left margin to 1".
2. Set the right margin to 1.5".
3. Set the top margin to 2".
4. Set line spacing to one-and-one-half.
5. Select the first paragraph of the document.
6. Select *Creative*.
7. Select the second line of the first paragraph.
8. Italicize *The Magical Forest*.
9. Place a blank line between each paragraph.
10. Bold *Congratulations!* (Do you understand why this word is considered a paragraph?)
11. Save this newly edited file as correct1.wri on the wpfiles directory on the DISK1 floppy disk.
12. Print the document and exit the Write program.

3. Changing the correct1.wri document

1. Start Write and open correct1.wri.
2. Change the line spacing of all paragraphs to single spacing.
3. Using the Ruler, indent the first line of each paragraph to 0.5".
4. Replace the sentence that begins *To claim your prizes...* with To claim your prizes, please feel free to contact us at the above address or phone number at your earliest convenience.

5. Move the paragraph that begins *We have selected you...* to the end of the document. Print the document.
6. Reverse the last change you made to the document.
7. Copy the paragraph that begins *We would like...* to the end of the document. Print the document.
8. Using Delete, reverse the last change you made to the document.
9. Save the document as correct2.wri in the wpfiles directory on the DISK1 floppy disk and exit Windows.

4. Using Windows and Write

1. Start Windows, and open the Accessories, StartUp, and Main windows.
2. Start the File Manager and display the Directory Contents List for the System subdirectory in the Windows directory.
3. Restore the File Manager window to the desktop.
4. Minimize the StartUp window.
5. Start Write, open correct2.wri, and make the following changes:
6. Add the following heading to the top of the document and center it: The Read Alot Group.
7. Use a large font size and change the font type for the heading.
8. Save the file using the same name.
9. Reduce the Write document window to an icon.
10. From the File Manager window, search for all files on DISK1 in the wpfiles directory that end in .doc.
11. Replace this extension with the extension .txt.
12. Sort files in the wpfiles directory by size.
13. Close all windows and exit Windows.

In-Depth Projects

1. Working in Windows

1. Start Windows, open the Games window, and start Minesweeper.
2. Open the Accessories window and start Write and CardFile.
3. Resize and move each of the opened document windows so you can view the contents of each.
4. Make a copy of the Write icon and place it in the StartUp group window.
5. Minimize each open document window to an icon on the desktop.
6. In the Program Manager window, open the Main window and start the File Manager.
7. Close the Main group window.

8. Display the Directory Tree and Directory Contents List for the PROJECTS floppy disk in one window, and then display the Directory Tree and Directory Contents List for the DISK1 floppy disk in a separate window.
9. Change the displays for both directories to two different font sizes and types.
10. Reduce the File Manager window to an icon on the desktop.
11. Fill the entire screen with a blank Write document window.
12. Create left tabs at the 2" and 4.5" marks on the Ruler.
13. Create a decimal tab at the 6.5" mark.
14. Type the following text, pressing TAB and ↵ ENTER as needed:

```
Designer Name       Item        Price
Charles             Dress       $120.00
Chic Extreme        Jumper      $150.00
Fashion Hype        Vest        $20.00
```

15. Save the file as fashion.wri, and print the document.
16. Close all windows and exit Windows.

2. Changing the fashion.wri document

1. Start Windows, and open the Accessories, Main, and Games group windows.
2. Tile the windows.
3. Open the fashion.wri file, if it is not already open.
4. Make the three column titles bold, and increase the font size of all three.
5. Add a header to the document that displays your name on the first line and your class name on the second line. Italicize and underline both lines of the header.
6. Save the file as fashion2.doc on the DISK1 floppy disk in the wpfiles directory. Print the document.
7. Minimize the Write document window.
8. Start the File Manager and make a copy of fashion2.doc on DISK1 and place it on the PROJECTS disk.
9. Delete the Write icon in the StartUp window.
10. Close all windows and exit Windows.

3. Using Windows

1. Start Windows, and open the Accessories window.
2. Start Write and open the horses.wri file.
3. At the bottom of the document, set left-tab markers at the 0.5", 2.5", and 4.5" marks using the Tabs dialog box.
4. Type the following text, pressing TAB and ↵ ENTER as needed:

```
Future Meeting Dates
Place                   Date        Time
Hebron Country Club     5/14/95     6:00 P.M.
Angelo's Banquet Hall   6/22/95     7:00 P.M.
Country Kitchen         7/5/95      8:00 P.M.
```

5. Bold and underline the heading *Future Meeting Dates*. Bold the titles of the three columns.
6. Save the document as horses7.doc.
7. Print the document.
8. Exit Write.
9. Open the Accessories, Games, Main, and StartUp windows.
10. Resize all four windows to 1.5" wide and 2" high. Position them on top of one another on the far right side of the screen. (If they don't fit, make each window smaller.)
11. Create a group window and name it Work Files.
12. Select an icon to represent the Write program and place it in the Work Files group window.
13. Rename the Work Files group window Task Files.
14. Copy the following icons into the Task Files group window: Notepad, CardFile, and Solitaire.
15. In the Task Files group window, rename the Notepad icon Memos, rename the CardFile icon Roladex, and rename the Solitaire icon Cardgame.
16. Delete the Task Files group window.
17. Close all windows and exit the program.

Acumen Critical Thinking Milestone

Individual Project:

Configuring Windows, Printing, and Using Accessories

The two most important reasons for configuring your Windows environment are to optimize your computer system and improve your efficiency. Using the Control Panel and the programs in the Accessories group improves your skills and your knowledge of how the Windows components work together to maximize your productivity.

To configure your Windows environment, do the following:

1. Open the Control Panel, which is located in the Main window.
2. Choose Settings, then choose Fonts.
3. Choose True Type and verify that Enable True Type Fonts is selected in the True Type dialog box.
4. Return to the Control Panel and double-click the Desktop icon.
5. Select a screen saver and set the delay to fifteen minutes.
6. Check the system's date and time and verify that both are correct.
7. Close the Control Panel.

Your manager has informed you that your job at Premier Systems Consulting (PSC) involves a large number of printed reports, memos, and schedules. To learn more about the operations of the Print Manager, do the following:

1. Open the Print Manager, which is located in the Main window.
2. Open the Help menu and choose What Is Print Manager?
3. When the help topic appears, choose File, then choose Print Topic.
4. Close the Help window.
5. Use the Print Manager to schedule and print the document readme.wri in the directory A:\myinfo on your data disk.
6. Close the Print Manager.

Company policy at PSC requires that all employees maintain a file management system that is consistent throughout the company. Your next task is to create and organize your operational files according to the following directions:

1. Use Cardfile to set up a database for the vendors that supply the computer equipment and software that you recommend to your clients. Create a separate card for each vendor with the name of the vendor at the top of the card. When you complete the cards, save the file as vendors in the A:\cardfile directory of your personal data disk. Your cards should resemble the following:

   ```
   Info USA
   133 Main Street
   Central City, PA 19004
   (215) 222-5511
   ```

   Include the following vendor information in your database:

   ```
   Info USA, 133 Main Street, Central City, PA 19004,
   (215) 222-5511

   PropellerHead Software, 8761 East College Avenue,
   Hagerstown, MD 21740, (305) 112-2212

   Bits & Chips, Inc., 1000 Corporate Way, Carmel, IN
   31123, (317) 345-6765

   Computers International, 400 Universal Avenue,
   Dallas, TX (535) 123-4543

   MemSoft Corp., 332 Hamilton Road, Louisville, KY,
   56775, (456) 345-6788
   ```

2. Use Calendar to set up a schedule of meetings for the coming week. Your manager has scheduled training sessions for next Tuesday and Thursday from 9:00 A.M. to noon and 1:00 P.M. to 4:00 P.M. Human Resources has requested a meeting for Wednesday at 10:00 A.M. to draw up your company benefits plan. A company-wide meeting is planned for Friday at 4:00 P.M. You also need to consult with the members of your team to schedule a regular weekly meeting. Save the Calendar file as agenda in the A:\myinfo directory.

3. Use Notepad to write and print a short memo informing your manager that you have completed your initial set-up and are now ready to begin work. Briefly describe what you have accomplished. Save the file as memo1 in the A:\memos directory of your personal data disk.

Team Project: Preparing a Group Campaign

Your team has been assigned the task of developing a computer system for the Mustard-of-the-Month Mail Order Company. Each month, the company sends a jar of gourmet mustard to each customer on its subscription list along with an invoice, which is payable within 15 days. Currently, the names on this list are stored on index cards, as is each customer's record of payments. The company's accountant, who currently keeps the financial records in a hand-entry ledger, is retiring at the end of the month. Financial records include billing and payment totals, vendor purchases and payments, and payroll information. When a customer is late on a payment, the company's clerical staff sends a typewritten request to the customer requesting payment. The company handles all its own shipping.

1. With your team members, decide what software the company requires and how the software will be used.
2. Decide what hardware is required to implement a computerized system.
3. Develop a preliminary agenda for installing the hardware and software and training the company employees.
4. Use Notepad to write and print your recommendations. Save the file as mustard in a new directory on your team disk A:\team.
5. Copy all new files from each team member's disk to the appropriate subdirectories on the team disk.

Part 3

Advanced Features

Chapter 8

Using Accessories

Objectives

- Using the Notepad Program
- Using the Clock Program
- Using the Calendar Program
- Using the Calculator Program
- Using the Cardfile Program

Key Terms

TERM	DEFINITION
Batch File	a file containing DOS commands that you can create to carry out repetitive tasks
Scratch Pad	an area at the bottom of a Calendar file that can be used to enter additional notes or comments regarding appointments
Database	a collection of related information that can be stored, sorted, and used to produce reports

In the previous chapter, you learned how to use the Write program, which is located in the Accessories program group. The Accessories program group contains many tools to increase your personal productivity. You can use them while you are working in other applications or by themselves to help you do your work. You can transfer data from any Accessories program into the application with which you are currently working by cutting, copying, and pasting the information. In this chapter, you will work with the following programs located in the Accessories program group: Notepad, Clock, Calendar, Calculator, and Cardfile.

Objective 1: Using the Notepad program

The Notepad program is represented by an icon in the Accessories window and is used to create small text files that do not need special formatting. Many of the techniques you used in Write apply when you use Notepad. For example, selecting, moving, copying, and pasting text are performed in the same manner when using Notepad. However, Notepad has few editing and formatting capabilities.

batch files

Notepad is a perfect tool for writing short memos and notes or creating and editing DOS batch files or Windows .ini files. A *batch file* is a file containing DOS commands that you can create to carry out repetitive tasks. Information that is keyed into a Notepad document can be copied and pasted into other documents.

Exercise 1: Starting Notepad and entering text

To start Notepad and enter text, perform the following steps:

1. Open the Accessories window.
2. Double-click the Notepad icon 

.

   The Notepad document window appears (see Figure 8-1).

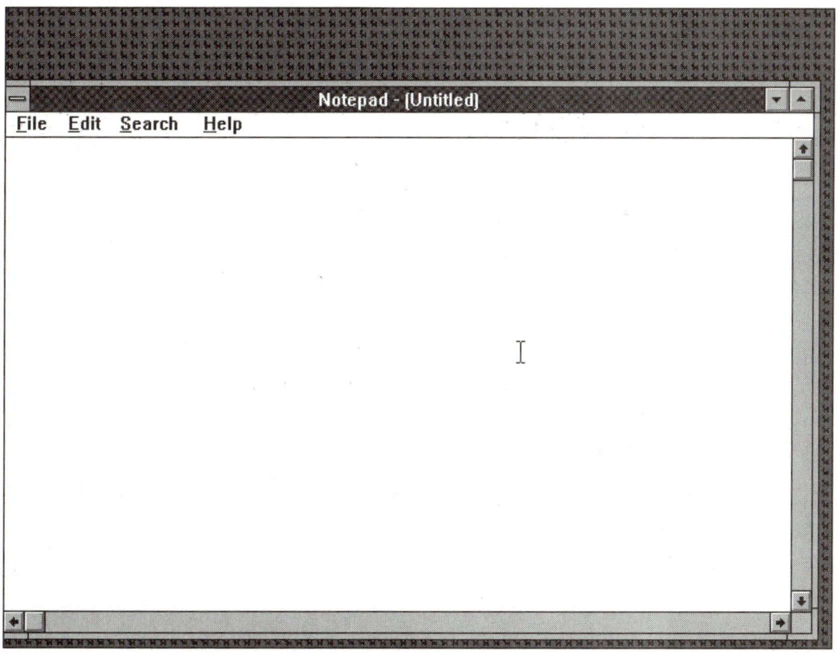

Figure 8-1 The Notepad document window

3. Choose Edit, and then choose Word Wrap.
4. Type the below text. Press TAB and ↵ ENTER as indicated. To correct errors as you type, use ← BACKSPACE and DELETE.

```
MEMO ↵ ENTER
To: TAB All Staff Members ↵ ENTER
From: TAB Cameron Mark, President ↵ ENTER
Re: TAB New Company Logo ↵ ENTER
I have assigned Mr. Thomas Martin to design a new com-
pany logo for me. I am proposing that the new design
take effect immediately once it is in place throughout
all our regional stores. Mr. Martin welcomes any cre-
ative suggestions that you may have regarding the design,
since it is still under development. Please feel free
to contact him at his office or though his e-mail
account. ↵ ENTER
```

Exercise 2: Saving and printing a Notepad document

The first time a Notepad document is saved, you must use the Save As command. Any subsequent time you save the file, you can use the Save command. To save the file you created and print a copy, perform the following steps:

1. Insert the PROJECTS floppy disk in drive A.
2. Choose File, and then choose Save As.

   The Save As dialog box appears (see Figure 8-2).

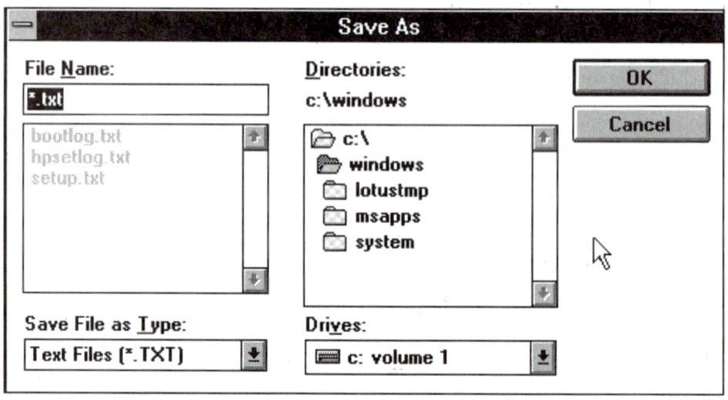

Figure 8-2 The Save As dialog box

3. Click the down arrow next to the Drives text box and choose drive A.
4. In the File Name text box, type logo.

   Notepad automatically attaches the extension .txt unless you specify a different extension.

5. Choose OK to return to the Notepad document window.
6. Choose File, and then choose Print.

   A message box displays telling you that the document is being printed.

Moving through a Notepad document

To move around a Notepad document, you can use the same methods you used when moving around a Write document. Both the keyboard direction keys and mouse can be used to reposition the insertion point at various places in a document. You cannot insert the insertion point in any space that does not contain text. The horizontal scroll bar is used to move to the right and left of a document, and the vertical scroll bar is used to move up and down in a document.

Searching for specific text in a document

To search for text strings in a Notepad document, you use the Find or Find Next options in the Search menu. You can quickly search forward or backward through text beginning from the insertion point.

Exercise 3: Searching a document

To search for all occurrences of *design* in the logo document, perform the following steps:

1. Display the logo document on the screen.
2. Position the insertion point at the top of the document.
3. Choose Search, and then choose Find.

   The Find dialog box appears (see Figure 8-3).

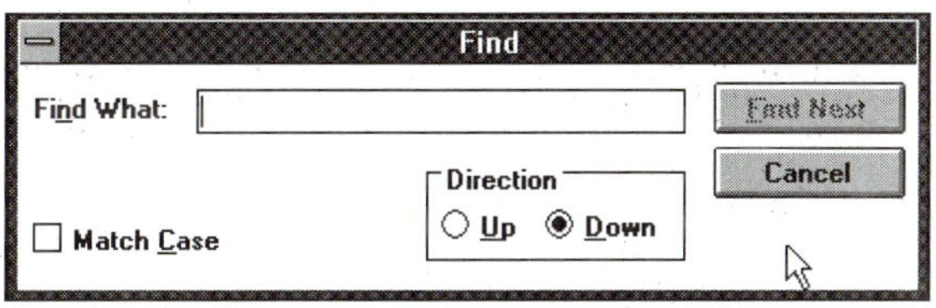

Figure 8-3 The Find dialog box

4. In the Find What text box, type design.
5. In the Direction option box, select Down, if it is not already selected.

   This selection causes Notepad to search from the insertion point to the end of the document. (Alternatively, selecting Up causes Notepad to search from the insertion point to the beginning of the document.)
6. Choose Find Next.

   The first occurrence of *design* in the document is highlighted (see Figure 8-4).

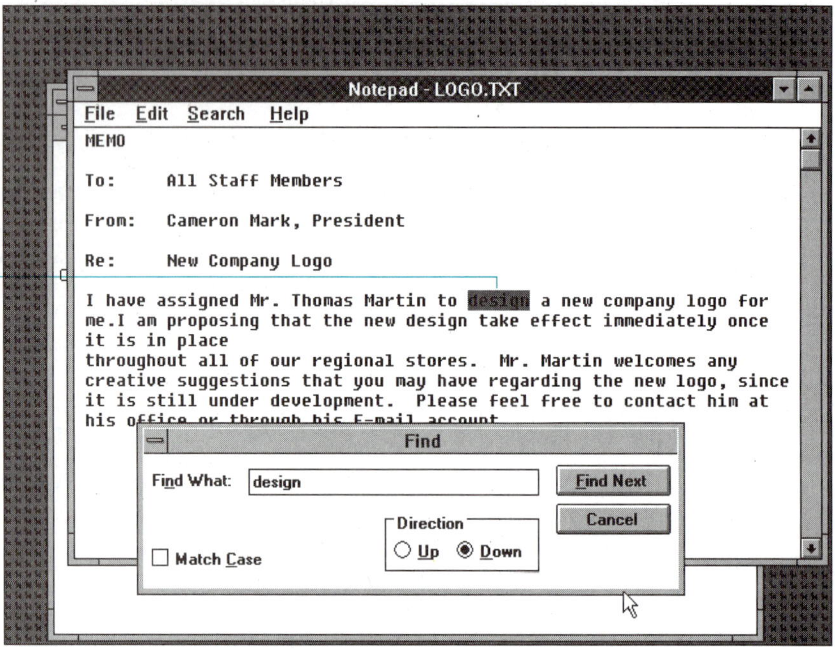

Figure 8-4 The first occurrence of *design* is highlighted

TIP You may have to reposition the Find dialog box so you can see the highlighted word.

7. Choose Find Next.

   The next occurrence of *design* is highlighted.

8. Choose Find Next.

   A message box appears informing you that Notepad cannot find any other occurrences of *design* in the document (see Figure 8-5).

Figure 8-5 A Notepad message box

9. Select OK.

   The Match Case option in the Find dialog box can be selected to limit a search to match the case of the text that you type in the Find What text box. If you do not choose the Match Case option, the search finds matching text that includes both uppercase and lowercase characters.

CD-ROMs Rock 'n Roll

It should be no surprise that desktop computers and the world of rock 'n roll have joined forces. Rock stars such as Peter Gabriel, Bob Dylan, Prince, and the Wilson sisters of the group Heart are but a few of the famous names using the world of CD-ROM to sell their creativity. The CD-ROM format provides many advantages to music artists, including enhanced sound, interactive video, elaborate visuals, and the chance to create virtual reality, which enables the listener to feel the music as well as hear and see it. Many musicians are involving their own production companies with this new technology in hopes of encouraging record sales for a new era of music-making.

For example, when searching for *the* with the Match Case option deselected, Notepad finds occurrences of *THE*, *the*, and *ThE*.

Exercise 4: Exiting Notepad

To exit Notepad and return to the Program Manager window, perform the following steps:

1. Choose File.
2. Choose Exit.

   If you haven't saved the latest changes to the document, you will be prompted to do so. Otherwise, you are returned to the Program Manager window.

Objective 2: Using the Clock Program

The Clock program is located in the Accessories window and can be used to display the current time on the desktop as you work in other applications. Clock can display the time in a digital or analog view and has several settings that can be adjusted to suit your personal preferences. Table 8-1 defines the options on Clock's Settings menu.

Table 8-1 Options on Clock's Settings menu

OPTION	DESCRIPTION
Analog	Displays the time on a clock with a round face and moving hands
Digital	Displays the time in a digital format
Set Font	Enables you to choose a font for the digital display
No Title	Removes Clock's menu and title bars
Seconds	Displays the time, including seconds, in Digital view
Date	Displays the date in a digital format
About Clock	Provides licensing information about the Clock program

Exercise 5: Displaying the time

Clock displays the time of your computer's system clock. You can set the system clock with the Control Panel, as discussed in Chapter 6. To change the display of the clock and place it on the desktop, perform the following steps:

1. Double-click the Clock icon 

in the Accessories window.

   The time is displayed in a digital or analog format depending on the option that is selected on the Settings menu (see Figures 8-6 and 8-7).

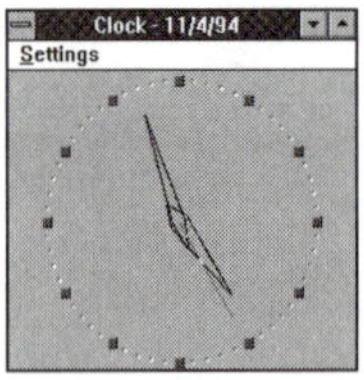

Figure 8-6 Analog format

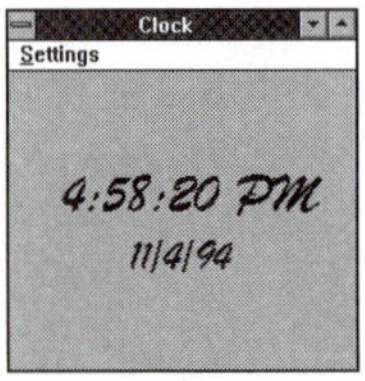

Figure 8-7 Digital format

2. Choose Settings, and then choose Digital, if it is not already chosen.
   The time is displayed in digital format.
3. Choose Settings, and then choose Seconds, if it is not already chosen.
   The clock includes seconds in its display.
4. Choose Settings, and then choose Date, if it is not already chosen.
   The clock includes the date in its display.
5. Choose Settings, and then choose Set Font.
   The Font dialog box appears (see Figure 8-8).

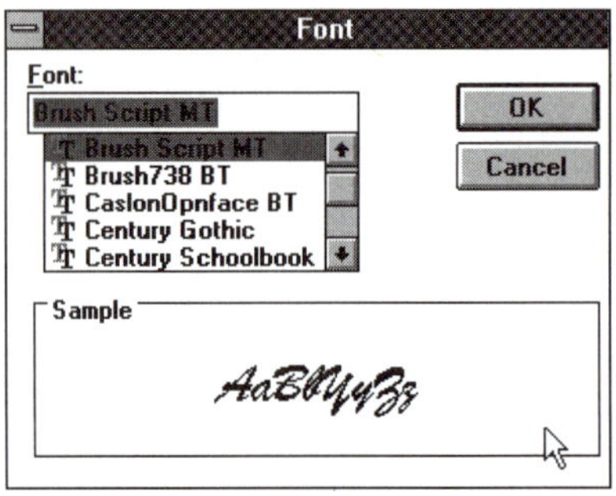

Figure 8-8 The Font dialog box

6. Select a font from the Font list box, and then choose OK.
   The font on the clock display is the font you selected.
7. Choose Settings, and then choose No Title.
   The clock is displayed without a menu bar.

8. Double-click anywhere on the clock.

   The menu bar reappears.

9. Click the Minimize button.

   The clock is reduced to an icon on the desktop.

Objective 3: Using the Calendar Program

The Calendar program enables you to keep track of appointments, meetings, and other scheduled events. Some of Calendar's options include viewing a single day or an entire month, setting an alarm to remind you of a scheduled appointment, adjusting time-interval settings, using the scratch pad, and marking special days with symbols. The *scratch pad* is an area at the bottom of a Calendar file that can be used to enter additional notes or comments regarding appointments.

scratch pad

Calendar, like other desktop accessories, can be reduced to an icon while you work in other applications. Calendar files can be saved and edited.

Exercise 6: Displaying the calendar in Day view

To display the calendar in Day view, perform the following steps:

1. Double-click the Calendar icon in the Accessories window.

   The Calendar window opens, displaying the calendar in Day view (see Figure 8-9).

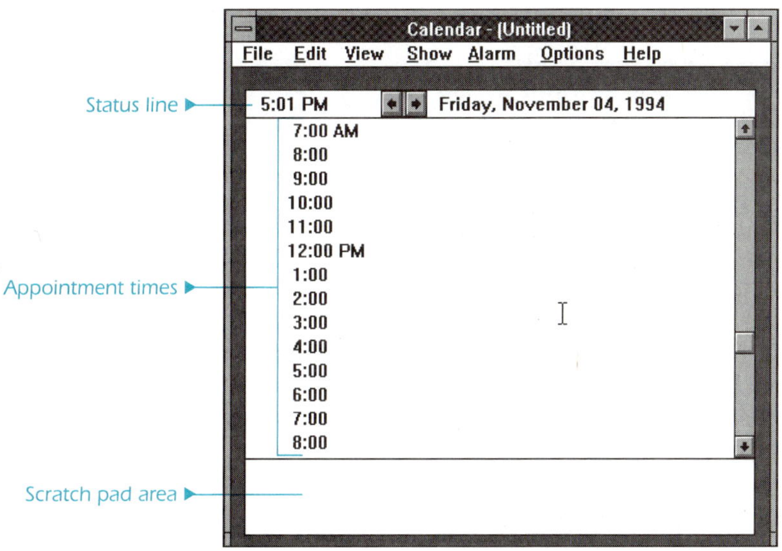

Figure 8-9 The calendar displayed in Day view

The status line displays the current date and time, using information from the computer's system clock.

2. Click the right arrow on the status bar.

   The date advances one day.

3. Click the left arrow on the status bar.

   The date moves back one day.

4. Click the up or down arrow on the vertical scroll bar.

   The calendar display moves up or down.

TIP Calendar's latest date is December 31, 2099.

Exercise 7: Changing time intervals and setting special times

By default, the calendar displays time intervals of one hour. You can change these intervals to half-hour or quarter-hour intervals. You can also display a special time on the appointment time area; this is useful if you want to display one-hour intervals but have an appointment that does not meet on the hour.

1. Choose View, and then choose Day.
2. Choose Options, and then choose Day Settings.

   The Day Settings dialog box appears (see Figure 8-10).

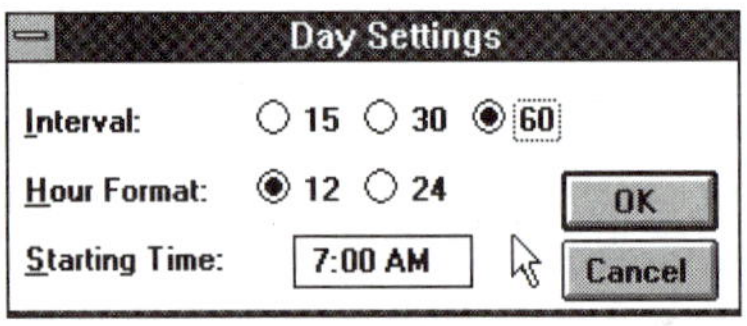

Figure 8-10 The Day Settings dialog box

3. For Interval, select 30.
4. In the Starting Time text box, type 9:00 AM.

   The Hour Format option can be used to display the time in a 12- or 24-hour format. The default is 12.

5. Choose OK.

   The calendar is divided into half-hour intervals, with 9:00 as the starting time at the top of the calendar.

6. Choose Options, and then choose Special Time.

   The Special Time dialog box appears (see Figure 8-11).

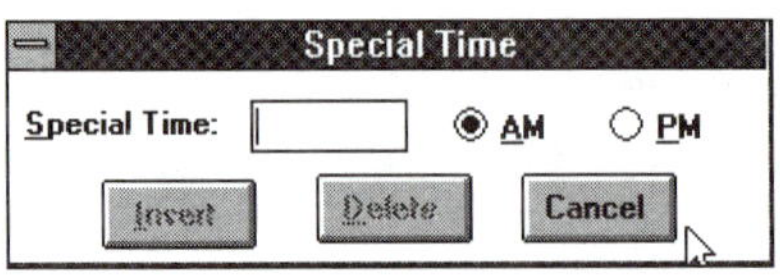

Figure 8-11 The Special Time dialog box

7. In the Special Time text box, type 9:22. Leave the AM button selected.
8. Choose Insert.

   The calendar inserts the special time of 9:22 A.M.

Exercise 8: Making appointments in Day view

To make an appointment while in Day view, you type appointment information (up to 80 characters) in the blank space to the right of the appropriate time. The scratch pad at the bottom of the calendar can be used to store additional text regarding the currently displayed date's appointments. To make an appointment, perform the following steps:

1. Position the insertion point to the right of 9:22.
2. Type Staff Meeting, and press ↵ ENTER.
3. Press TAB.

   Your insertion point jumps to the scratch pad at the bottom of the calendar.
4. Type Tom Martin will present new company logo. Ask staff members to take a vote on the design of the logo.

   The note is assigned to the currently displayed date.
5. Position the insertion point to the right of 11:30.
6. Type Lunch with corporate office, and then press ↵ ENTER.

Exercise 9: Setting an alarm

You can set an alarm to remind you of an appointment time. When the time is reached, the computer will beep (if its sound is activated) and a message box will appear, reminding you of the appointment. If Calendar is minimized to an icon on the desktop when the appointment time arrives, the icon will flash. To set the alarm perform the following steps:

1. Position the insertion point at 11:30.
2. Choose Alarm, and then choose Set.

   A small bell symbol appears to the left of 11:30 (see Figure 8-12).

FEATURE

Dialing Phone Numbers with Cardfile
Although Cardfile is a simple database program and not considered to be extremely powerful, it does include some attractive options that can simplify many of your daily tasks. For example, if you have a modem, Cardfile can automatically dial a phone number for you. You can also link, embed, and insert pictures (created in a program such as Paintbrush) on a Cardfile card.

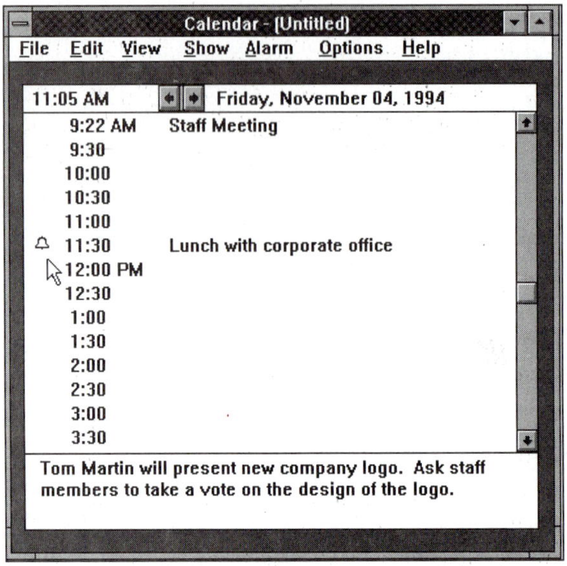

Figure 8-12 The alarm bell symbol

Exercise 10: Editing appointments

You can edit or change appointments by selecting them and then deleting, moving, or copying them. To change an appointment, perform the following steps;

1. Select the 11:30 appointment labeled *Lunch with corporate office.*
2. Choose Edit, and then choose Cut.

   The appointment is removed from the calendar.
3. Position the insertion point at 1:00.
4. Choose Edit, and then choose Paste.

   The Lunch with corporate office appointment appears in the 1:00 time slot.

Exercise 11: Tracking appointments in Month view

You might like the idea of having the entire month displayed at one time. When you want to see the entire month you can easily switch from Day view to Month view. You can use the mouse or the direction keys on the keyboard to move to different days when using Month view. The current day of the month will appear in angled brackets. To understand how to move and enter appointments in Month view, perform the following steps:

1. Choose View, and then choose Month.

   The calendar displays an entire month (see Figure 8-13).

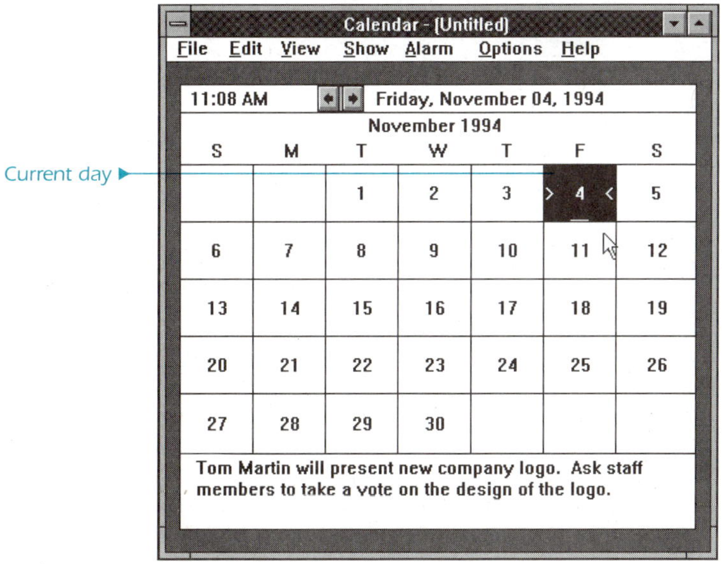

Figure 8-13 The calendar displayed in Month view

2. Place the mouse pointer on the third day of the month and click.

   The third day of the month becomes the active day and is highlighted.

3. Press the right arrow once.

   The fourth day of the month becomes the active day and is highlighted.

Exercise 12: Marking special days with symbols

To remind yourself of special dates or events, you can mark dates with one of five symbols provided by Calendar. The scratch pad is also available for you to add comments about a particular date in the month. To place a symbol on a date, perform the following steps:

1. Make sure your calendar is displayed in Month view.
2. Click the fifth day.

   The insertion point appears on the fifth day.

3. Choose Options, and then choose Mark.

   The Day Markings dialog box appears (see Figure 8-14).

Figure 8-14 The Day Markings dialog box

4. Choose Symbol 2, and then press OK.

   The calendar displays Symbol 2 on the fifth day of the month.

5. Press TAB.

   Your insertion point moves to the scratch pad.

6. Type Book report due.

   This note is attached to the fifth day of the month.

7. Highlight the seventh day of the month.
8. Choose Options, and then choose Mark.
9. In the Day Markings dialog box, choose Symbol 4, and then press OK.

   The calendar displays symbols for the fifth and seventh days of the month (see Figure 8-15).

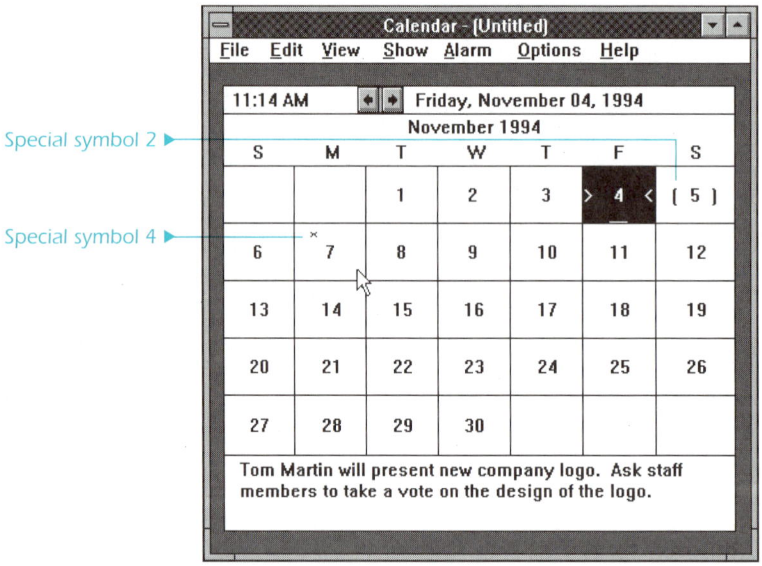

Figure 8-15 The calendar with special symbols

Exercise 13: Removing appointments from the calendar

To remove an appointment from the calendar, perform the following steps:

1. Activate the fifth day of the month.
2. Choose Edit, and then choose Remove.

   The Remove dialog box appears (see Figure 8-16). Notice that the From text box displays the active date.

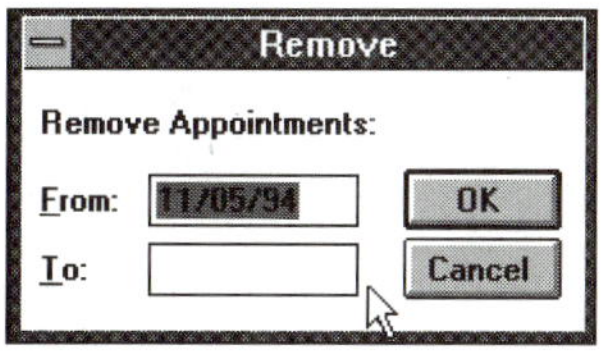

Figure 8-16 The Remove dialog box

3. Choose OK.

   The special symbol and the scratch-pad note are removed from the calendar.

TIP You can remove more than one appointment by entering a range of dates in the Remove dialog box. In the From text box, enter the first date in a range. In the To text box, enter the last date of the range.

Exercise 14: Saving and printing a calendar file

You can save and print a calendar file. To print a listing of appointments and save the current file, perform the following steps:

1. Choose File, and then choose Print.

   The Print dialog box appears (see Figure 8-17).

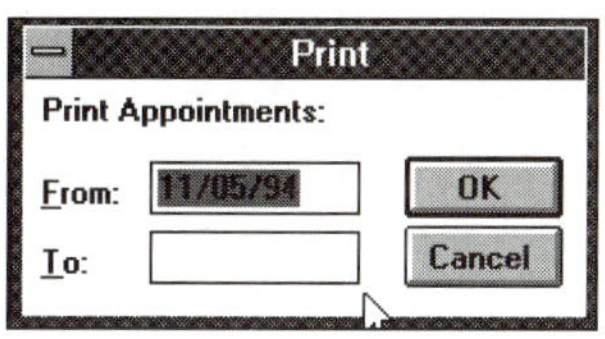

Figure 8-17 The Print dialog box

2. In the From text box, type *today's date*, and then choose OK.

   The listing of appointments for the current date is sent to a printer.
3. Place the PROJECTS floppy disk in drive A.
4. Choose File, and then choose Save As.

   The Save As dialog box appears.
5. Click the down arrow next to the Drives text box and choose drive A.
6. Type mycal in the File Name text box, and then choose OK.

   Calendar automatically attaches the extension .cal to a calendar file.

7. Choose File, and then choose Exit.

   You are returned to the Accessories window.

Objective 4: Using the Calculator Program

The Calculator program operates in much the same way as a hand-held calculator. Calculator has its own window, but it cannot be resized like other desktop accessory windows. Calculator's Edit option includes Copy and Paste commands, but not Cut. You can enter numbers into the calculator using the keyboard or the mouse. The calculator uses two displays: Standard and Scientific. Standard view is used for simple calculations; Scientific view is used for more complicated calculations.

One major advantage of the program is that you can move information generated in Calculator to other applications. You will learn how to do this type of data transfer in Chapter 11.

Table 8-2 defines the various calculator keys and how to activate each using the keyboard.

Table 8-2 Calculator keys

KEY	ACTION OF KEY	KEYBOARD METHOD
+	Adds	+
*	Multiplies	*
/	Divides	/
-	Subtracts	-
%	Generates the percentage	%
sqrt	Generates the square root	@
+/-	Changes the sign of a number	F9
1/x	Calculates the reciprocal	R
C	Clears all numbers or functions entered	ESC
CE	Clears only the last number or function entered	DELETE
Back	Deletes the last number of a displayed value	←

Exercise 15: Entering numbers in the calculator

The calculator in Standard view is used to perform simple mathematical calculations such as adding, subtracting, multiplying, dividing, and calculating percentages and square roots. You can use the mouse or keyboard to enter numbers. To make some simple calculations, perform the following steps:

1. Double-click the Calculator icon  in the Accessories window.

   The Calculator window opens, displaying the calculator in one of two views (see Figures 8-18 and 8-19).

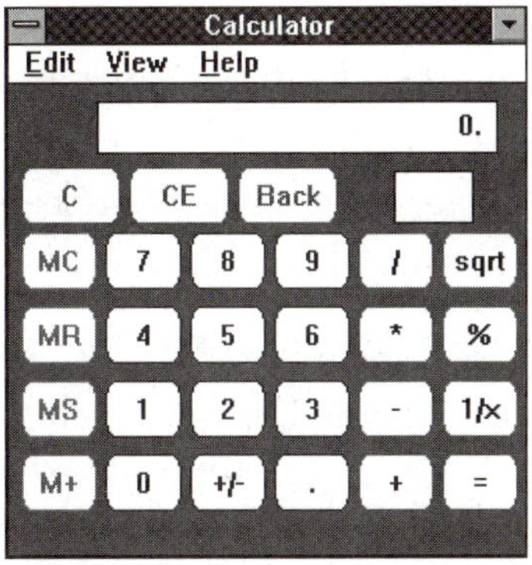

Figure 8-18 The calculator in Standard view

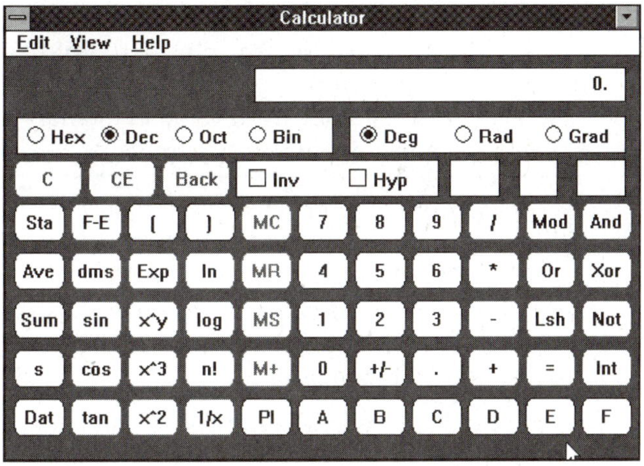

Figure 8-19 The calculator in Scientific view

2. Choose View, and then choose Standard, if it is not already chosen.
3. Using the mouse, click the following numbers and symbols on the calculator pad:

   40 + 50 =

   The sum *90* appears in the calculator's display box.
4. With the mouse, click C on the calculator pad to clear the display box.
5. Using the keyboard, type the following numbers and symbols:

   20 / 4 =

   The quotient *5* appears in the calculator's display box.
6. Press ESC to clear all functions and numbers from the display box.
7. Using the mouse, click the following numbers and symbols:

   15 * 25 =

   The product *375* appears in the display box.

8. Click Back.

   The last digit of 375 is removed so that 37 appears in the display box.
9. Using the keyboard, press F9.

   The sign of the number changes, so that –37 appears in the display box.
10. Click C to clear all numbers and functions.

Understanding Calculator's memory

You can perform mathematical calculations on several numbers by storing them in Calculator's memory. Table 8-3 defines the memory keys on the calculator pad and how to activate each one using the keyboard.

Table 8-3 Memory keys

KEY	KEYBOARD METHOD	ACTION OF KEY
MC	CTRL + L	Clears all numbers and functions in memory
MR	CTRL + R	Display a value in memory
MS	CTRL + M	Stores a displayed value in memory
M+	CTRL + P	Adds the displayed number to current value in memory

Exercise 16: Using Calculator's memory to perform calculations

To demonstrate how the memory of the calculator works, you will add three separate calculations together: (234 + 116 + 917), (5 × 10), and (60 ÷ 5). To do this, perform the following steps:

1. Using the keyboard, type the following numbers and symbols:

   234 + 116 + 917 =
2. The sum *1267* appears in the display box.
3. Click M+ to store the sum in memory.

   Note that *M* appears in the box above the sqrt button.
4. Using the mouse, enter the following numbers and symbols:

   5 * 10 =

   The product *50* appears in the display box.
5. Press CTRL+P to add this number to the number already stored in memory.
6. Using the keyboard, type the following numbers and symbols:

   60 / 5 =

   The quotient *12* appears in the display box.
7. Click M+ to add this number to the number already stored in memory.
8. Click MR to see the results of your calculations.

   The sum *1329* appears in the display box.
9. Close Calculator by double-clicking its control menu box.

Objective 5: Using the Cardfile Program

database The Cardfile program is a simple database program. A *database* is a collection of related information that can be stored, sorted, and used to produce reports. Databases are used to store a wide variety of information in an organized fashion. Cardfile is often used to maintain lists, such as a customer list, Christmas card list, or employee list.

Exercise 17: Starting Cardfile and creating a master card

The Cardfile icon is located in the Accessories window and resembles a stack of index cards. Once opened, Cardfile displays a card with two sections for entering information. The Index Line section determines the alphabetical order in which a card is displayed. You can include up to 40 characters on the index line. The Information area can be used to include any additional information you may want to record. In this exercise, you will create a Cardfile database that contains information on the owners and horses that qualified for national competition in 1994. To start Cardfile and create a master card, perform the following steps:

1. Double-click the Cardfile icon Cardfile in the Accessories window.

   The Cardfile window appears (see Figure 8-20).

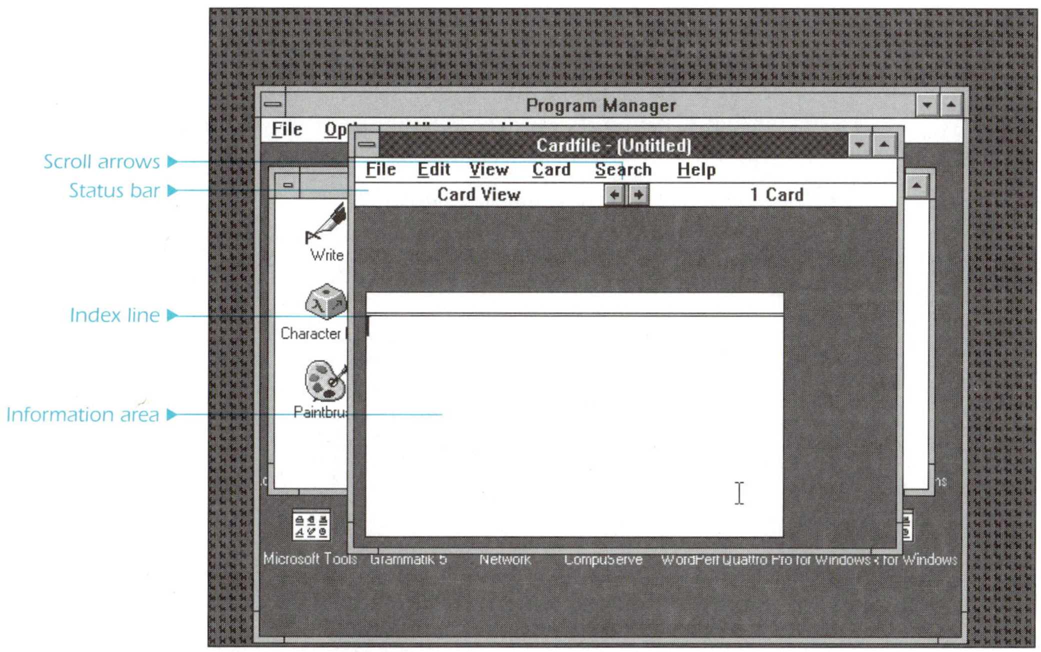

Figure 8-20 The Cardfile window

2. Press F6 (or double-click the index line).

   The Index dialog box appears (see Figure 8-21).

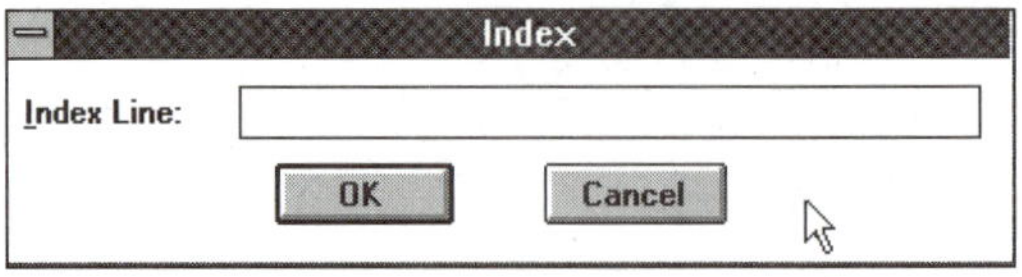

Figure 8-21 The Index dialog box

3. Click OK, leaving the index line for the first card blank.

   Your insertion point will be flashing in the Information area.

4. Type the following information, pressing ENTER at the end of each line:

   Owner Name:

   Name of Farm:

   Breed Classification :

   Gender:

   Age:

   Placement:

   This is your master card; you can duplicate it to create the rest of the cards in your Cardfile database.

Exercise 18: Duplicating the master card and entering information

You will now duplicate the master card you created and enter the information for each horse in the Information area. Do not enter information on the master card. If you do, you will have to retype the text in the Information area for each card you create.

1. Choose Card, and then choose Duplicate.

   A new blank card appears displaying the master card information. The original master card is behind the new card (see Figure 8-22).

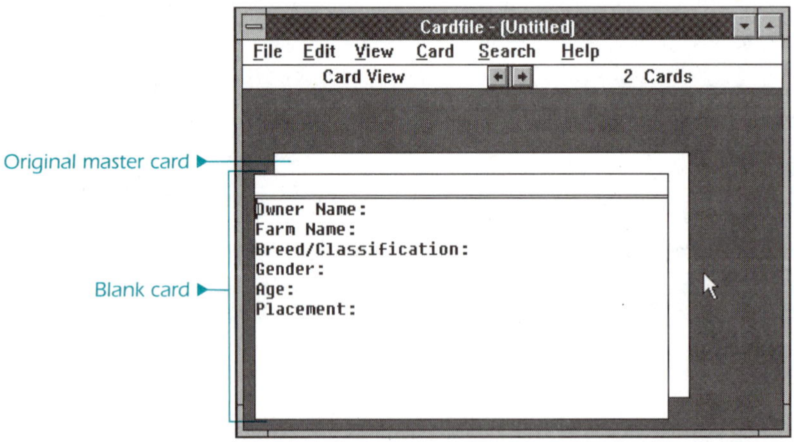

Figure 8-22 A duplicate blank card displaying the master card information

2. Double-click the index line of the blank card.
3. Type In The Skye, and then choose OK.

   The name *In the Skye* is entered on the index line.
4. Place the insertion point after Owner Name in the Information area and type Mary Mark.
5. Place the insertion point after Farm Name and type Tumbling Valley.
6. Place the insertion point after Breed/Classification and type 3-Gaited Show.
7. Place the insertion point after Gender and type Gelding.
8. Place the insertion point after Age and type 7.
9. Place the insertion point after Placement and type 1st.
10. Repeat Steps 1–9 to add three additional cards with the following data:

```
Index line: Forever Sunshine
Owner Name: Samantha Frazier
Farm Name: Willowdale Farm
Breed/Classification: 5-Gaited Pleasure
Gender: Mare
Age: 5
Placement: 1st

Index line: Friendly Persuasion
Owner Name: Rose Williams
Farm Name: Windy Hills
Breed/Classification: 3-Gaited Pleasure
Gender: Stallion
Age: 2
Placement: 2nd

Index line: Sir Aristocrat
Owner Name: Norma Paskash
Farm Name: Rolling Timbers
Breed/Classification: 3-Gaited Show
Gender: Gelding
Age: 3
Placement: 3rd
```

TIP You can add new cards to an existing file by choosing Card, and then Add. You then type in the name of the new card in the Add dialog box.

Exercise 19: Saving and printing a Cardfile database

You can save multiple Cardfile databases, and you can choose to print a single card or all the cards in a Cardfile database. To save and print the database you created, perform the following steps:

1. Make sure the PROJECTS disk is in drive A.

2. Choose File, and then choose Save As.

   The Save As dialog box appears (see Figure 8-23).

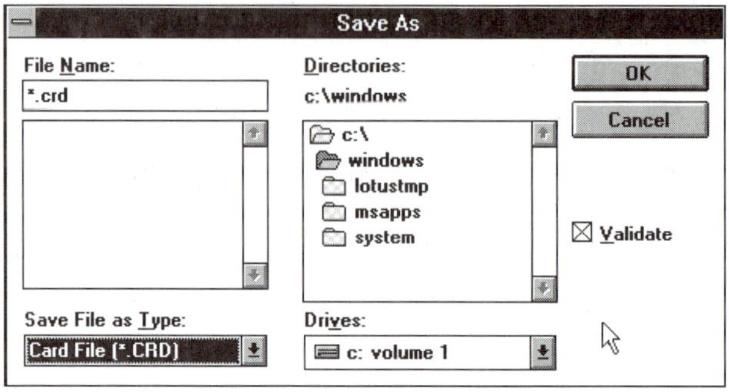

Figure 8-23 The Save As dialog box

3. Click the down arrow next to the Drives text box and choose drive A.
4. In the File Name text box, type finalist.
5. Choose OK.

   The file is saved to the PROJECTS disk in drive A. Cardfile automatically assigns the extension .crd to all files.
6. Choose File, and then choose Print All.

   All the cards in the file are printed.
7. Click the card *In the Skye*.
8. Choose File, and then choose Print.

   Only the *In the Skye* card is printed.

Exercise 20: Changing views and deleting a card

You can change the way the cards are displayed with the View option, and you can delete a card that you no longer want as part of a file. To change the view and delete a card, perform the following steps:

1. Choose View, and then choose List.

   The Cardfile window displays a list of index lines for existing cards; the active card's index line is highlighted (see Figure 8-24).

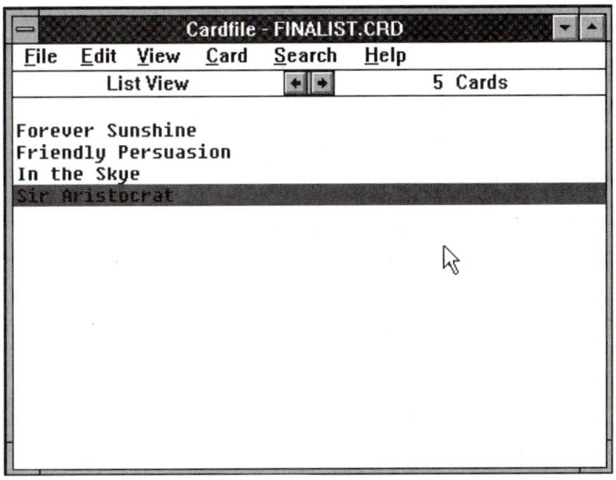

Figure 8-24 The Cardfile window in List view

2. Select the *Friendly Persuasion* card.
3. Choose Card, and then choose Delete.

   The Delete warning box appears, asking you if you want to delete the card.
4. Choose OK.

   The card is removed from the Cardfile database.

Using the Search option

Your Cardfile database may grow to include many cards; this can make finding a particular card or set of cards difficult. Fortunately, the Search and Find options in the Search menu make it easy to locate cards.

Exercise 21: Searching through cards

To search for a card based on the information in the card's index line, you use the Go To option. To search for information in the Information area, you use the Find option. You can also use the scroll arrows in the status bar to move sequentially through a stack of cards.

1. Choose Search, and then choose Go To.

   The Go To dialog box appears (see Figure 8-25).

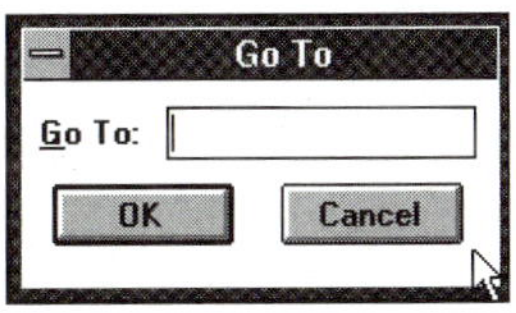

Figure 8-25 The Go To dialog box

2. Type In the Skye, and then choose OK.

The card with the index line In the Skye is displayed at the front of the stack.

3. Choose Search, and then choose Find.

   The Find dialog box appears (see Figure 8-26).

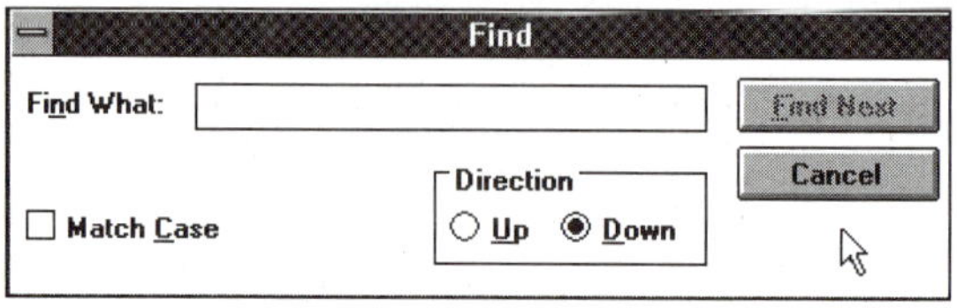

Figure 8-26 The Find dialog box

4. In the Find What text box, type Rolling Timbers, and then choose Find Next.

   The card that includes Rolling Timbers in its information area is displayed at the front of the stack, with *Rolling Timbers* highlighted. You may have to move the Find dialog box to see the highlighted text.
5. Choose Cancel to close the Find dialog box.
6. Click the right arrow in the status bar.

   The next card in the stack moves to the front.
7. Click the left arrow in the status bar.

   The last card in the stack moves to the front.
8. Choose File, and then choose Exit.
9. Choose Yes to save your changes.

Chapter Summary

In this chapter, you learned how to use the many utility programs located in the Accessories window to help you complete a variety of tasks. Notepad can be used to record short memos and notes. Clock places a clock on the desktop, which you can view as you work on other tasks. Calendar can help you keep track of appointments. Calculator performs a variety of mathematical computations. And Cardfile maintains simple databases. Each of these programs has its own window and can be used while you are working in other applications.

Review Questions

True/False Questions

_____ 1. Notepad is used to track appointments.

_____ 2. Notepad includes many of the same formatting features as Write.

_____ 3. To restore the title bar to the clock once it has been removed, you double-click anywhere on the clock face.

_____ 4. There are five different special symbols that you can use to mark days on the calendar.

_____ 5. You can attach a scratch-pad note to a specific time.

Multiple-Choice Questions

_____ 6. In Calendar's Month view, the current date appears in

A. square brackets.

B. angled brackets.

C. parentheses.

D. quotation marks.

E. none of the above

_____ 7. All the following commands can be found in one of Notepad's menus except

A. Cut.

B. Copy.

C. Paste.

D. Bold.

_____ 8. When working in Calculator, pressing @

A. generates the reciprocal.

B. computes the square root.

C. clears all numbers and functions.

D. calculates the percentage.

_____ 9. To display a value in memory using the keyboard, press

A. CTRL+L.

B. CTRL+R.

C. CTRL+M.

D. CTRL+P.

_____ 10. Cardfile is a simple
- A. spreadsheet program.
- B. analytical program.
- C. database program.
- D. productivity program.

Fill-in-the-Blank Questions

11. To print all cards in a Cardfile database, choose the ______________ ______________ command.
12. You can view the Cardfile database as a ______________ or as a ______________ of cards.
13. The ______________ ______________ option enables you to change the digital display of the clock.
14. When you set the alarm in Calendar, a small ______________ symbol appears to the left of the appointment time.
15. The default time interval used by Calendar is ______________.

Acumen-Building Activities

Quick Projects

1. Opening Windows accessories

1. Open the Accessories window, and start Notepad.
2. Minimize the Notepad document window to an icon on the desktop.
3. Start Cardfile, which is located in the Accessories window.
4. Minimize the Cardfile document window to an icon on the desktop.
5. Start Calculator, which is located in the Accessories window.
6. Minimize the Calculator window to an icon on the desktop.
7. Maximize the Notepad window to fill the entire screen.
8. Activate the option that causes text to drop automatically to the next line.
9. Type the following text:

```
Things to Do
1.Go to the grocery store. Don't forget to pick up:
   milk, bread, Kleenex, dog food, butter.
2.Go to the pharmacy to pick up the kids' medicine.
3.Wash and wax the car.
```

10. Save the file as todo.
11. Print the file.

12. Beginning at the top of the document, search for the text string *kids' medicine.*
13. Exit Notepad.

2. Using the Clock program

1. Start Clock, and display the clock with a digital face.
2. Minimize the clock to an icon on the desktop.
3. Use the Control Panel option to change your computer system's date and time to July 5, 1994, 11:20 PM.
4. Reduce the Control Panel window to an icon.
5. Maximize the clock window so that it is no longer an icon on the desktop. Check to be sure that the time displayed is 11:20 PM (or shortly thereafter).
6. Change the display of the clock to show the date but not the seconds.
7. Use a new font for the clock.
8. Remove the title of the clock.
9. Reduce the clock to an icon on the desktop and move it to the lower, left corner of the screen.
10. Reset the system's date and time to the current date and time.

3. Using the Calculator program

1. Restore the Calculator window to fill the screen.
2. Restore the Cardfile window to fill the screen.
3. Resize the Cardfile window so that it is very small and place it in the upper, right corner of the screen.
4. Display the Standard view of the calculator.
5. Using the keyboard to enter numbers and symbols, perform the following calculations:

   Find the remainder of $3045 - 266$.

   Find the sum of $12999 + 45007$.

   Find the product of 123×50.

   Find the quotient of $500 \div 4$.
6. Using Calculator's memory, compute the following:

   $(120 + 765 + 330) + (30 - 25) + (3 \times 6) + (100 \div 4)$
7. Close Calculator and minimize the Accessories window.

4. Using the Cardfile program

1. Resize the Cardfile document window so that is large (but do not maximize it).
2. Move the clock to the upper, left corner of the screen.
3. Open the Main window.
4. Start Write.

5. Resize all open windows so that each is visible on the screen.
6. Activate the Cardfile window, and create six cards; on each card, type the following information as indicated:

```
Index line: Aerosmith
Name of Song: Love in an Elevator
Medium: CD

Index line: Melissa Etheridge
Name of Song: Bring Me Some Water
Medium: CD

Index line: Rolling Stones
Name of Song: Brown Sugar
Medium: Cassette

Index line: Pink Floyd
Name of Song: The Wall
Medium: LP

Index line: Eagles
Name of Song: Hotel California
Medium: LP

Index line: Fleetwood Mac
Name of Song: Rhihannon
Medium: Cassette
```

7. Save the file as records.
8. Print all the cards in the file.
9. Search for *Hotel California*.
10. Print only the Hotel California card.
11. Change the name of the Rolling Stones song to Ruby Tuesday.
12. Save the Cardfile database and exit Cardfile.

In-Depth Projects

1. Using Windows accessories

1. Start Windows and open the Accessories and Main windows.
2. Cascade the windows.
3. Make the Main window active, and start the File Manager.

   Using the File Manager, copy files between the PROJECTS and DISK1 floppy disks until both disks contain the same files. (All the file names you have assigned so far have been unique; therefore, you won't accidentally overwrite a file by copying files between disks.) When finished, close the File Manager.
4. Start Calendar and change the date on the status bar so that it is five days later than the current date.
5. Change to Month view.

6. Exit Calendar and close all windows except the Program Manager window.

2. Using the Calendar program

1. Open the Accessories window and start Calendar.
2. Display the Day view, and make sure that the current date is displayed.
3. Set the time intervals to every 15 minutes.
4. Set a special time for 10:24 AM.
5. At the 10:30 appointment slot, type Meet with the Chancellor.
6. Set the alarm to go off at 10:15 AM and include the message *Don't be late!!!*
7. Move the 10:30 appointment to 11:15 AM.
8. Reset the alarm and its message to go off at 11:00 AM.
9. At the 1:00 appointment slot, type Meet the Coach.
10. Print the Calendar file.
11. Save the file as school.cal and exit Calendar.

3. Working in Windows

1. Start Windows.
2. Make the following changes to the floppy disks. Change the volume label of the PROJECTS disk to BACKUP. Change the volume label of the DISK1 disk to ORIGINAL.
3. Split the File Manager window so that the Directory Tree measures one inch across.
4. Remove the status bar from the File Manager window.
5. Place the BACKUP disk in drive A and display a window for it.
6. Display only the Directory Contents List for the BACKUP disk.
7. Sort the files in the root of the BACKUP disk by date.
8. Minimize the File Manager window.
9. Start Write and open the horses document. Make the following changes:

   Set the top, bottom, left, and right margins to 1".

   Create a header and type Meeting in Minutes as the header text. Make this text bold and italic.

   Change the size of the text in the document to 16 points; change the font to any of your choosing.
10. Save the file as horses8.doc.
11. Start Cardfile and display the records file.
12. Delete the record for Fleetwood Mac, and then duplicate the record for the Rolling Stones.
13. Save the new file as record8.crd.
14. Close all windows and exit the program.

Chapter 9

The Print Manager

Objectives

- Using the Print Manager
- Understanding the Print Manager's Options

Key Terms

TERM	DEFINITION
Print Queue	a listing of files waiting in a print spooler to be printed
Background	a figurative area in Windows in which lower-level operations, such as printing, are performed invisibly while you work with applications in the foreground
Foreground	a figurative area in Windows in which primary tasks, such as working in an application, take precedence over lower-level operations, such as printing
Print Spooler	a program that stores files in a specified order and causes the files to print in that order

By now, you realize that Windows is an environment in which you can accomplish many tasks at once. The Print Manager is an option in Windows that handles your printing in the background while you continue to work with other applications in the foreground. (Windows differs from DOS in this way. When you print a file from a DOS application, you must wait until the file finishes printing before you can work in another application.) The

background *background* is a figurative area in Windows in which lower-level operations, such as printing, are performed invisibly while you work with applications

foreground in the foreground. The *foreground* is a figurative area in Windows in which primary tasks, such as working in an application, take precedence over lower-level operations, such as printing. Tasks occurring in the foreground are generally displayed on the screen as you perform them.

In previous chapters, you printed various files by choosing the Print command. In this chapter, you will learn how the print jobs you request are handled by the Print Manager and the many ways you can control the

print spooler

print spooler and queuing. The *print spooler* is a program that stores files in a specified order and causes the files to print in that order.

Objective 1: Using the Print Manager

The Print Manager icon is located in the Main window. The Print Manager window provides information about files that you have sent to the printer, their order in the print queue, and how close each print job is to completion.

print queue

A *print queue* is a listing of files waiting in a print spooler to be printed. The Print Manager also alerts you to problems the printer may be having—for example, when the printer runs out of paper or is jammed. As long as files are stored in the print queue waiting to be printed, the Print Manager icon is displayed on the desktop (see Figure 9-1).

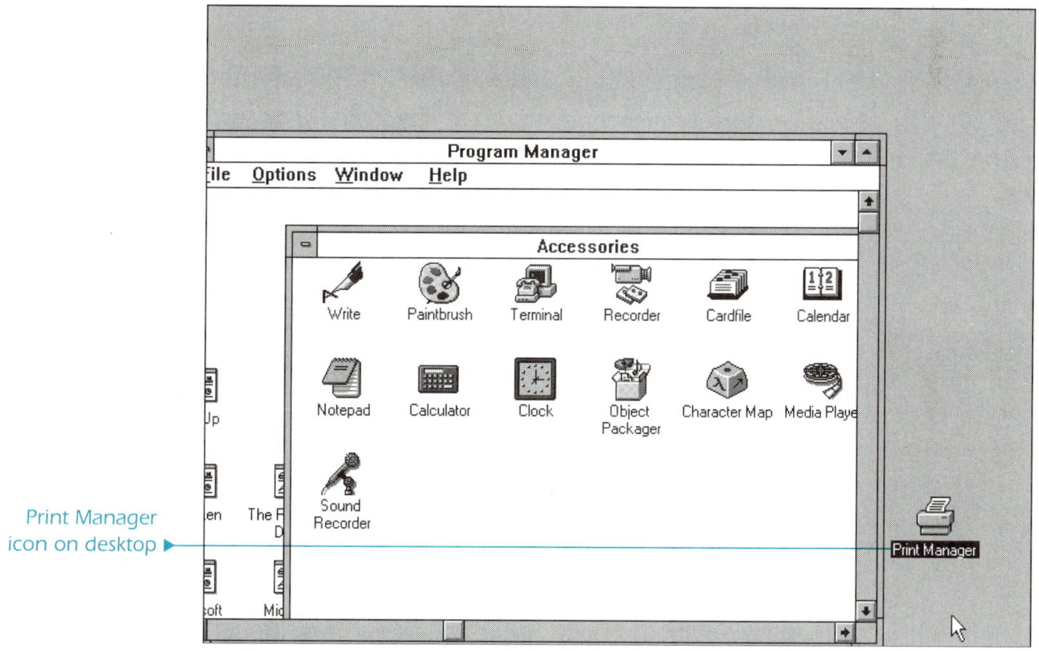

Figure 9-1 The Print Manager icon on the desktop

Exercise 1: Understanding the Print Manager window

The Print Manager starts printing a file automatically when you choose Print from the file's document window and the Print Manager check box is enabled. The Print Manager check box appears in the Print dialog box which you activate with the Control Panel window. Once you select a file to print from within an application, the file is sent to the Print Manager. If the file is very large, you may have to wait a few seconds until the Print

Manager places the requested file in the print queue before you continue with your work. You will need to turn your printer off before beginning the following exercise.

1. Place the disk labeled ORIGINAL in drive A.
2. Start Write from the Accessories window, open horses7.doc, and print the file.

   A message box appears, indicating that the file is printing.
3. Open story.txt and print the file.

   A message box appears, indicating that the file is printing.
4. Minimize the Write window to an icon.
5. Start Cardfile from the Accessories window, open finalist.crd, and print the file.
6. Minimize the Cardfile window.
7. Start Calendar from the Accessories window, open mycal.cal, and print the file.
8. Minimize the Calendar window.
9. Open the Main window and double-click the Print Manager icon .

   The Print Manager window appears (see Figure 9-2).

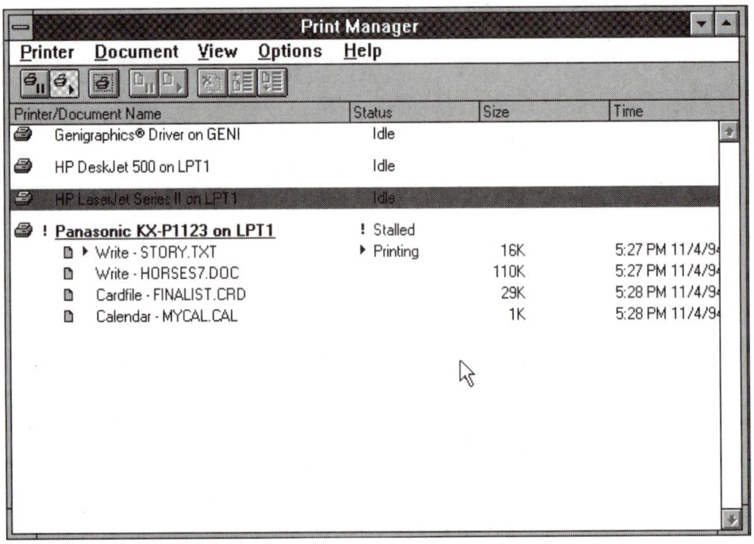

Figure 9-2 The Print Manager window

The information in the Print Manager window includes the name of the active printer and its status, the list of files that are waiting in the print queue, and the names of any additional printers that are configured with the Windows program. The word *Stalled* appears next to the active printer because you turned the printer off.

Objective 2: Understanding the Print Manager's Options

The Print Manager window includes a variety of options. You can pause and then resume printing a file, change the order in which files are listed in the print queue, change the speed of the Print Manager, remove a file from the print queue, and display a variety of information in the Print Manager window.

Exercise 2: Using the Pause and Resume buttons

You can temporarily stop a file from printing and then resume printing using the Pause and Resume buttons located under the Printer option in the menu bar. To pause and resume printing the files in the queue, perform the following steps:

1. Turn your printer on.
2. Select the active printer. (The name currently has *Stalled* next to it.)
3. Choose Printer, and then choose Resume Printer.

   The printer resumes printing.
4. Select the active printer.
5. Choose Printer, and then choose Pause Printer.

   The printer pauses printing.
6. Select the active printer.
7. Choose Resume Printer.

   The printer resumes printing.

Exercise 3: Changing the order of files to print

When several files are in the print queue, you can change the order in which they will print. You cannot reorder a file if it is already printing. The first file has a printer icon next to it instead of a number; this means its order cannot be changed because it is already printing. However, you can change the order of the numbered files by performing the following steps:

1. Drag story.txt to the last position in the list of files.
2. Release the mouse button.

   The order of the file is changed in the queue.

Exercise 4: Changing the printer's priority level

While you work on application tasks in the foreground and print in the background, the resources of your system (RAM and disk space) are allocated to handle both operations. You can control the allocation of system resources that are shared by the printer and running applications by setting priority levels in the Print Manager. Priority levels include Low, Medium, and High. When printing is given a low-priority setting, the system spends its resources on running applications, and printing slows. When printing is given a high-priority setting, printing proceeds faster, but it will take longer for running

Automating Performance Reviews

Writing effective, analytical job performance reviews for each employee in a company can be a time-consuming task that managers and bosses dread. Software is now available to help with this task. The software helps you define the role of the employee and assess his or her skills using a rating system that ranges from unsatisfactory to outstanding. Some of the programs include a database that can be used to track an employee's performance throughout the year and write a descriptive performance analysis of the accumulated information. Suggestions on how to improve performance and approach performance problems are also included in the software.

applications to perform tasks. The Medium setting assigns the printer and applications even amounts of system resources; this is often the best choice. To change priority levels, perform the following steps:

1. Choose Options from the menu bar.

   The Options menu appears (see Figure 9-3).

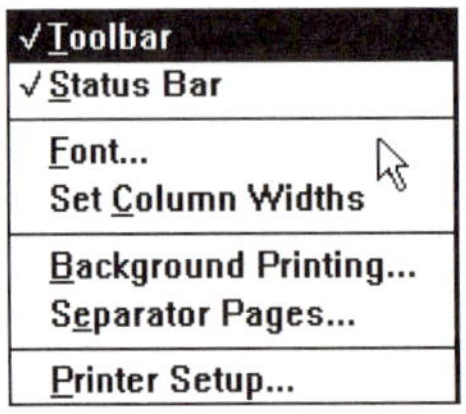

Figure 9-3 The Options menu

The Medium option is the default and includes a checkmark indicating that it is active. For this exercise, leave the default activated.

2. Choose Background Printing.

   The Background Printing dialog box displays (see Figure 9-4).

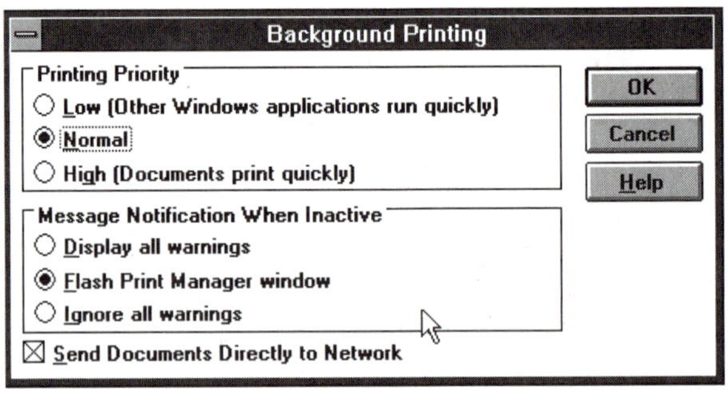

Figure 9-4 The Background Printing dialog box

The Normal option is the default + 3' and is a bulleted option.

3. Close the Options menu.

Exercise 5: Deleting a file from the print queue

If you change your mind about printing a file, you can remove it from the print queue. To delete a file from the print queue, perform the following steps:

1. Select story.txt.
2. Choose Delete.

   A message box appears asking if you want to delete this file from the print queue.
3. Choose Yes.

WARNING If the file you are deleting contains graphics, you may have to turn the printer off and on to clear the printer's memory.

Displaying printer messages

You can have the printer alert you to different situations using the Options menu. Table 9-1 defines the options in the Options menu.

Table 9-1 Printer message options

OPTION	DESCRIPTION
Display All Warnings	Displays a message box when the printer needs to be checked.
Flash Print Message Window	Beeps and causes the Print Manager icon to flash when the Print Manager is an icon or the Print Manager window is inactive and the printer needs to be checked. To learn more about the status of the printer, activate the Print Manager window.
Ignore All Warnings	Does not alert you in any way when the Print Manager is an icon or the Print Manager window is inactive and the printer needs to be checked.

Exercise 6: Displaying file queue details

Using the View menu in the Print Manager window, you can choose to display the time and date you sent a file to the printer, as well as the size of the file in bytes. A checkmark appears next to an option when it is activated. To view the time and date of each print request and the size of each file in the print queue, perform the following steps:

1. Choose View from the menu bar.
2. Choose Time/Date Sent.
3. Choose Print File Size.

Exercise 7: Canceling all print jobs

You can cancel all print jobs listed in the print queue by performing the following steps from the Print Manager window:

1. Choose View, and then choose Exit.

   A message box appears asking for confirmation to stop all printing.
2. Choose Yes.

Chapter Summary

This chapter introduced you to the Print Manager, which enables you to work in other applications while printing documents. You can control and adjust settings in the Print Manager window, and have messages displayed to alert you to any problem the printer may be experiencing. The Print Manager is another tool that helps you use your time more efficiently.

Review Questions

True/False Questions

_____ 1. The Print Manager icon is located in the Control Panel window.

_____ 2. The check box used to enable or disable the Print Manager is located in the Print dialog box.

_____ 3. The Print Manager is a time-saving tool that you can use to print files to disk or hard copies.

_____ 4. You can specify how many copies you want printed in the Print Manager window.

_____ 5. The Print Manager numbers all files in the print queue except the file that is currently printing.

Multiple-Choice Questions

_____ 6. The command buttons in the Print Manager window include all the following except

A. Pause. C. Resume.
B. View. D. Delete.

_____ 7. You can change the order in which files will print by

A. double-clicking the file name.
B. typing a new number next to the file name.
C. dragging the file name to a new position in the print queue.
D. none of the above

_____ 8. Setting a printer's priority level affects

A. the allocation of system resources.
B. the speed at which a file will be printed.
C. the sequence in which a file will be printed.
D. all of the above
E. A and B only

_____ 9. All the following options are located on the View menu except:

A. Time/Date Sent. C. Exit.
B. Print File Size. D. Flash If Inactive.

_____ 10. To cancel all print jobs in the print queue you choose

A. File, Close. C. Options, Delete.
B. View, Exit. D. none of the above

Fill-in-the-Blank Questions

11. When you set the priority option to Low in the Print Manager window, the system resources focus more on ______________ than on printing.
12. When a file that you are deleting contains graphics, you may have to ______________ the printer.
13. The ______________ option causes a message to appear whenever the printer needs to be checked.
14. You can display the number of ______________ a file contains by activating the Print File Size option.
15. You can ______________ or ______________ the Print Manager option from the Printer dialog box.

Acumen-Building Activities

Quick Projects

1. Using Windows accessories

1. Start the following programs: Write, Calendar, Cardfile, and Notepad.
2. Arrange and resize the document windows so each can be seen.
3. Insert the disk ORIGINAL in drive A.
4. Print the following files from the Write window: correct2.txt, fashion.doc, and horses.wri.
5. Print todo.txt from the Notepad window.
6. Print school.cal from the Calendar window.
7. Print records.crd from the Cardfile window.
8. Minimize all document windows to icons on the desktop so you can see the Print Manager icon.
9. Maximize the Print Manager icon.
10. When correct2.txt is partly printed, pause the printer.
11. Adjust the printer so that it will begin a new page when it resumes printing, and then resume printing.
12. Reposition horses.wri so that it is the last file in the print queue.
13. Reposition records so that it is the third file in the print queue.
14. Change the priority level to High and allow one more file to print. (Do you notice a difference in the speed of the printer?)
15. Cancel all remaining print jobs.

2. Using the Print Manager

1. Send the following files to the printer: horses.wri, logo.txt, mycal.cal, and finalist.crd.
2. Minimize each document window to an icon.
3. Display the Print Manager window and choose the option that causes the computer to beep or the Program Manager icon to flash when the printer needs to be checked.
4. Minimize the Print Manager window so you can see it on the desktop.

5. Turn the printer off.
6. When the computer signals you that the printer needs to be checked, turn the printer on and maximize the Print Manager window.
7. From the Print Manager window, choose the option to restart the printer.
8. Change the priority level to Low.
9. Exit Windows and cancel all print jobs.

3. Practicing with Windows

1. Start Windows.
2. Display Scotties on the desktop.
3. Speed up the keyboard repeat rate.
4. Display mouse trails.
5. Turn off the warning beep when an error is made.
6. Disable the Print Manager.
7. Create a color scheme and name it color9.
8. Start Notepad and open todo.txt.
9. Add the text to the end of the document:

   4. Do the laundry.

   5. Scrub and wax the floor.
10. Save the file as todo2.txt.
11. Reverse the order of the listed items.
12. Save the file as todo3.txt.
13. Make a copy of the list and place it at the bottom of the page.
14. Save the file as todo4.txt.
15. Send todo.txt, todo2.txt, todo3.txt, and todo4.txt to the printer.
16. Start the Print Manager and delete todo3.txt from the print queue.
17. Display the times and dates of the remaining file requests.
18. Reset all settings to their original status.
19. Close all windows.

4. Using File Manager and Cardfile

1. Place the ORIGINAL disk in the drive A.
2. Start the File Manager and open two display windows for the ORIGINAL disk.
3. Tile them on the screen.
4. Start Cardfile from the File Manager.
5. Choose the option that will reduce the File Manager to an icon so you can easily switch between the Cardfile and File Manager windows.
6. Make the default printer a different printer.
7. Create a Cardfile database that includes the names, addresses, phone numbers, and birthdays of at least six friends.
8. Name the file friends.crd and print it.
9. Reset all settings to their original status, and exit Windows.

In-Depth Projects

1. Using the Calculator, Calendar, and Print Manager

1. Start Windows.
2. Start Calculator and compute (3421 + 7765) – (4 × 12).
3. Minimize the Calculator window.
4. Open the Accessories window and place all the icons on the left side of the window.
5. Make a copy of the Cardfile and Write icons and place them in the StartUp window.
6. Start Calendar and display the Month view.
7. Use one special symbol to mark the 10th, 12th, and 13th days.
8. Use a different special symbol to mark the 5th, 6th, and 8th days.
9. Save the file as mycal9.cal.
10. Turn off the printer, and then send all files with a .crd extension to the printer.
11. Turn on the printer, display the Print Manager window, and delete the last file in the queue.
12. Choose the option that automatically rearranges icons in all windows.
13. Close all windows and exit Windows.

2. Using the Calendar, Clock, and Print Manager

1. Start Windows, and then start Calendar.
2. Open mycal9.cal and change the symbols for the 5th, 6th, and 8th days.
3. Remove the symbols for the 10th, 12th, and 13th days.
4. Set a special time for 1:07 AM and set an alarm for 2:00 PM.
5. Save the file as mycal9a.cal.
6. Change the clock to an analog display without a title.
7. Request three printed copies of correct1.txt.
8. Cancel all print jobs.
9. Place a comment on the Help topic Window Menu Commands.

3. Using Print Manager and Write

1. Open the Print Manager window and reduce it to an icon.
2. Remove the color9 color scheme.
3. Start Write from the File Manager window.
4. Open story.txt.
5. Bold the first paragraph.
6. Italicize the salutation and increase the font size.
7. Set line spacing to 2 and indent the first line of each paragraph using the ruler.
8. Save the file as story9.txt.
9. Send all files created in Write to the printer.
10. Using the Control menu in Write, switch to the Print Manager window.
11. Print the help topic Printing to a File.
12. Close all windows and exit Windows.

Chapter 10

Paintbrush

Objectives

- Using Paintbrush
- Using Paintbrush's Drawing Tools
- Manipulating Images
- Using Text
- Printing a Drawing

Key Terms

TERM	DEFINITION
Bitmapped File	a file that contains an image created by pixels (or screen dots) arranged on the screen
Cutout	an image or portion of an image that has been cut with the Scissors tool

In previous chapters, you learned about some of Windows' productivity tools. In this chapter, you will learn about Paintbrush, another productivity tool that you can use to enhance a document or express your creativity. Paintbrush is a drawing program, and you can cut, copy, and paste a Paintbrush drawing into documents created in Write, Notepad, and Cardfile.

Objective 1: Using Paintbrush

Paintbrush can be used to create and edit drawings, which can then be included in greeting cards, newsletters, posters, brochures, and other documents. Paintbrush provides a set of drawing tools, a color palette, text capabilities, and predesigned shapes. Table 10-1 describes the components of the Paintbrush window.

Table 10-1 Components of the Paintbrush window

COMPONENT	DESCRIPTION
Toolbox	Contains the tools used to create drawings; the toolbox is displayed on the left side of the Paintbrush window.
Line Width Box	Provides a variety of widths that you can apply to lines and brushstrokes.
Color Palette	Provides a collection of colors that you can apply to objects.
Drawing Area	The blank area in the window where you create your drawings.

Exercise 1: Starting Paintbrush

Paintbrush is located in the Accessories window. To start Paintbrush, perform the following steps:

1. Double-click the Paintbrush icon  in the Accessories window.

   The Paintbrush window appears (see Figure 10-1).

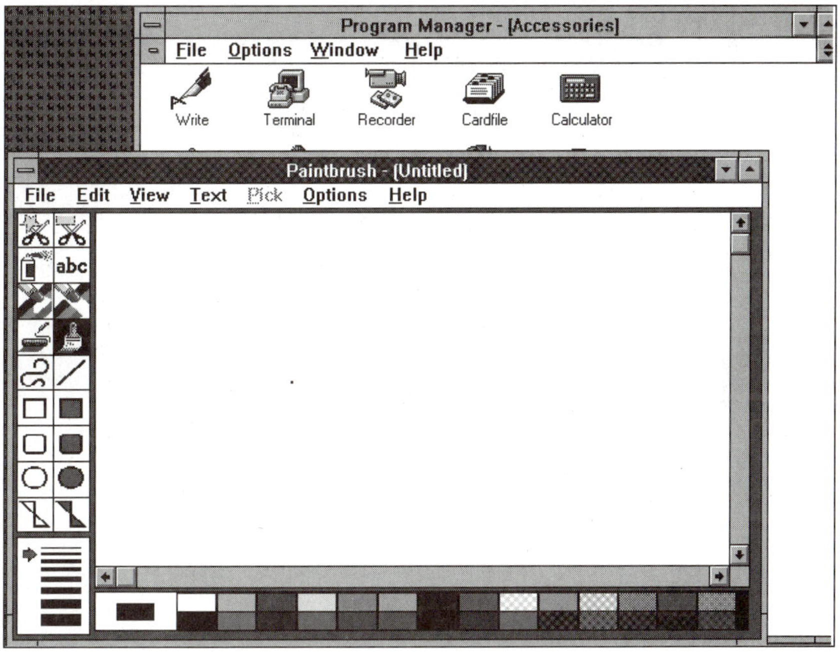

Figure 10-1 The Paintbrush window

2. Maximize the Paintbrush window.
3. Move the mouse pointer to the drawing area.

   The mouse pointer changes to a small, black square.
4. Hold down the left mouse button and drag the mouse pointer in a circle within the drawing area. Release the mouse button.

   A circle is drawn on the screen.

5. Choose Edit, and then choose Undo to remove the circle from the drawing area.

TIP The Undo function in Paintbrush operates in the same manner as it does in Write, Notepad, and Cardfile: Selecting Undo reverses your last action on screen.

6. Select the thickest line in the line width box.

   An arrow appears next to the chosen line width.

7. Move the mouse pointer to the drawing area.

   The mouse pointer changes to a large, black square.

8. Drag the mouse pointer back and forth across the drawing area (see Figure 10-2).

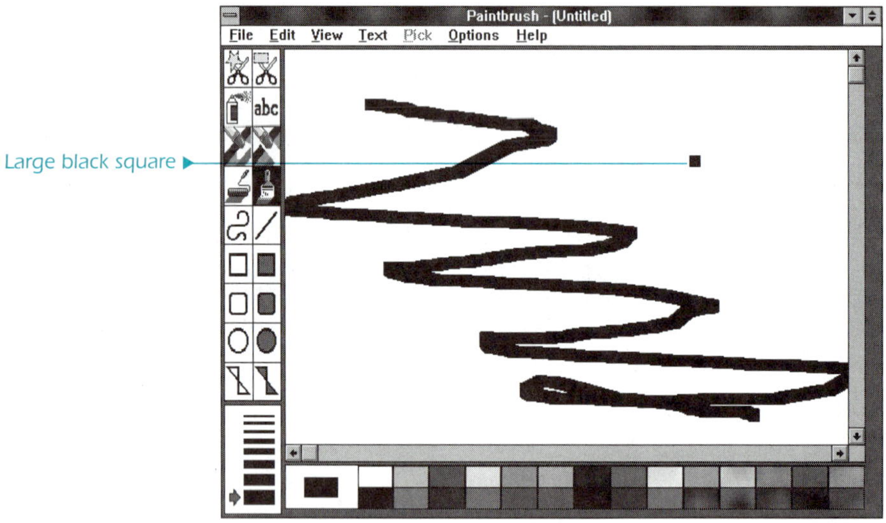

Figure 10-2 The drawing area displaying the selected line width

9. Choose Edit, and then choose Undo to clear the screen.

Objective 2: Using Paintbrush's Drawing Tools

The Paintbrush program includes a toolbox that contains eighteen tools (see Figure 10-3).

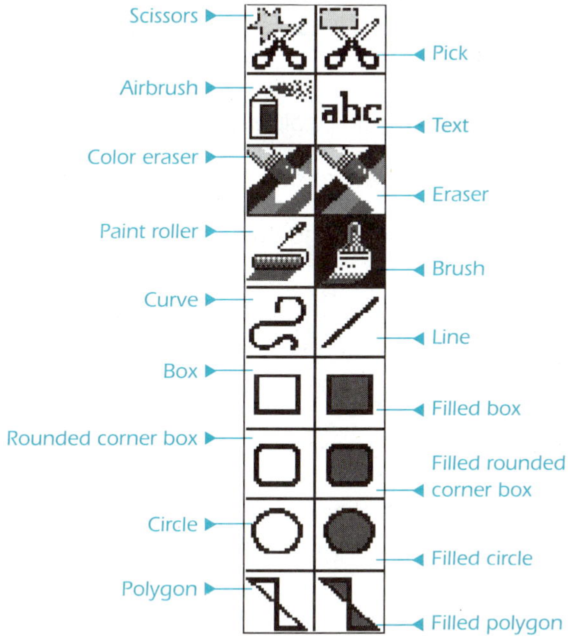

Figure 10-3 Paintbrush's drawing tools

The tools fall into three categories: graphics, text, and editing. The graphics tools enable you to draw objects freehand or using predesigned shapes. The editing tools enable you to move, cut, copy, and paste an object in the drawing area. With the Text tool, you can insert text into a drawing.

To use a tool, you must select it from the toolbox and then position the mouse on the drawing area. The mouse pointer changes shape, depending on the tool that is selected. Table 10-2 describes the actions performed by each tool.

Table 10-2 Actions of toolbox tool

TOOL		FUNCTION
Scissors		Use to select an irregularly shaped portion of a drawing for editing.
Pick		Use to select a rectangular-shaped portion of a drawing for editing.
Air Brush		Use to create a spray-paint effect. The Air Brush tool leaves a mist of color on the drawing area.
Text		Use to include text in a drawing. The Text tool does not have a word-wrap option or any text-editing features.

continued

Table 10-2 continued

TOOL	FUNCTION
Color Eraser	Use to switch foreground and background colors over an area. When you drag the Color Eraser tool over an area, you switch the currently selected foreground color to the currently selected background color. When you double-click the Color Eraser, you switch all the selected foreground colors to the selected background color.
Eraser	Use to erase a portion of an image from the screen.
Paint Roller	Use to fill in an enclosed area with a selected color.
Brush	Use to paint a solid brushstroke of color.
Curve	Use to create curved lines and detailed shapes.
Line	Use to draw a straight line.
Box	Use to create an unfilled square or rectangle.
Filled Box	Use to create a filled square or rectangle.
Rounded box	Use to create an unfilled square or rectangle with rounded corners.
Filled Rounded Box	Use to create a filled square or rectangle with rounded corners.
Circle/Ellipse	Use to create an unfilled circle or oval.
Filled Circle/Ellipse	Use to create a filled circle or oval.
Polygon	Use to create an unfilled polygon (a multisided shape made of straight lines).
Filled Polygon	Use to create a filled polygon.

Exercise 2: Using the toolbox

To use the tools in the Paintbrush toolbox, perform the following steps:

1. Change the line width to thin.
2. Choose the Filled Rounded Box tool.
3. Position the mouse on the top, left side of the drawing area.

   The mouse pointer turns into a cross-hair cursor.
4. Drag the mouse to the right 1.5" and down 1.5". Release the mouse button.

TIP To draw a perfect square, hold down SHIFT while you drag the mouse pointer.

A filled, rounded-corner square is displayed on the screen. It reflects the default colors of black and white.

5. Select the Circle tool. Place the mouse pointer to the right of the box in the drawing area.

   The mouse pointer turns into a cross-hair cursor.

6. Drag the mouse pointer down 2" and to the right 2". Release the mouse button.

TIP To draw a perfect circle, hold down SHIFT while you drag the mouse pointer.

Your drawing area should resemble Figure 10-4.

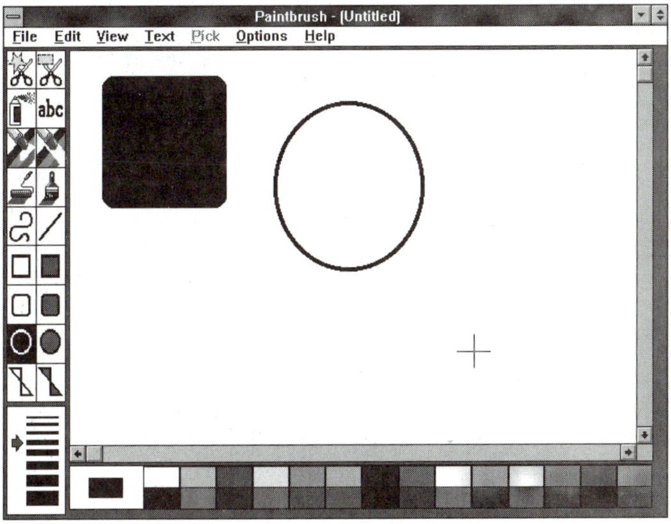

Figure 10-4 A filled, rounded-corner square and unfilled circle

Exercise 3: Saving a drawing

bitmapped file

You can save Paintbrush drawings the same way you save other types of files. Files saved in Paintbrush are bitmapped files and have the extension .bmp. A *bitmapped file* is a file that contains an image created by pixels (or screen dots) arranged on the screen. To save the drawing you created, perform the following steps:

1. Choose File, and then choose Save As.

   The Save As dialog box appears.

2. In the File Name text box, type shapes.
3. Choose OK.

Exercise 4: Adding color to a drawing

You can use the Paint Roller, Air Brush, and Brush tools to add color to your drawings by choosing a color from the color palette and then applying it with one of these tools. Foreground colors are selected using the left mouse button, while background colors are selected with the right mouse button.

1. Select pink from the color palette, using the left mouse button.

   The small, inner box on the color palette turns pink. The inner box indicates the foreground color, which is used to color objects.

2. Select the Paint Roller tool  and position the mouse pointer over the circle in the drawing area.
3. Click inside the circle.

   The inside of the circle is pink.

4. Select blue from the color palette, using the left mouse button.

   The small, inner box on the color palette turns blue.

5. Select the fourth line width in the line width box.
6. Select the Brush tool  and move the mouse pointer to the drawing area.

   The mouse pointer changes to a large, black square.

7. Drag the mouse pointer to print the word *cool* in the lower, right portion of the drawing area.

   Cool is displayed on the screen using the foreground color of blue (see Figure 10-5).

Figure 10-5 The drawing area displaying predesigned shapes and the word *cool*

8. Click bright green from the color palette, using the right mouse button.

   The background color in the indicator box turns green.

9. Choose File, and then choose New.

   A message box displays, asking if you want to save your changes.

10. Choose Yes.

    The current screen is replaced by a new screen with a green background. The selected background color appears on screen when you open a new file.

11. Change the background color to white.
12. Choose File, New.

    The screen is returned to white.

13. Choose red as the foreground color from the color palette.
14. Choose the Air Brush tool  and move the mouse pointer to the drawing area.

    The mouse pointer turns into a cross-hair cursor.

15. Drag the mouse from left to right across the drawing area.

    Dragging the Air Brush tool creates a spray-paint effect (see Figure 10-6).

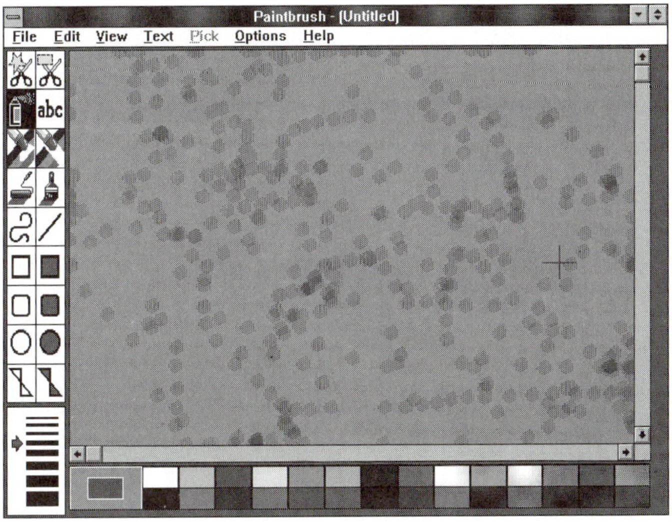

Figure 10-6 The Air Brush tool's spray-paint effect

Objective 3: Manipulating Images

cutout

It may take several attempts before a drawing looks the way you want it to. For this reason, Paintbrush includes tools you can use to edit and manipulate images: the Scissors, Pick, Color Eraser, and Eraser tools. The portion of a drawing that is cut or copied is called a *cutout*. The Edit menu also contains an Undo command so that you can reverse your last change to a drawing.

Exercise 5: Copying and moving a drawing

To copy, paste, and move a drawing, perform the following:

1. Choose File, and then choose Open.

   A message box appears asking if you want to save the current file.
2. Choose No.

   The Open File dialog box appears.
3. Select shapes.bmp from the File Name list box, and then choose OK.

   The current file closes and the shapes.bmp file is displayed on the screen.
4. Choose the Scissors tool  and move the mouse pointer to the drawing area.

   The mouse pointer becomes a cross-hair cursor.
5. Drag the cross-hair cursor around the word *cool* on the screen. Release the mouse button.

   Cool is enclosed in dotted lines.

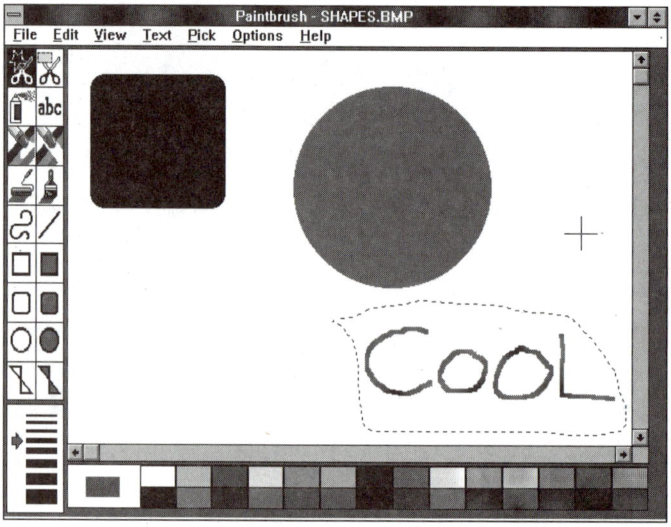

Figure 10-7 ***Cool* is enclosed in dotted lines**

6. Drag the dotted-line box to the lower, left portion of the drawing area and release the mouse button.

   Cool is relocated (see Figure 10-8).

Figure 10-8 ***Cool* is relocated on the drawing area**

TIP If you select the wrong object when drawing a dotted-line box, release the mouse button, place the cross hair cursor on a blank portion of the drawing area, and click to deselect the object.

7. Click the mouse button on a blank portion of the drawing area to deselect the drawing.
8. Choose the Pick tool .
9. Drag the cross-hair cursor around the filled circle on the screen. Release the mouse button.

   The filled circle is enclosed in a dotted-line box.

Figure 10-9 **The circle enclosed in a dotted-line box**

10. Choose Edit, and then choose Copy.
11. Choose Edit, and then choose Paste.

    A second, filled circle appears enclosed in a dotted-line box. This filled circle is a copy of the filled circle you selected.
12. Drag the dotted-line box to the lower, right portion of the drawing area and release the mouse button.

    The copy of the filled circle is relocated (see Figure 10-10).

Figure 10-10 The copy of the filled circle relocated on the drawing area

Exercise 6: Removing an image

You can remove an image from the screen with the Eraser tool. You can also use the Undo command to reverse the last change you make to an image. To practice using the Eraser tool and Undo, perform the following steps:

1. Choose the Eraser tool .

   The mouse pointer turns into a small, clear box.
2. Place the mouse pointer on the filled circle that appears in the lower, right portion of the drawing area.

> **FEATURE**
>
> **Importing Graphics Files into Paintbrush**
> You can import graphics files from other drawing programs into Paintbrush. Paintbrush accepts files with the extensions .bmp, .msp, and .pcx. To import a file, you simply select the file in Paintbrush's Open File dialog box. You can then manipulate and change the file as you would a Paintbrush file.

3. Click and hold down the mouse button as you move the mouse pointer back and forth inside the filled circle.

   The color inside the filled square is partially erased (see Figure 10-11).

Figure 10-11 The color partially erased from the filled circle

4. Choose File, and then choose New.

   A message box appears asking if you want to save your changes.
5. Choose No.

Objective 4: Using Text

The Text tool enables you to add text to a drawing. Characters appear in the current foreground color. Certain restrictions exist when adding text to a drawing. For example, unlike a word processing program, which enables you to format existing text, Paintbrush requires that you choose the font and attributes you want assigned to text before you enter the text. Also, word-wrap is not an option in Paintbrush, so you must press Enter to create a line break.

Exercise 7: Adding text to an image

To add text to an image, perform the following steps:

1. Choose File, and then choose New, if a new file is not already displayed on the screen.
2. Choose the Box tool. (Do *not* choose the Filled Box tool.)

3. Drag the mouse 4" to the right and 2.5" down. Release the mouse button. Your drawing area should look like Figure 10-12.

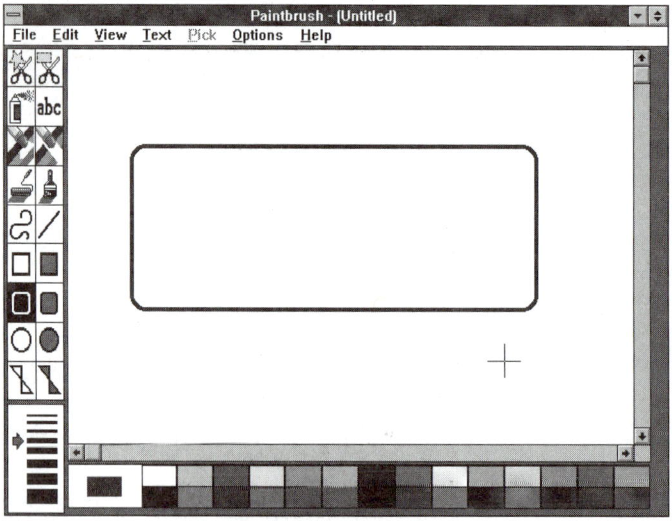

Figure 10-12 An unfilled rectangle

4. Choose the Text tool .
5. Choose a foreground color.

   This foreground color will be applied to the characters that you type.
6. Position the mouse pointer inside the rectangle.

   The mouse pointer turns into an I-beam.
7. Choose a color for the background.
8. Choose Text, and then choose Shadow.

   A shadow effect will be applied to the text you type. The shadow will appear in the selected background color.
9. Choose Text, and then choose Fonts.

   The Font dialog box appears.
10. Choose a font. Choose 24 for the point size. Choose OK.
11. Position the I-beam in the center of the rectangle.
12. Type *your name*.

    The text appears in the unfilled rectangle (see Figure 10-13).

WARNING Do not press ENTER or click the mouse button as you type. The colors, font type, and size of the text can be changed until you press ENTER or click the mouse button.

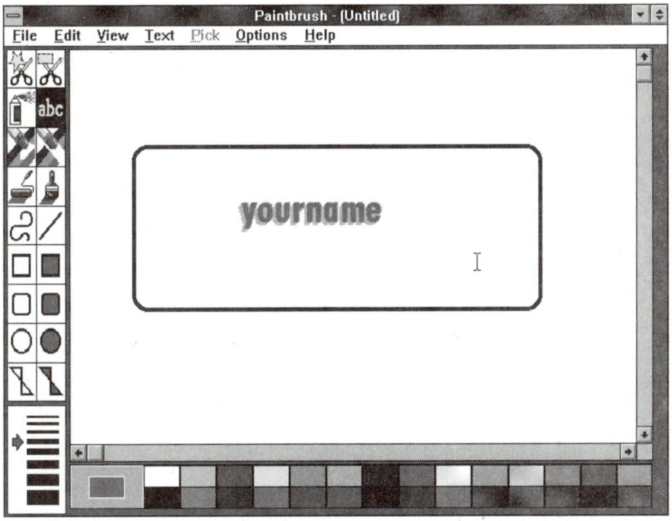

Figure 10-13 Text inside the unfilled rectangle

13. Use the mouse and color palette to change the colors of the text and shadow.

Objective 5: Printing a Drawing

When you are ready to print your drawing, you can choose from several options in the Print dialog box. You can print the entire drawing or just part of the drawing. You can choose to print a rough draft or a final copy of the drawing. And you can choose to scale the printed copy of the drawing.

Exercise 7: Printing a drawing

To print a copy of the file you created in Exercise 6, perform the following steps:

1. Choose File, and then choose Print.

   The Print dialog box appears (see Figure 10-14).

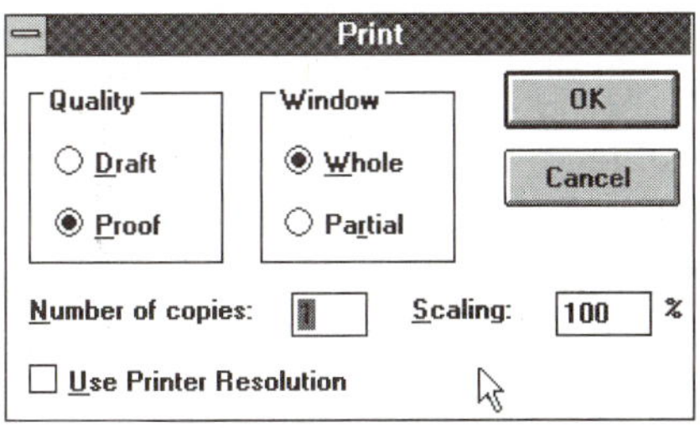

Figure 10-14 The Print dialog box

2. In the Quality portion of the Print dialog box, select Proof, if it is not already selected.
3. In the Window portion of the Print dialog box, select Whole, if it is not already selected.
4. Choose OK.
5. When the file is finished printing, close Paintbrush. Do not save your changes.

Chapter Summary

In this chapter, you learned about the three categories of tools that are included in the Paintbrush program. Paintbrush's graphics, editing, and text tools enable you to create, change, and manipulate images, as well as add text to an image. Paintbrush can be used to express your creativity or to enhance and enliven a document created in another application.

Review Questions

True/False Questions

_____ 1. The inner box on the left side of the color palette is the foreground indicator.

_____ 2. The Pick tool can be used to copy, cut, or paste information.

_____ 3. The Text tool is a graphics tool.

_____ 4. When you choose the Color Eraser, the mouse pointer becomes a small, clear box that you can use to remove objects from the drawing area.

_____ 5. You can change the font and size of text in a drawing.

Multiple-Choice Questions

_____ 6. To copy a selected portion of a drawing, you would choose the
- A. Pick tool.
- B. Text tool.
- C. Paint Roller tool.
- D. Scissors tool.

_____ 7. To change the foreground color of a drawing, you would
A. click the desired color, and then click the inner box.
B. click the left mouse button while pointing to the desired color.
C. click the outside box, and then click the desired color.
D. click the right mouse button while pointing to the desired color.

_____ 8. The line width box determines the width(s) of
A. lines.
B. brushstrokes.
C. lines and brushstrokes.
D. lines, brushstrokes, and the outside frames of unfilled shapes.

_____ 9. When adding text to a drawing, you can apply all of the following except
A. more than one font style at a time.
B. shadow effects.
C. the bold attribute.
D. the underline attribute.

_____ 10. When you first start Paintbrush, the mouse pointer appears on the drawing area as
A. a cross-hair cursor.
B. a small, black square.
C. an I-beam.
D. none of the above
E. any of the above

Fill-in-the-Blank Questions

11. Fonts and attributes must be selected __________ you enter text in Paintbrush.
12. The portion of a drawing that is cut or copied is referred to as a __________.
13. The __________ tool is used to create multisided shapes with straight sides.
14. You must __________ a tool before you can use it in the drawing area.
15. You can print a __________ or __________ copy of a drawing.

Acumen-Building Activities

Quick Projects

1. Using the Brush tool

1. Start Paintbrush.
2. Using the Brush tool, draw a different line for every line width available.
3. Place the different lines directly under one another and make each 3.5" long.
4. Make each line a different color.
5. Under the lines, draw a small, freehand image. (This image can be very simple—for example, a flower or leaf.)
6. Print the drawing in Draft mode.

2. Using colors

1. On a new Paintbrush screen, choose a background color of blue and a foreground color of red.
2. Create and place a filled rectangle in the top right corner of the drawing area.
3. Choose a background color of white and a foreground color of green.
4. Create and place an unfilled circle to the left of the filled rectangle.
5. Choose a foreground color of yellow and a background color of black.
6. Create and place an unfilled rounded-corner rectangle to the left of the unfilled circle.
7. Move the circle to the lower left side of the drawing area.
8. Save the file as variety on your ORIGINAL disk.

3. Changing the variety file

1. Start Paintbrush and open the file variety.
2. Remove the color inside the filled rectangle.
3. Move the upper right corner of the unfilled rounded-corner rectangle to the lower middle of the drawing area.
4. Change the background color to a bright pink, and then open a new file.
5. Spray a mist of black paint across the new drawing area.
6. Save the file as mist.
7. Exit Paintbrush.

4. Working in File Manager

1. Start Windows and open the Main and Accessories windows.
2. Start the File Manager.
3. Display two windows in the File Manager: one for your ORIGINAL disk and the other for your BACKUP disk.

4. Tile the display.
5. Open an additional window for the ORIGINAL disk.
6. Create a directory called drawings on the ORIGINAL disk and move all your .bmp files to this directory.
7. When finished, display all expandable branches in the root directory of the ORIGINAL disk.
8. Reduce the File Manager to an icon.
9. Start Write, and then start Paintbrush.
10. Use the Task Manager to switch back to the Write program.
11. On the variety drawing, type Variety of Shapes and Sizes.
12. Save the file using the same name.

In-Depth Projects

1. Creating a birthday card

1. Create a birthday card for one of your friends using Paintbrush.
2. Be sure to include a variety of colors.
3. Draw a simple freehand image or use the available shapes to create an image.
4. Save the file as birthday.

2. Changing the birthday card

1. Add text to the card you created in In-Depth Project 1.
2. Change the look of the card by manipulating the images.
3. Sign your name at the bottom of the card using the Brush tool.
4. Save the file as birth1.
5. Turn off the printer.
6. Request that the file be printed.
7. Use the Print Manager to restart the printer.

3. Creating a banner

1. In Paintbrush, create a banner using a rectangular box.
2. Type Welcome New Committee Members inside the banner.
3. Use attractive fonts, add shadow effects, and try out different colors for the banner.
4. Save the file as welcome.
5. Close Paintbrush and display the clock on the desktop using the following settings: digital face, Times New Roman font, and 24-point size. Do not display the date.
6. Change the screen saver and set a delay time of two minutes.
7. Cause an alarm to go off twenty minutes from the current time.

Chapter 11

Sharing Data

Objectives

- Using the Clipboard with Text and Numbers
- Using the Clipboard with Graphics
- Using the Clipboard with Screen Images
- Using the Clipboard with Data with DOS Applications

Key Terms

TERM	DEFINITION
386-Enhanced Mode	an operating mode that uses conventional and extended memory and can use part of the hard disk for virtual memory; this mode is able to utilize the power of 80386 (and higher) computers that have at least 2MB of RAM; it is especially useful when running DOS applications in the Windows environment
Standard Mode	an operating mode that uses only extended memory on 80286 (and higher) computers; unlike 386-enhanced mode, standard mode cannot use part of the hard disk for virtual memory

In this chapter you will explore the Clipboard. As we discussed in Chapter 7, the Clipboard is a temporary storage area in RAM that holds text or graphics that have been copied from another location. In this chapter, you will learn how to use the Clipboard to cut, copy, and paste text, numbers, and graphics from one location to another. You will also see how the Clipboard can be used to capture screen displays. Screen captures have many uses: They can provide a hard copy of an error message and are often used as training aids. Finally, you will see how to use a DOS program with the Clipboard.

Objective 1: Using the Clipboard with Text and Numbers

One of Windows' greatest advantages is that you can transfer data quickly and easily from one Windows-based program to another. The data is held temporarily in the Clipboard, which is a feature of the Windows environment that is shared by all Windows-based programs. You may have noticed that all Windows applications include an Edit menu. The commands on the Edit menu facilitate the use of the Clipboard. In Chapter 7, you learned how to cut, copy, and paste text from one area in a document to another area in the same document. In this chapter, you will learn how to transfer data via the Clipboard from one application to another.

Exercise 1: Transferring data using the Clipboard

In the following exercise, you will use the Clipboard to cut and paste text from one application to another by performing the following steps:

1. Start Write.
2. On the blank document screen, type You can use the Clipboard to cut and copy text.
3. Select the sentence.
4. Choose Edit, and then choose Cut.

   The sentence is removed from the document window.
5. Close the Write document window without saving the changes.
6. Start Notepad.
7. Choose Edit, and then choose Paste.

   The sentence you typed in Write is displayed in the Notepad document window (see Figure 11-1).

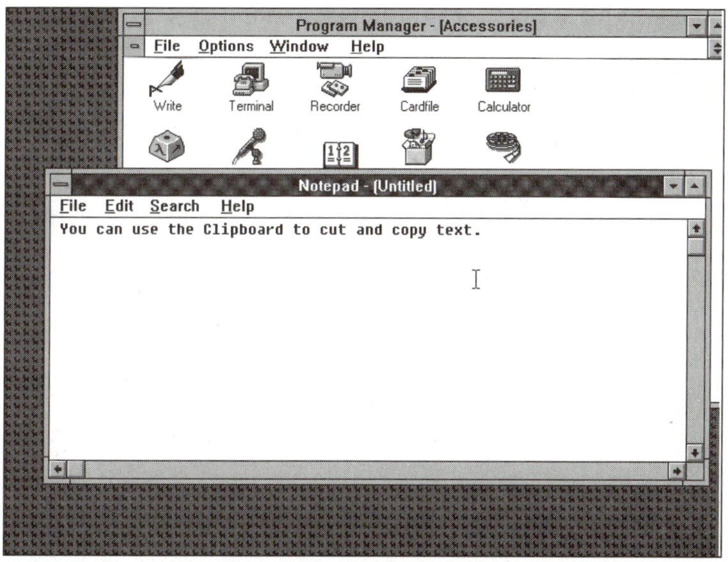

Figure 11-1 The sentence copied to the Notepad document

8. Close Notepad without saving the changes.
9. Start Calculator.
10. Multiply 10 × 5.

    The number *50* is displayed in the calculator window.
11. Choose Edit, and then choose Copy.

    Notice that the calculator does not include a Cut command.
12. Close the Calculator window.
13. Start Write and open horses.doc.
14. Highlight *30* in the last sentence of the third paragraph.
15. Choose Edit, then choose Paste.

    50 is transferred from the Clipboard to the horses.doc file and pastes over the previous text *30*.
16. Type .00 following the number 50.
17. Type $ in front of the number 50 (see Figure 11-2).

Result of calculation ▶

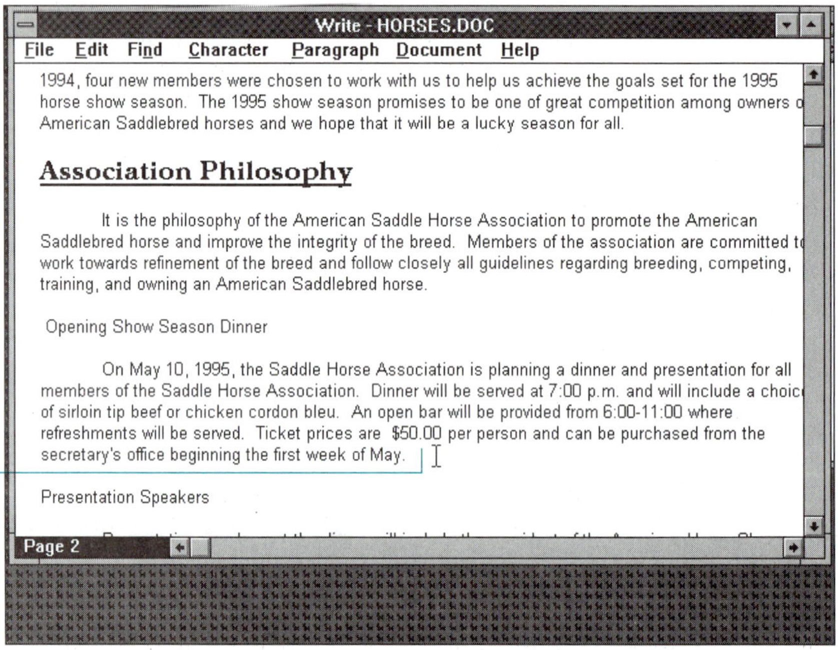

Figure 11-2 Data from Calculator pasted into a Write document

18. Exit Write and don't save your changes.

Exercise 2: Viewing and clearing the contents of the Clipboard

Information stays in the Clipboard until you do one of three things: (1) perform another cut or copy, which overwrites the current information stored in the Clipboard, (2) turn off the computer, or (3) delete the information in the Clipboard. You can repeatedly paste the same information to various applications until the Clipboard is cleared. You can view information stored in the Clipboard at any time. To view the contents of the Clipboard, perform the following steps:

1. Open the Main window.
2. Double-click on the Clipboard Viewer 

.

   The Clipboard Viewer window displays the number you copied from the calculator (see Figure 11-3).

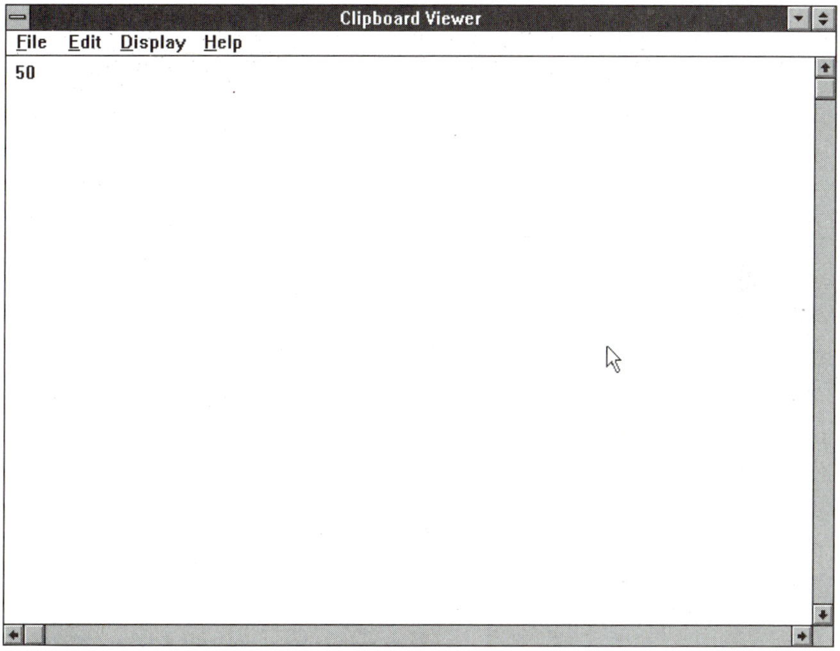

Figure 11-3 Contents of the Clipboard displayed in the Clipboard Viewer window

3. Choose Edit, and then choose Delete.

   A message box appears, asking you if you want to clear the Clipboard's contents.
4. Choose Yes.

   The information is removed from the Clipboard.

Objective 2: Using the Clipboard with Graphics

The Clipboard can be used to transfer a graphic created in a Windows-based drawing program to a word processing document created in a Windows-based word processing application.

> **Upgrading to Multimedia**
>
> The CD-ROM format can hold a vast amount of information and consequently is becoming more and more prevalent in a wide variety of areas, such as education, computer games, reference materials, and entertainment. To take advantage of the sound, graphics, and video provided by CD-ROMs, your system must have a sound board, speakers, and a CD-ROM drive. Older computers may not include these components.
>
> However, there are a number of multimedia upgrade kits that you can install yourself on your current system. Buying an upgrade kit—versus buying newer components—has several advantages. The manufacturers of upgrade kits have usually worked out any compatibility problems between their product and yours. This is not always true of new components that you purchase separately from your original system. Of course, the biggest advantage is price: It is much less expensive to buy an upgrade kit than it is to purchase new components.

Exercise 3: Copying and pasting a graphic

In the following exercise, you will create a graphic in Paintbrush and copy it a Write document.

1. Start Notepad.
2. Open memo.txt.
3. Select the entire document.
4. Choose Edit, and then choose Copy.
5. Close Notepad and don't save your changes.
6. Start Write.
7. Choose Edit, and then choose Paste.

   The memo.txt file is copied into the Write document window.
8. Minimize the Write document window.
9. Start Paintbrush.
10. Choose the Rounded Box tool.
11. In the drawing area, create a large rounded-corner box with a smaller box inside it (see Figure 11-4).

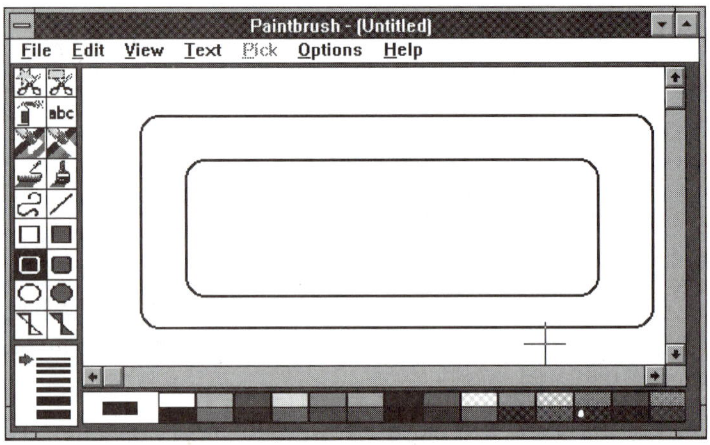

Figure 11-4 The Paintbrush drawing

12. In the smaller box, type:

    S & J Hardware Stores
    For all your building and remodeling needs
13. Enhance the text by applying a font of your choice and a shadow effect. Apply contrasting colors to the background and foreground (see Figure 11-5).

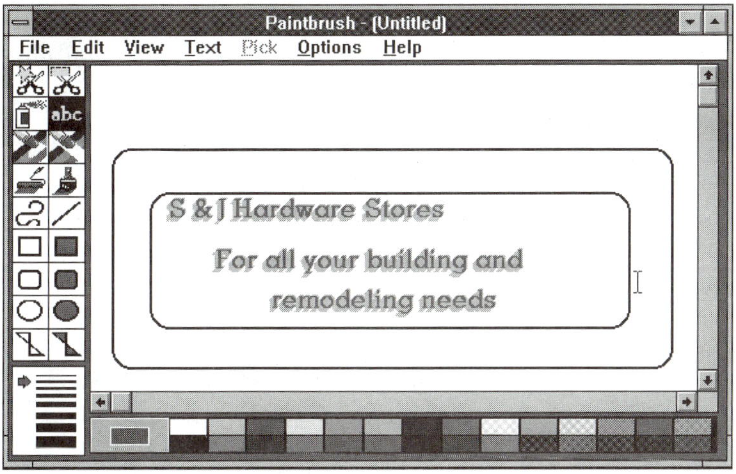

Figure 11-5 **The enhanced text**

14. Choose the Scissors tool and enclose the entire drawing within a dotted-line box.
15. Choose Edit, and then choose Copy.
16. Close Paintbrush and don't save your changes.
17. Maximize the Write document window.
18. Position the insertion point after *development* in the third sentence. Type Included is an image submitted by the purchasing department for our new logo. Please take a moment to review it and call Mr. Martin at his office or contact him through his e-mail account about any ideas you may have regarding this project.
19. Press ENTER.
20. Delete any remaining text.

FEATURE

Recording Macros in Windows

The Windows Recorder enables you to create macros—small pieces of program code that contain lists of commands that perform specific tasks. For example, you could create a macro to start Paintbrush; retrieve, copy, and paste a Paintbrush file into a Write document; and then print the document. Normally it would take several keystrokes and mouse actions to complete this series of tasks. By recording all the steps you use and placing them in a macro, you can quickly perform all the tasks by pressing a single keyboard combination that you assign to the macro. The macro can then be played back whenever you need it.

21. Choose Edit, and then choose Paste.

    The logo you created in Paintbrush appears in the memo document (see Figure 11-6).

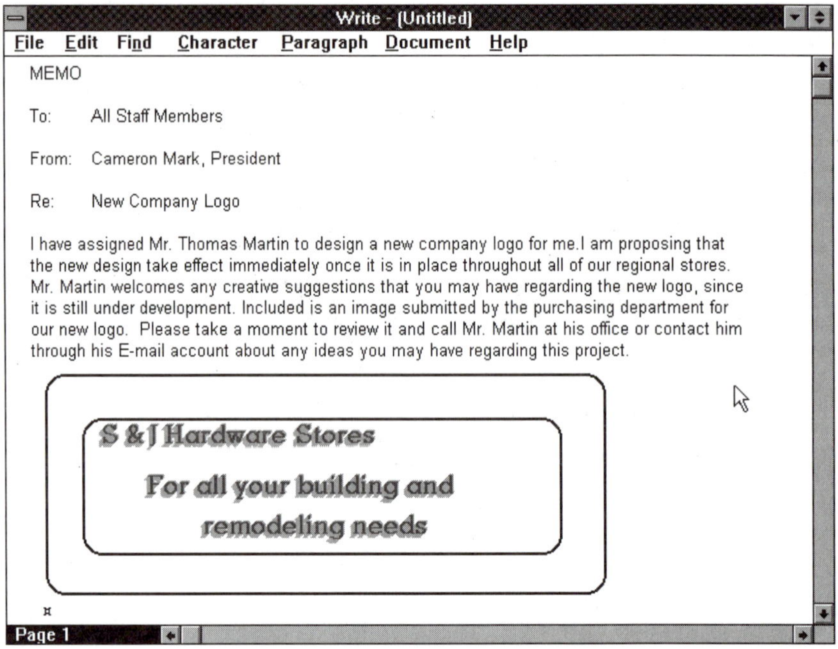

Figure 11-6 The logo created in Paintbrush copied to memo.txt

22. Close the document, naming it memo.txt.

Objective 3: Using the Clipboard with Screen Images

Entire screen images can be captured as bitmapped files, and then transferred to the Paintbrush program. You can also limit the capture selection to an active window. The Print Screen key on your keyboard is used to capture a screen. Captured screens are especially useful when you want a picture of a screen for training documentation. For example, most of the figures in this textbook are screen captures.

Exercise 4: Capturing a screen

To capture a Windows screen, perform the following steps:

1. Open the Accessories window.
2. Press ALT + PRINT SCREEN.

   The active window is captured, and the screen capture is placed in the Clipboard.

TIP Pressing PRINT SCREEN captures the entire screen.

3. Maximize the Paintbrush application window.
4. Choose Edit, then choose Paste.

   The screen capture appears in the Paintbrush drawing area (see Figure 11-7).

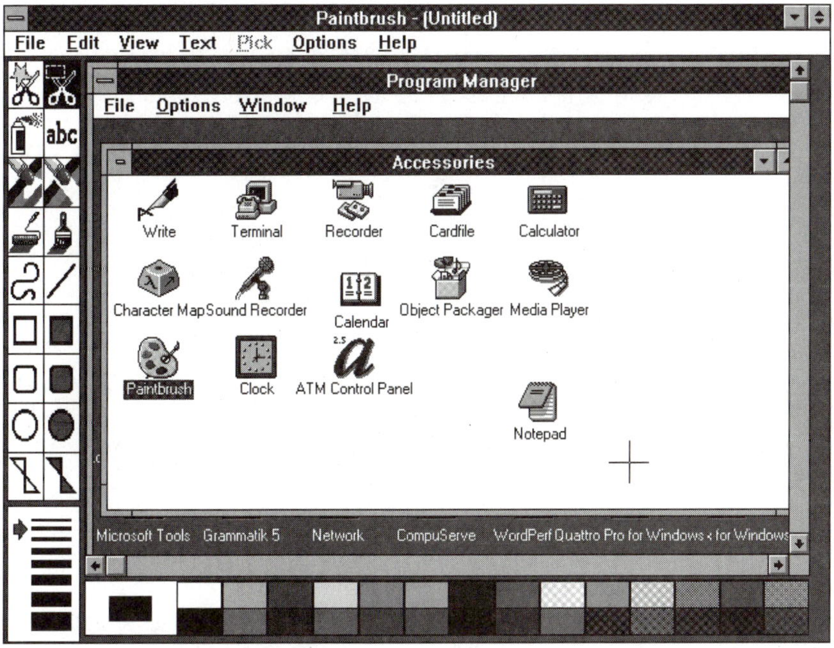

Figure 11-7 A screen capture of the Accessories window in the Paintbrush drawing area

5. Choose File, and then choose Print.
6. Choose OK.

   The screen capture is printed.
7. Close Paintbrush without saving your changes.

Objective 4: Using the Clipboard with DOS Applications

An application that is not based in the Windows environment is called a DOS application. You can use the Clipboard to copy and paste text and numbers from a DOS application to a Windows-based application or another DOS application. For this process to work correctly, you should be operating in 386-enhanced mode. The *386-enhanced mode* is an operating mode that uses conventional and extended memory and can use part of the hard disk for virtual memory. This mode is able to utilize the power of 80386 (and higher) computers that have at least 2MB of RAM. It is especially useful when running DOS applications in the Windows environment.

386-enhanced mode

standard mode In contrast, *standard mode* is an operating mode that uses only extended memory on 80286 (and higher) machines. Unlike 386-enhanced mode, standard mode cannot use part of the hard disk for virtual memory. If you are operating in standard mode, you will have to capture the entire screen of a DOS application instead of just the text you want copied.

Exercise 5: Copying DOS information to a Windows application

The following exercise shows the steps used to copy information from a DOS application (in this case, Lotus 1–2–3) to the Write program. Depending on the programs on your computer, you may or may not be able to follow this exercise exactly.

1. From the Program Manager window, open the Main window.
2. Double-click the MS-DOS icon .

   You are temporarily returned to the DOS prompt.
3. Start Lotus 1–2–3 and open a Lotus 1–2–3 file. (If you do not have Lotus 1–2–3 on your computer, simply use another DOS application for the remainder of this exercise.)
4. Press ALT+↵ ENTER.

   The Lotus 1–2–3 document appears in a window of its own (see Figure. 11-8).

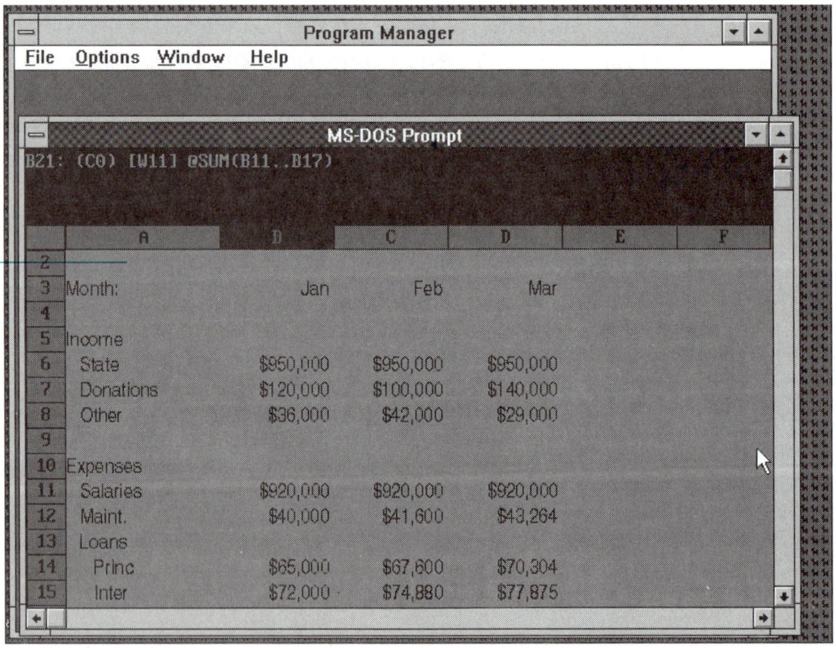

Figure 11-8 A Lotus 1–2–3 document in its own window

5. Locate the information in the Lotus 1–2–3 document that you want to copy to the Clipboard.
6. Click the control menu box of the Lotus 1–2–3 application window.
7. Choose Edit, and then choose Mark.
8. Drag the mouse pointer across the text or numbers you want to copy.
9. Choose the control menu box of the Lotus 1–2–3 window, and then choose Edit.
10. Choose Copy Enter.

    The text or numbers you selected are copied to the Clipboard.
11. Start Write.

    A blank Write document window opens.
12. Choose Edit, and then choose Paste.

    The Lotus 1–2–3 text appears in the Write document window (see Figure 11-9).

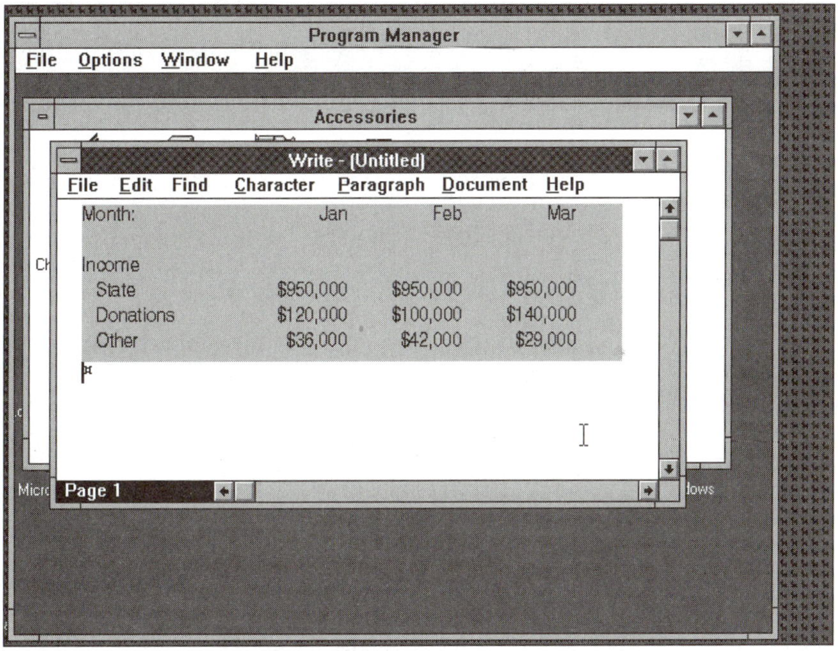

Figure 11-9 Text copied from a Lotus 1–2–3 document to a Write document

Chapter Summary

You should now understand how versatile Windows is. You have learned how to transfer text, numbers, and graphics between Windows programs, as well as text and numbers between DOS applications and Windows programs.

Review Questions

True/False Questions

____ 1. You can paste the information stored in the Clipboard as many times as you want.

____ 2. You can copy and paste text, numbers, and graphics between DOS applications and Windows applications.

____ 3. 386-enhanced mode utilizes the power of 80386 (and higher) computers.

____ 4. Screen images can be captured as bitmapped files.

____ 5. Pressing Print Screen captures the active window only.

Multiple-Choice Questions

____ 6. All the following Windows programs include the Cut command except

A. Write.

B. Calculator.

C. Notepad.

D. Calendar.

____ 7. Applications that are not based in the Windows environment are often called

A. system applications.

B. standard mode applications.

C. DOS applications.

D. none of the above

_____ 8. To use 386-enhanced mode, a computer must have at least
   A. 2MB of RAM.
   B. 1MB of RAM.
   C. 4MB of RAM.
   D. any of the above

_____ 9. When you transfer information between a DOS application and a Windows application in standard mode,
   A. a portion of the screen is captured.
   B. the entire screen is captured.
   C. highlighted text is captured.
   D. none of the above

_____ 10. Pressing Alt+Print Screen
   A. captures an entire screen.
   B. cancels a capture.
   C. captures a portion of the screen.
   D. limits the capture to the active window.

Fill-in-the Blank Questions

11. The ______________ is a Windows feature that temporarily stores information.
12. To place in a document information that has been copied to the Clipboard, you ______________ the information.
13. ______________ ______________ utilizes extended memory only.
14. The ______________ option places text, numbers, or graphics in a new location.
15. 386-enhanced mode utilizes extended and conventional memory and can also use part of the hard disk for ______________ ______________.

Acumen-Building Activities

Quick Projects

1. Using Windows

1. Start Windows and open at least five different group icons on the desktop, including the Games window.
2. Cascade the windows, and then resize them so that they use a small portion of the screen.
3. Make the Games window the active window.
4. Capture the Games window screen and copy it into a Paintbrush document.
5. Print a copy of the entire Paintbrush document in Final mode.

2. Using Write and Notepad

1. Start Write and open horses7.doc.
2. Copy the second heading and paragraph to a Notepad document.
3. Open the todo file and copy all its contents into a Write document.
4. Make the following changes in Write:

   Underline each listed item, increase the font size, and adjust all margins to 2".
5. Print the file, but do not save your changes.

3. Using Windows accessories

1. Using Calculator, divide 150 by 5.
2. Copy the result into Write, Cardfile, and Calendar documents.
3. Have each document window displayed in its own window.

4. Using DOS and Windows

1. Start a DOS application from your system and retrieve a DOS file.
2. Select a portion of the DOS file and copy it to a Write document.
3. Print the Write document.

In-Depth Projects

1. Pasting a Paintbrush file

1. Start Paintbrush and open welcome.
2. Place a copy of the banner at the top of horses7.doc.
3. Print the document from Write.
4. View the contents of the Clipboard.
5. Close all windows.

2. Creating and Using a Paintbrush file

1. Start Paintbrush and create a drawing of a musical tape cassette and record.
2. Save the file as songs.
3. Copy the drawing to the Cardfile file called records.
4. Place the drawing on each card in the database.
5. Print the top card.
6. View the image in the Clipboard and make a screen capture of it.
7. Print the screen capture.
8. Open the finalist file and search for the card that includes Windy Hill as the farm name.
9. Make a screen capture of the card and print it.
10. Close all windows except the Program Manager.

Chapter 12

Advanced Features

Objectives

- Understanding Operating Modes
- Understanding Object Linking and Embedding

Key Terms

TERM	DEFINITION
Conventional Memory	the first 640K of memory that is used by DOS and available for DOS applications
Extended Memory	memory available on 286 (and higher) computers that can utilize memory above 1MB
Multitasking	running more than one program at a time
Object	data in the form of pictures or text
Linking	creating a relationship between two or more files that share common data; linked files may be created in the same program or different programs; when files are linked, common data that is changed in one file is automatically changed in the linked file
Embedding	placing an object created in one program in another

Windows includes a number of advanced features for making the best use of your system's resources. In this chapter, you will begin to understand how Windows uses memory in different ways, depending on your system's hardware. In Chapter 11, you learned how you can place information from a document in one program to a document in another program using the Clipboard. In this chapter, you will learn about Windows object linking and embedding (OLE) technology, which enables you to link documents created in different programs. When documents are linked, you can change the information found in one document, and this change will be incorporated in all other linked documents.

Objective 1: Understanding Operating Modes

Depending on the system hardware you are using, Windows can run in standard or 386-enhanced mode. You can determine your system's operating mode by choosing Help from the Program Manager menu bar, and then choosing About Program Manager. Your computer's current mode will be displayed at the bottom of the Help screen.

When running in 386-enhanced mode, Windows can use virtual memory when necessary. This chapter describes both standard and 386-enhanced modes, as well as virtual memory. Operation modes affect the way Windows and DOS applications use your computer's RAM.

Standard mode

extended memory; multitasking

Standard mode is used on 286 (and higher) computers that have less than 2MB of RAM. Standard mode uses *extended memory*, which can utilize memory above 1MB, and can perform *multitasking*, which means running more than one program at once, with Windows applications only. Your computer will operate much faster in standard mode than it will in 386-enhanced mode, but standard mode cannot run DOS and Windows applications at the same time.

386-enhanced mode

conventional memory

The 386-enhanced mode utilizes the full power of 386 (and higher) computers that have more than 2MB of RAM. The 386-enhanced mode enables Windows to access all available conventional memory and extended memory. *Conventional memory* is the first 640K of memory that is used by DOS and available for DOS applications. When necessary, 386-enhanced mode is able to use virtual memory as well. Unlike standard mode, 386-enhanced mode enables multitasking with DOS and Windows applications.

Virtual memory

Some applications demand a great amount of memory while running, which can leave you with a shortage of available RAM. When this happens, a 386 (or higher) computer can use portions of the hard drive's memory as a substitute for RAM; this "borrowed" memory is called *virtual memory*. Although the advantage of virtual memory is obvious, it does have a significant drawback. Applications using virtual memory must access the hard disk, which is a very slow process compared to retrieving information from RAM; therefore, the speed at which the computer operates is greatly decreased.

Objective 2: Object Linking and Embedding

embedding; object

OLE technology gives you great versatility when sharing data between documents. OLE technology enables *embedding*, which means placing an object created in one program in another. (An *object* is data in the form of pictures or text.) For example, you could take a graph created in Lotus and place it in a WordPerfect document. Embedded objects can be edited in the programs to which they are imported. As an example, you could edit a graph created in Lotus from within a WordPerfect document.

linking

OLE technology also enables linking. *Linking* means creating a relationship between two or more files that share common data. Linked files may be created in the same program or different programs. When files are linked, common data that is changed in one file is automatically changed in the linked file.

Some applications can only receive data in a link; these are called client applications. Write and Cardfile are client applications. They cannot send data in a link, they can only receive data. There can be several client applications involved in a link. Other applications can only send data in a link; these are called server applications. Paintbrush is a server application. It cannot receive data in a link; it can only send data. Still other applications can send *and* receive data in a link; these are called client-server applications.

Conducting Business Online

The next time you feel like going on a shopping spree, you may be able to satisfy the urge without leaving your home. A new cyberspace mall may soon be available as an on-line service. Currently an estimated 20 million users have access to the Internet, and that number is expected to increase dramatically within a year. Entrepreneurs and merchants are ready to jump on the information super highway as a way to market a variety of products. After all, what better way to sell your product than electronically to a global audience?

Although the possibilities for such marketing strategies are endless, the experts agree that certain issues need to be resolved before the grand opening of the cyberspace mall. For example: How will customers pay for their purchases? And how will companies identify their customers through the Internet?

Exercise 1: Embedding data in a document

In the following exercise, you will embed a Paintbrush drawing in a Write document. To understand how the embedding process works, perform the following steps:

1. Start Write.

   A new, blank document window opens.
2. Type Balloons.
3. Enlarge the font of Balloons three times and make the text bold.
4. Press ENTER three times.
5. Choose Edit, and then choose Insert Object.

   The Insert Object dialog box appears (see Figure 12-1).

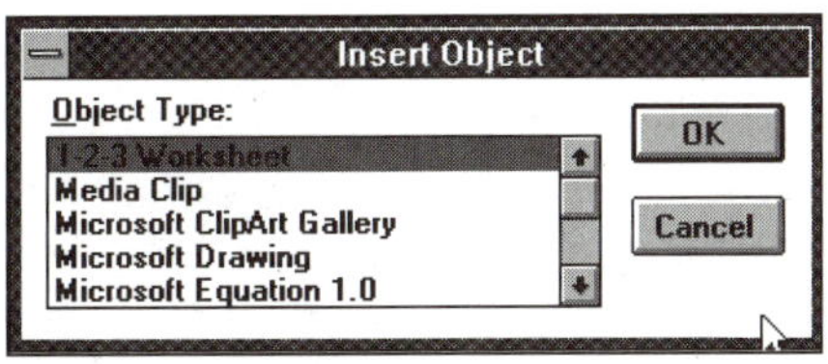

Figure 12-1 The Insert Object dialog box

6. Choose Paintbrush Picture, and then choose OK.

   A Paintbrush window opens. Notice that the title bar reads "Paintbrush - Paintbrush Picture in [Untitled]."

7. Use the Circle/Ellipse and Curve tools to draw three balloons in the drawing area. Color each balloon (see Figure 12-2).

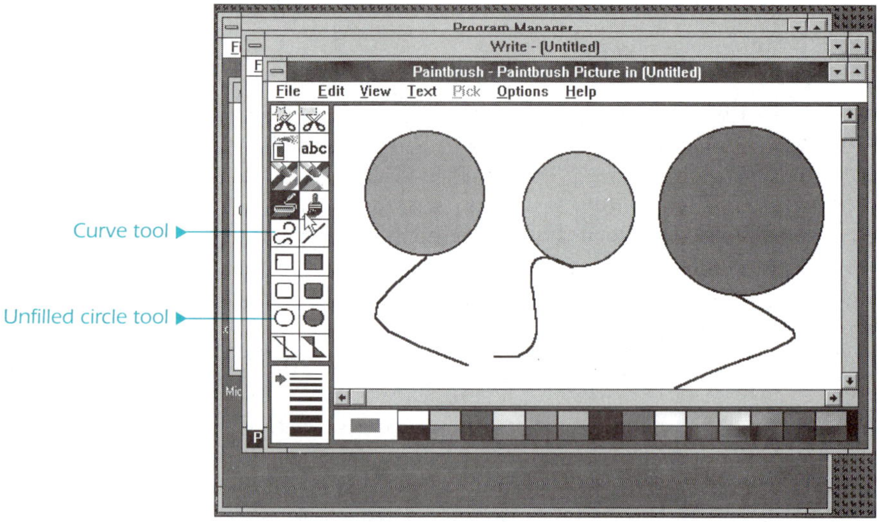

Figure 12-2 A Paintbrush drawing of three balloons

8. Choose File, and then choose Exit & Return to [Untitled].

   A message box appears, prompting you to update the open embedded object before proceeding.

9. Choose Yes.

   You are returned to the Write document where the balloon drawing is placed at the insertion point (see Figure. 12-3). You may need to press PAGE UP to see the picture of the balloons.

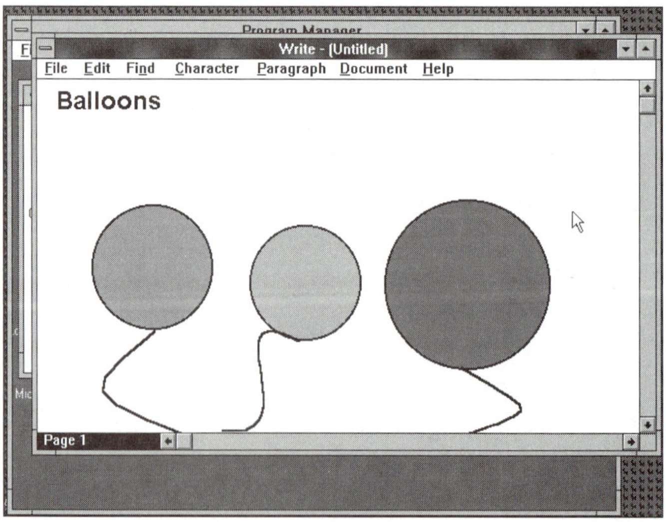

Figure 12-3 The balloon drawing inserted in the Write document

Exercise 2: Moving and sizing an embedded picture

After a picture has been placed in a document, it can be moved to another location in the document or resized. To move and resize the balloons picture, perform the following steps:

1. Place the pointer on the balloons and click the left mouse button to select the picture, if it is not already selected.

   The balloons become highlighted.
2. Choose Edit, and then choose Size Picture.

   The cursor becomes a small square enclosing a smaller square.
3. *Do not click the mouse button.* Move the mouse pointer across the drawing area 1.5" to the right to decrease the size of the picture (see Figure 12-4).

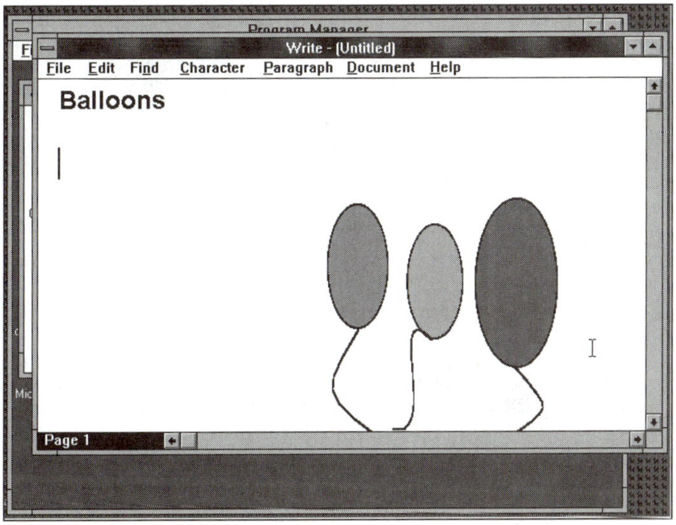

Figure 12-4 The size of the balloons picture is decreased

4. Click the mouse button.
5. Select the balloons picture, if it is not already selected.
6. Choose Edit, and then choose Move Picture.

   The cursor becomes a small square enclosing a smaller square.
7. *Do not press the mouse button.* Move the mouse pointer across the drawing area until the balloons picture is centered on the document page.
8. Click the left mouse button.

   The picture is repositioned in its new location.
9. Deselect the picture.
10. Choose File, and then choose Save As.
11. Type balloons as the file name.

Exercise 3: Editing an embedded object

You can change a Paintbrush drawing that is embedded in a Write document from within the Write program by performing the following steps:

1. Double-click the balloons.

   The drawing is highlighted momentarily, then the Paintbrush window appears. Note that the title bar reads "Paintbrush - Paintbrush Picture in BALLOONS.WRI."
2. Maximize the Paintbrush window.
3. Add a smiling face to the drawing and paint it yellow (see Figure 12-5).

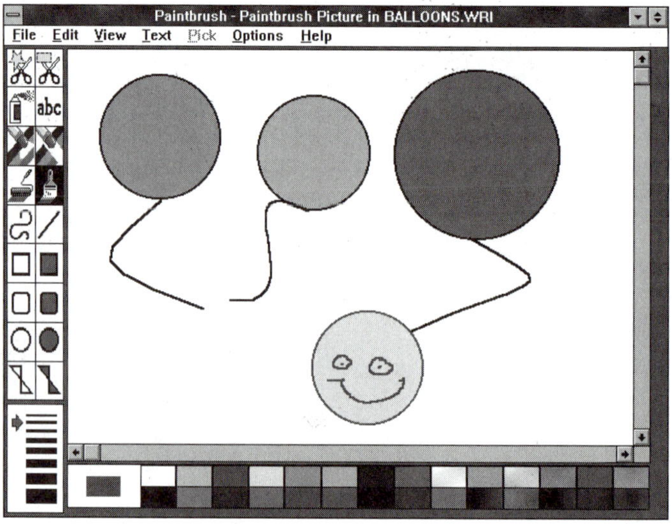

Figure 12-5 Balloon drawing with smiling face

4. Choose File, and then Exit & Return to balloons.wri.

   A message box appears, asking if you want to update the open embedded object before proceeding.
5. Select Yes.

   You are returned to the Write document; the balloons picture includes the smiling face.
6. Choose File, and then choose Print.
7. Save the file as balloon1.
8. Exit Write.

Exercise 4: Linking applications

In the following exercise, you will link data that is located in Paintbrush (the server application) to information in Cardfile (the client application). Changes made in the document in the server application are included automatically in the document in the client application.

1. Start Cardfile and open the finalist file.
2. Minimize the Cardfile window.
3. Start Paintbrush.
4. Draw a small red barn.
5. Choose File, and then choose Save As.
6. Type barn as the file name, and then choose OK.
7. Use the Pick tool to enclose the drawing of the barn within a dotted-line box.
8. Choose Edit, and then choose Copy.
9. Minimize the Paintbrush window.
10. Maximize the Cardfile icon.
11. Choose Edit, and then choose Picture.
12. Position the Forever Sunshine card at the top of the stack.
13. Choose Edit, and then choose Paste Link.

    The barn is placed on the Forever Sunshine card (see Figure 12-6).

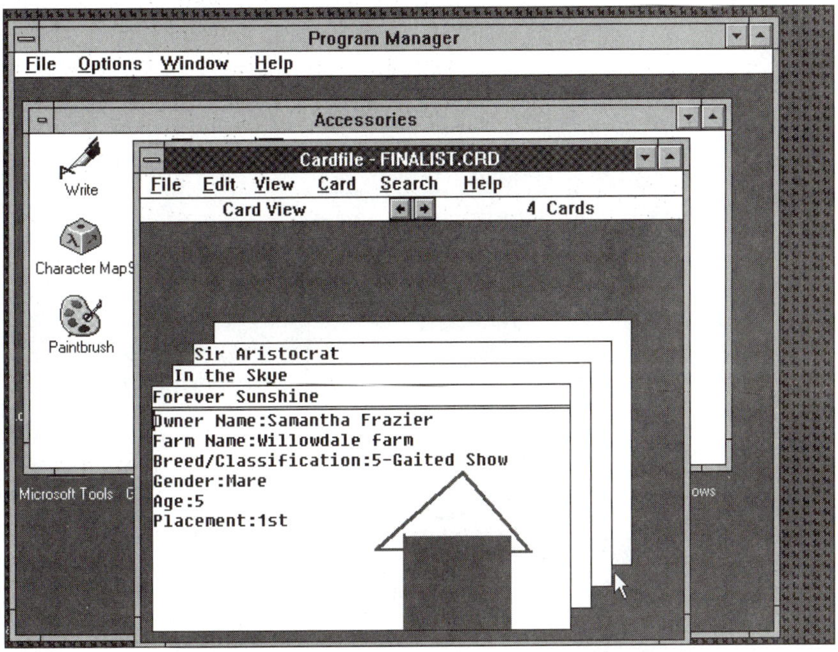

Figure 12-6 **The barn drawing copied to the Forever Sunshine card**

14. Drag the barn to an open area on the card.
15. Choose File, and then choose Save.
16. Minimize the Cardfile window.
17. Maximize the Paintbrush window.
18. Erase the roof of the barn using the Eraser tool.

FEATURE

Computer Talk
Windows Terminal application enables you to share information with other computers via a modem. You can also transfer files back and forth between your computer and mainframes or electronic bulletin boards. Modems use telephone lines to send information from one computer to another. Electronic bulletin boards, such as Compuserv, America Online, and Delphi, provide a number of services to which users can subscribe. Some of these services catalog sales, health forums, stock market reports, and groups for computer users.

19. Choose File, and then choose Save.
20. Choose File, and then choose Exit.
21. Maximize the Cardfile window.

    Notice the change you made in Paintbrush is included in the Cardfile document (see Figure 12-7).

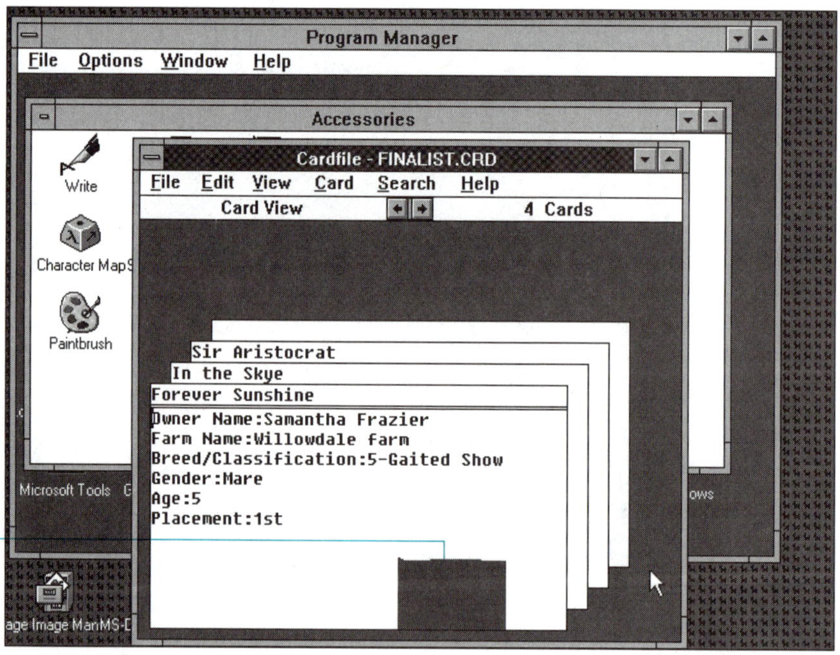

Figure 12-7 The edited drawing displayed in the Cardfile document

22. Save the file as barn1.
23. Exit Cardfile.

Chapter Summary

In this chapter, you learned how Windows operates differently, depending on the type of hardware your system uses. You learned how you can use OLE technology to place an object in a document in a program other than the program in which the object was created. You also discovered how linking files can save time and reduce errors.

Review Questions

True/False Questions

_____ 1. Linking can be used to update data stored in several different documents by changing the data in one document in the link.

_____ 2. Text or graphics that are cut, copied, and pasted are called objects.

_____ 3. Virtual memory can be used on 286 (or higher) computers.

_____ 4. Extended memory can access only memory higher than 2MB.

_____ 5. An embedded object can be edited from its pasted location.

Multiple-Choice Questions

_____ 6. Which of the following statements is not true? 386-enhanced mode

A. utilizes machines that include at least 1MB of RAM.
B. enables Windows to access all available conventional memory.
C. enables Windows to access all available extended memory.
D. enables multitasking for DOS and Windows application.

_____ 7. An object can be

A. text.
B. graphs.
C. pictures.
D. all of the above

_____ 8. An application that can send but not receive data in a link is called a

A. client application.
B. server application.
C. file server.
D. object application.

_____ 9. The Exit & Return command is located on which of the following menus?

A. Edit
B. File
C. Insert
D. none of the above

_____ 10. To cause data changes in one document to be included automatically in another document, you would use which of the following commands?

A. Edit, Paste
B. Copy, Paste link
C. Paste Special
D. Edit, Paste Link

Fill-in-the-Blank Questions

11. The type of memory that can be used depends on your particular system __________.
12. Paintbrush acts as a __________ __________ only.
13. Conventional memory is the first __________ of memory used by DOS.
14. There can be several __________ applications involved in a link.
15. To embed a picture, you must go through the __________ dialog box to identify the application of the picture to be embedded.

Acumen-Building Activities

Quick Projects

1. Summarizing the Chapter

1. Determine your computer system's type and operating mode.
2. Create a Write document that summarizes the information you learned in this chapter.
3. Name it summary.
4. Use Paintbrush to create a large, unfilled box with *Book Summary* printed inside.
5. Make the box large enough so that you will be able to add a drawing later.
6. Choose an attractive font and color for the text.
7. Save the file as paintsum.
8. Print the drawing.

2. Linking Files

1. Link paintsum to the summary document you created in Write.
2. Edit the paintsum file by placing a drawing of a book in the unfilled box.

3. Place the drawing at the top of the summary document and resize it if necessary.
4. Save the file, and then print the document.

3. Managing files

1. Display a separate window in the File Manager for each of the following: the root directory of the BACKUP floppy disk, the root directory of the ORIGINAL floppy disk, and the subdirectory called drawings of the ORIGINAL disk.
2. Create a new directory on the BACKUP disk and call it finish.
3. Using the mouse, copy two files from the drawings directory to the finish directory.
4. Then move two files from the drawings directory to the finish directory.
5. Reduce the windows to icons on the desktop.
6. Create a Paintbrush drawing that includes your name, class name, instructor's name, and school name.
7. Call this file heading.
8. Embed heading in all your Write files that have the extension .txt.
9. Place the heading at the top of each file.
10. Examine the contents of the Clipboard.

4. Editing linked files

1. Link heading with all your Write files with the extension .doc.
2. Place the heading at the bottom of each file.
3. Use Copy, Cut, and Paste to transfer the heading file from Paintbrush to your Write files with the extension .wri.

In-Depth Projects

1. Embedding files

1. Use a spreadsheet program to create a financial profit/loss statement for a fictitious company.
2. List expenses and earnings for four quarters.
3. Subtract the expenses from the earnings.
4. Create a document in a word processing program that explains to the company's manager why the company made or lost money over the past four quarters.
5. Embed the spreadsheet information in the word processing document to give a visual representation of the company's profit or loss.
6. Print a copy of the new document.

2. Linking files

1. Start Windows.
2. Open the Accessories, Main, and Games windows.

3. Display them as overlapping windows.
4. Make the Accessories window the active window.
5. Minimize the Games and Main windows.
6. Maximize the Accessories window.
7. Start Write. Access Help on Finding Text and print this help topic.
8. Create a Write document that includes the following list of items: apples, bananas, coconuts, grapes, kiwi, oranges, peaches pineapples, and watermelon. (Press ENTER after each item in the list.)
9. Save the document as fruits.
10. Print the document.
11. Use Cut and Paste to arrange the fruits in reverse alphabetical order.
12. Save and print the document.
13. Create a Paintbrush drawing of the listed fruits.
14. Save this file as paintfrt.
15. Link the paintfrt drawing to the fruits document.

3. Editing Linked Files

1. Start Write and open the fruit file.
2. Enhance each fruit name by applying different font types and sizes.
3. Create a header called Produce List.
4. Set up tab stops in the fruit file at 2" and 4".
5. Place the various fruits at the 2" tab stop and add the following amounts at the 4" tab stop:

```
apples     $2.49/lb.   oranges     $1.59/lb.
bananas     $.69/lb.   peaches     $1.89/lb.
coconuts   $1.49 each  pineapples  $2.59 each
grapes     $2.79/lb.   watermelon  $3.00 each
kiwi       $1.19 each
```

6. Under the columns of fruits and their prices, type The total of your produce is
7. Use the calculator to figure out the cost of 2 lbs. of apples, 3 coconuts, 2 lbs. of peaches, and 3 kiwis.
8. Copy the calculated amount from the calculator and place it at the bottom of the fruit document.
9. Save the file, and then print the document.

Acumen Advanced Features Milestone

Windows includes a variety of programs that you can use to create documents and illustrations, as well as share data between programs and computer systems.

Individual Project:

Creating Documents and Illustrations

1. Most of Premier Systems Consulting's current clients are attorneys, accountants, and doctors. However, your team is developing a project for a mail-order company. Your manager has asked you to explore other opportunities for new business and recommend types of businesses that would benefit from PSC's services. You may select one type of company or several, as long as your recommendations are logical and compelling.

   Use Write to write and print your recommendations. Save the file as newbus in the A:\memos directory of your personal data disk.
2. One of the executives in your company has an idea: She wants to create an electronic classroom in your company that would teach clients how to use their computer systems. She feels this would serve as an excellent marketing tool. Use Paintbrush to design and lay out an electronic classroom suitable for training up to six people at a time. You can use boxes and rectangles to represent desks and equipment and circles to represent chairs. Save your file as layout in the A:\shows directory of the personal data disk. Print a copy of your design.
3. Use Write to write a memo to your manager that explains your particular design for the electronic classroom. Include your reasons for designing the room as you did. Copy the layout design into your memo. Save the memo file as laymemo in your A:\memos directory on your personal data disk.

Team Project: Sharing Information among Team Members

1. With your team members, write a recommendation to the Mustard-of-the-Month Mail Order Company's managers that explains the benefits of computerization. Use Write to write and print your recommendation. Save the file as plan1 in the A:\team directory of your team disk.
2. Working with the members of your team, design and lay out a computer system for the various departments of the mail-order company. These departments are warehouse, shipping, billing, accounting, clerical, and administration. Use Paintbrush to create a schematic diagram and label each item in the diagram. Save the file as system1 in the A:\team directory of the team disk. Print a copy of the diagram to attach to your recommendation letter.
3. Update your team disk with all new files from each of your team member's disks.

Index